INTERPRETATION OF NARRATIVE

EDITED BY MARIO J. VALDÉS
AND OWEN J. MILLER

Interpretation of Narrative

UNIVERSITY OF TORONTO PRESS
Toronto Buffalo London

© University of Toronto Press 1978
Toronto Buffalo London
Printed in Canada

Library of Congress Cataloging in Publication Data

International Colloquium on Interpretation of Narrative, University of Toronto, 1976.
Interpretation of narrative.

1. Criticism – Congresses.   I. Valdés, Mario J.
II. Miller, Owen J.   III. Toronto. University.
IV. Title.
PN80.5.I5   1976   809'.92'3   78-23683
ISBN 0-8020-5443-9

qr 10-11

Contents

MARIO J. VALDÉS

Preface

Literary theory is an area of inquiry where one finds agreement infrequently. Most literary theory attempts to state the case for a given position in opposition to another. In spite of this penchant for polemics there are interesting and difficult problems in literary theory which could be taken as common ground. But what is most significant is that the understanding of these problems can grow in depth and sophistication with commentary from opposing sides. The area of inquiry of this volume – interpretation of narrative – is one such region of common concern. Our task has been to explore the commentary of various text-oriented approaches as distinct from that of reader-based approaches.

In linguistics and philosophy the study of interaction leads logically to holistic concepts. In literary theory we have seldom considered that the opposing sides of an issue could be related to each other in opposition and thus could implicitly interact on the same issue. Text-oriented and reader-oriented approaches to interpretation make contradictory claims and deny validity to each other, but in the broader perspective of a theory of systems they have all the properties of subsystems in interaction within a system. In logical terms textual analysis and the aesthetics of reception are necessary and essential to each other. If we do not have a text and the possibility of textual analysis within the self-imposed discipline of formal relations, there is no possibility either of a reader or of his reception of the messages inherent in reading. The whole of the system thus encompasses both positions and the interaction between them, a fact sometimes lost sight of because of concentration on what is but a subsystem of the whole. I would thus begin by establishing the domain of critical inquiry to be a text considered 'literary' by a reading community and a reader, which together establish their mutual interaction. Both the text and the reader are subsystems in their own right, and each is a subject of inquiry.

There is, of course, a basic disagreement between formalist and hermeneutic critics. Critics of a formalist persuasion hold that the function of criticism is to examine and comment on the text and its context and not on the reader. The exclusion of the reader is made not because there is any lack of interest in the reception process but because of the mode of study which an inquiry into reception presupposes. Consequently the formalist makes a basic assumption that while investigation into the textual systems of signs and symbols is legitimate, inquiry into the reading experience is not.

The reader-oriented critic on the other side of this issue holds that all inquiry into textual elements develops within a set of norms which have arisen in the critic's readings of the text. Consequently, the task of criticism for this critic is not to search for empirical evidence to substantiate an objective description, but rather to inquire into the functions of the text as a reader's text. Specifically, there is a proposal here to go beyond structural or other formal modes of analysis and turn to the functional questions of how the text is experienced. Such a notion has been implicit for a long time in much of the more sophisticated criticism which seeks to go beyond analysis; its advent has had to wait for critics to come to grips with modernism from Beckett and Borges to Nabokov and Vargas Llosa.

If we accept that an increase in knowledge is an increase in the certitude with which we can claim to understand phenomena and a corresponding decrease in the probability of error in our understanding, can we claim that interpretation of literary texts contributes to an increase in knowledge? I believe we can make such a statement, for certitude or diminution of error is only the measure of how well we know what we know. And we will always know more about certain domains of inquiry than about others. But this is only part of the issue, for we must still determine what is worth knowing. The wider the realm of inquiry the more elegant and simple the theory will be. A theory of the universe contains multiple theories of physics, and although the degree of certitude in micro-physical theory is much higher than in the theory of the creation and destruction of planets, both are essential facets of knowledge. In the same way textual analysis has a much higher degree of certitude than theories of reception, but both are essential. I disagree with the view that literary theory must be a theory of history and literary criticism must be exclusively descriptive, for a reader exists and creates as much as he re-creates.

Receptionist and formalist theories of literary criticism are two characteristic perspectives in contemporary criticism which are also related outside literary criticism to a particular style of scientific reflection and of course to philosophy. It is not uncommon to find mutually divergent conceptions in all forms of reflective inquiry closely connected with phenomenology and analytical philosophy. It is a simple task to identify the divergence of these two perspectives in terms of reader-oriented theories as against text-oriented theories, but it is quite another matter to show the convergence which I believe these two directions have now begun to manifest. This convergence is not a kind of compromise but rather is a development in response to similar questions discovered by each perspective within the field of its presuppositions.

Reception theories remain grounded in methods which analyse objective structures in the text from the position of the reading subject. By 'objective' let us understand a method which tries to describe structures unambiguously in terms of their plan of action in the reading encounter of the reader's experience. Reception methodology seeks to establish the plan of the text through logical rules which centre on the functional concept.

In contrast, formalist theory holds meaning to be the result of logical operations which are defined in the text itself. Therefore a concept of dual meaning is inevitable: a self-evident textual meaning must be gained by the reader in relating his own version of the text to the author's text.

If we continue to map the contrast between the two theories we could say that formalism is operationalist, while reception theory is an integrationist approach which seeks to establish a place for logical reduction within a broader context of experience. Thus, broadly speaking, formalist criticism is linguistically inspired in its logical reduction of the text to a describable system and an elusive epiphenomenon which cannot be considered. Reception criticism seeks to establish a dialectic inquiry which encompasses both the horizon of experience and the logical reduction of analysis.

This contrast, I suggest, is to be thought of as a heuristic model intended for purposes of demonstration, permitting finer characterization for an inquiry into the more central features of the ideas and developments of the respective theories. To do this we must look at two things: first, the similarity of methodological approach behind the idiosyncratic vocabularies of the varying tendencies within reception theory and formalism; second, the surprising fact that both schools contrive to escape the ultimate consequences of idealism in the case of reception theory and of behaviourism in the case of formalism. The best criticism today is typified by a more open methodology.

I would outline the convergence of the two approaches as follows: 1/ both are concerned with the text and what is analytically available therein, so that in the critical inquiry and in the interpretation which derives from it an 'a priori' base is rejected as untenable; 2/ both formalism and reception theory are open systems in the sense that even in principle they cannot be completed; 3/ both reception theory and formalism come together in their consideration of meaning as something more than personal experience; and 4/ both schools of criticism point to the model-character of systemized knowledge. Knowledge of the literary text is seen as relational, that is, as relating to the wider contexts from which this knowledge itself has arisen. But it is precisely in this wider context that the value of theoretical schematization becomes evident as an instrument for critical orientation.

This convergence in textuality has developed out of a common methodological hypothesis which holds that the objects of study (i.e. written texts) constitute a process of everchanging texts which each reader seeks to decipher and to interpret. The opposition this methodological hypothesis offers to the older views of the objects of study as substances which the reader through correct instruction must know is obvious.

Recent interest in reception theory and formalism perhaps arises out of dissatisfaction with historical reconstruction of the author which is not the same as the philological search for the historical context of the literary work. In the best of cases author historicism created a careful patchwork of biographical and textual data held together by speculation. In the worst cases the critic indulged in speculative impressionism under the guise of interpreting what the author was really like. Both reception theory and formalism have disengaged from the biographical hunt for keys to the text and concentrate on close reading of the text; but they nevertheless seek distinct goals. For reception theory seeks intersubjective (i.e. suprapersonal and interpersonal) evidence of meanings as the source of logical operations, whereas the various types of formalist criticism seek to find meaning, or at least a level of meaning, as a result of logical impersonal operations.

This volume contains an edited selection of the papers read at the International Colloquium on *Interpretation of Narrative* held at the University of Toronto, 24 to 27 March 1976 by the Graduate Programme in Comparative Literature. From 1970 to 1976 Toronto has been one of the most exciting centres of Comparative Literature in North America. A succession of major voices have given their support to that endeavour: Hans Georg Gadamer, Paul Ricœur, Hillis Miller, Robert Wiemann, Wolfgang Iser, Hans Robert Jauss, Hayden White, Fredric Jameson, and Tzvetan Todorov. The articles in this collection have been selected for publication because they represent the positions taken at the colloquium and offer the best written re-creation of the dialectic exchange which characterized this meeting.

The papers in the first part by McDonald, Miller, Riffaterre, and Fitch all deal with the methodology of text-oriented criticism. Reiss's paper addresses the assumptions which stand behind these approaches. Reading the five papers together one is immediately struck by the mutual coherence of the authors' positions in their search for a more adequate means of analysis. But there is no question of the importance and the primacy of analysis in the critical inquiry. The first part of the proceedings provides us with an excellent demonstration of expert readers concerned with their methodology and its implicit claims.

The papers in the second part by Martínez Bonati, Iser, Vance, and Hamlin bring to the discussion a fundamental agreement and acceptance of the hermeneutic method and reception theory. The agreement of basic principles gives this part of the proceedings a sense of unity and strength. The three writers are from Santiago, Constance, and Toronto, but they have in common Ingarden, Husserl, and Gadamer. The point I wish to make is that agreement on basic principles has made these papers complementary. The consequent united front gives the impression that the opposition is in disarray, though it does not win the debate.

It is most fitting that these proceedings should end with an attempt to find the holistic identity of interpretation of narrative. The papers in the third part were prepared for the colloquium, although both Hillis Miller's and Paul Hernadi's were published in part afterwards in *Critical Inquiry*. They were given in Toronto, and each in turn assisted in the inquiry. Jauss brought the philosophical questions of hermeneutics into view. Hillis Miller made perhaps the most radical statement, making us question the questioners, and, finally, Paul Hernadi provided us with a map of the intellectual landscape we had covered.

This book has been published with the help of grants from the Canadian Federation for the Humanities, using funds provided by the Social Sciences and Humanities Research Council of Canada, and from the Publications Fund of University of Toronto Press, and with the generous support of the Canadian Comparative Literature Association. We also wish to thank Professor M. Dimić, editor of the *Canadian Review of Comparative Literature*, for his enthusiastic support of this project.

University of Toronto

INTERPRETATION OF NARRATIVE

RALPH COHEN

Introduction: Remarks on Formalist and Hermeneutic Features of the Conference Papers

My subject is 'Formalist and hermeneutic criticism in conflict and concord'; I shall take as the data for examination some of the papers contained in this volume. That the papers present wide variations of subjects derived from the two criticisms should not surprise or dismay us. They are all, despite their variations, literary forms in which readers write analyses of their reading for other readers or in which readers write analyses of the problems involved in the act, process, or theory of reading for other readers. The papers are acts of composition about other acts of composition, or they are acts of composition that theorize about other acts of composition.

To ask whether these papers are examples of formalist or hermeneutic criticism is to treat them as abstracted content, not as the literary forms they obviously are. Literary forms demand of us as readers that we engage them, that we fill in interstices, recognize ambiguities, and seek to understand – though there is little reason to assume that we can complete these papers, any more than we can come to a complete and absolute understanding of Rousseau's *Dialogues* or a story by Flaubert or Balzac.

Every paper is engaged in an act of interpretation and itself needs to be interpreted. Every paper has as one of its features mixed methods of proceeding – logical, psychological, ontological, etc.; a range of data to which it refers; and a method of persuading the reader that the conclusions ought to be accepted. Every paper focuses on certain aspects of the reading of texts and is itself a text. Every paper is, inevitably, a mixture of formalist and hermeneutic criticism. It is itself a series of signs, and it interprets a series of signs. It interprets the objects of representation and is itself an object to be intepreted. If all papers are forms of this combination, what are we to say of Félix Martinez Bonati's paper, which argues that formalist and hermeneutic criticisms represent two incompatible views? This paper develops by antithesis or contrast, so that the two views are seen as resisting fusion. Hermeneutic interpretation, he declares, focuses on natural events as the basis of representation, whereas formalist interpretation focuses on *representation* itself. This reasonable distinction, it should be noted, neglects the function of the choices. For 'to focus' on the events as the basis of representation or as representation itself is not antithetical at all. The two foci are not a logical contradiction.

What if we press this point further and ask whether the distinction between poetic language and natural language does not involve an irreconcilable conflict? If the hypothesis is that poetic language is opposed in function to referential language, then a contradiction it is. But members of the conference do not write in non-poetic, purely referential language. Not only do the papers deny the notion of language as divisible in this manner, but I might point to Hillis Miller's paper as an example of a critical fiction, using the term in the same way that Brian Fitch refers to Bataille's novel as the story of a word. The occasional references to critical metaphors reveal grave doubts about the poetic-natural language distinction. My point here is that verification or support of the 'irreconcilable conflict' depends on very narrow evidence; when Owen Miller argues that referential statements can function with some elements of symbolism, or when Christie McDonald demonstrates that Rousseau's autobiographical dialogues function as fictive entities, then there seems a body of evidence which makes the so-called conflict too narrow to be retained as a useful concept.

What agreements do we find among the two groups of critics with regard to reading? Both assume that the literary work is an event achieved by the interaction of author, text, and reader; that the literary work is a whole (though never completable by readers); and that, although there may be mistaken readings, there is no one correct reading. Both recognize rhetorical, grammatical, and semantic features as systems of relations, hierarchically organized. These systems are identified as groups of conventions, which change in time, and these changes are the result either of changes in the horizon of expectations of readers or in the language codes which they use or understand in reading literature. Thus both groups see as one of the central problems the reading of literature.

The analysis of the process of reading or of a particular reading has resulted in some of the most subtle agreements in the conference. Michael Riffaterre argues that the reader (a critic knowledgeable about literary conventions) experimentally establishes implications of the code of the narrative by observing repetitions and how they function. These functions make it possible for the reader to interrelate description, characters, and objects so that the work as a whole becomes a single sign. Riffaterre has argued elsewhere that such decoding becomes more difficult for later readers and that they have to reconstruct the code with reference to a network of codes. If Riffaterre sees the novel as a sign, Brian Fitch analyses the Bataille novel as the story of a word. Christie McDonald applies a similar code analysis to dialogue. Still another version of code transformations reappears in Hillis Miller's paper when he argues for the transformation of images into each other. The stability of the code is determined by imagistic transformation, by hierarchical interrelation, and by a part-whole network.

In Wolfgang Iser's paper we have an attempt to describe this process of decoding, of hypothesis-making and developing, of the reader's engagement with the text, his selection of a reading construct, and the manner in which this construct is modified. Although he gives no extended examples, the process involves selection of a construction, interpretation, and reinterpretation of background and foreground; indeed a demonstration of how character, imagery, and action relate to the interpretative end. Paul Hernadi shares with Wolfgang Iser the idea that each text has an implied reader and that such a reader must be engaged by the actual reader. And even when Hillis Miller remarks that there is no foreground or background because everything fuses into everything else, he means, I assume, that each image is transformed not at once but in different perspectives. Thus, he does not disagree with Wolfgang Iser's foreground-background distinction; he merely prefers his own way of stating it.

Why, it may be asked, if there is such considerable agreement, do the papers seem to be independent of one another? I think the first difficulty has to do with the nature of narrative. The papers do not make clear to what forms the reading procedures apply. Wolfgang Iser confines his discussion to novels and thus remains within this traditional genre, as do Michael Riffaterre and Brian Fitch. But Professor Fitch wonders whether his procedure of the metaphoric chain applies to all texts; Christie MacDonald refers to the analysis of dialogue as a method for reading narrative; and Paul Hernadi uses examples from the drama. I do not deny that procedures in the dialogue or drama can serve for procedures in narrative. I wish merely to argue that we must be conscious of the implications of our position. The critics may indeed urge that generic considerations are irrelevant in the analyses of narrative, but to do so involves important consequences in the role of forms.

At this point it seems relevant to draw attention to Hans Robert Jauss's argument about changing horizons of expectations in the reader resulting from changes in literary conventions. I have indicated that Michael Riffaterre, Paul Hernadi, Wolfgang Iser, and, I should add, Owen Miller and Eugene Vance, are cognizant of the need to discuss reading in the context of a given time. No model for reading or interpretation is outside time. It therefore becomes necessary to ask, to what extent Rousseau's character in the *Dialogues* is innovative or characteristic. Is Bataille's novel as the story of a word the consequence of all works or only of modern works? The analysis of consciousness or of tropes requires for its definition the diachronic as well as synchronic account.

The historical issue should, perhaps, be put more firmly. Jauss argues that, for readers, horizons of expectations change. Do these changes result in altering the boundaries of interpretation? Are these boundaries genre-bound or are they independent of genres? To what extent are boundaries in some way permanent? If they are not permanent, how do they change?

Many papers make very clear that they are examining tropes, and the subtlety with which they manage this is rewarding. If language is culture-bound, how does the examination of the trope relate to its particular culture? Can one deal with words and images as though the meanings pertinent to them exist outside time?

Eugene Vance suggests that in medieval literature an understanding of tropes is bound up with speech conventions of the period. His approach to strategies for understanding the text is tentative and unsystematic, but it represents an effort to combine historical understanding and an analysis of tropes. Thus the urging of Paul de Man that tropological structures be treated historically is precisely what some of the papers seek to do.

What are the expectations of those who attend a conference on formalist and hermeneutic procedures applied to narrative? They are, I suggest, in view of the varied formalist and hermeneutic practices and theories with regard to narrative, becoming conscious of the possibilities of one's own criticism and of some of the problems that need to be solved, responding to, engaging, enjoying, rejecting views of others: behaving, in other words, as readers grappling with texts. Perhaps it might be said that one of the shortcomings of the conference was the lack of interchange among partici-pants, the neglect of the texts of others. I see the present paper as an attempt to remedy this lack.

The purpose of the conference was not to create unity among critics or theorists, nor to abandon controversy, nor to set up ideal models for criti-cism. The purpose was to help all of us become conscious of what we as critics are doing and grasp the principles governing formalist and heremeneutic theory and practice; to become conscious of variations or innovation in the genres of critical and theoretical writing. Fifteen-minute position papers can do little more than assert positions which we as critical readers or hearers need to explore.

Although I agree that we need to make literary study as systematic as possible in order for it to be a body of knowledge, the concept of 'system' that includes the sentence, the poem, and all literary study as a system is too loose to be reliable. It implies models that do not properly distinguish 'implicit' from 'explicit' systems and do not distinguish assumptions from coherent and consistent interrelations. A poet's assumptions do not form a system in the sense that Frye's *Anatomy* does.

If we employ the concept of a system, the explanation of 'system' is a part of the system itself. This means that some embracing hypothesis is necessary to establish the relation of a system to what is to be explained. To offer such a hypothesis is to attempt to interrelate all parts, and this I suggest can be done by assuming, as I have throughout this paper, that all writing (I put aside oral discourse for the moment) is done in forms. Thus literary theory is itself a form and behaves as other forms by being historically conditioned and participating in interrelations with them. I offer this not as a third appendage to formalism and hermeneutics but as a procedure for dealing with statements such theories make.

To conceive of the papers as forms is central to our question because it raises doubt about some of the procedures for discussing narrative. Narrative is a form, or a part of a form, or both, but whatever it is, it needs to be distinguished from what it is not. What are the underlying assumptions that critics in their papers hold about narrative? Whether writing about codes or expectations, they rely on conventions. If conventions are culture-bound, can they be combined with certain absolutes that have stirred in some of the papers?

Neither codes nor conventions can be defined as self-contained, since by definition they are derived from other works or from non-literary systems. If we are not to deal with codes or conventions as words, but as words that are part of forms, then the shift of words or conventions from one poem to another involves a reordered relationship, a shift in form or style or rhetorical or lexical procedure. The grounds for such shifts – for the contrasting, harmonizing, resisting, supporting of literary interrelations – lie in the personal and social manipulation of forms. The interrelations of forms will thus provide a more systematic manner for doing what we do. Indeed, the repeated use of 'fictive discourse' in the papers, while indicating non-fictive features, suggests that an outmoded language can nest with descriptions that contradict it.

I want to conclude by drawing attention to one of the valuable developments in theory and practice presented to the conference. We have heard a series of papers in which the theories of the aesthetics of response as practiced by Hans Robert Jauss and Wolfgang Iser have led to attempts to relate their views to those of Gérard Genette in the paper of Owen Miller, to those of Austin and Searle in the paper of Paul Hernadi, to that of I.A. Richards in the paper of Cyrus Hamlin. We have thus had an opportunity to witness the papers of the theoreticians of a movement and the effort of others to apply it to formalist procedures. These are acts of generic continuity and theoretical self-consciousness. And they are examples of the kind of interrelations the conference set out to explore.

University of Virginia

PART ONE

VERIFICATION OF FORMALIST ANALYSIS

CHRISTIE V. McDONALD

The Model of Reading in Rousseau's *Dialogues*

Un texte n'est un texte que s'il cache au premier regard, au premier venu, la loi de sa composition et la règle de son jeu. (Jacques Derrida)

R: Je devine ... une contradiction, n'est-ce pas?
F: Non, j'en ai vu l'apparence. On dit que cette apparence est un piège que J.J. s'amuse à tendre aux lecteurs étourdis.
R: Si cela est, il en est bien puni par les lecteurs de mauvaise foi qui font semblant de s'y prendre pour l'accuser de ne savoir ce qu'il dit. (Jean-Jacques Rousseau)

The *Dialogues, Rousseau juge de Jean-Jacques,* is a work which confronts the problem of truth and method explicitly, a work which reflects upon the act of reading within the enclosure of the text itself, and which – because reading and writing are so intimately bound – strives to make language reflect the process of its own begetting. It is a work which thus postulates criteria for the interpretation of texts, and though literary works are important such criteria must also be valid for Rousseau's political and philosophical texts as well. Yet critics have tended to shun this work, which is 'autobiographical,' as either marginal or simply the product of a sick mind, perhaps due to the belaboured anguish it manifests towards the problem of the reader, perhaps due also to the obsessive concern with meaning and authenticity. Whatever the reason, the work entitled the *Dialogues* has been considered Jean-Jacques Rousseau's most eccentric and least approachable text. However, not only does he defend here the manifest core of his beliefs but also his acutely conscious exploitation of the dialogue form makes explicit presuppositions about the nature of language, specifically written language, as communication. Although the autobiographical works come towards the end of Rousseau's life, he indicates that it was only then that he came to the fundamental principles of his thought. In the spectrum of the Rousseau texts, from the early anthropological to the late autobiographical works, the *Dialogues* function as a curiously anachronistic and negative preamble in which Rousseau sets forth the ideals of his life and work and proceeds then to put them radically into question.

In describing the schematic movement of the *Dialogues* I propose to show how Rousseau posits a model of reading which is to reveal truth and how this model is then undermined through the practice of his own writing. One small but significant prefatory remark: Rousseau had been concerned with the problem of the reader throughout his *Confessions* (which precede the *Dialogues* chronologically), and although he had originally intended the work to be in three parts he cut short the project and ended the second – and now last – part with a description of his own disappointed reading of the manuscript: 'J'achevai ainsi ma lecture et tout le monde se tut. Madame d'Egmont fut la seule qui me parut émue; elle tressaillit visiblement; mais elle se remit bien vite, et garda le silence ainsi que toute la compagnie. Tel fut le fruit que je tirai de cette lecture et de ma déclaration.'[1]

Almost as if in response to this defeat, Rousseau opens the *Dialogues* with a preface (entitled 'Sujet et forme de cet écrit') in which he explains the object of the three dialogues that are to follow. The principle concern of the work will be to prove the unity of the author and the work, the unity of the author within himself, and, finally, the unity of the works themselves. Scriptor Rousseau explains how he will absent himself from the three dialogues and become the object of their exploration: he will refer to himself in the third person 'il' and use only his first name, Jean-Jacques. The first protagonist of the work, then, is Rousseau – the first interlocutor of the dialogue – who has read all the works of Jean-Jacques and finds them to be innocent and inspiring, but who does not know the man. The second interlocutor, called the Frenchman, neither knows the man nor has read the works, but he is the spokesman for all the gossip of Rousseau's contemporaries (what he calls public opinion). The goal of the dialogues between these two interlocutors is to uncover the real Jean-Jacques. Several suppositions are entertained: either Jean-Jacques is the innocent man who wrote innocent works, or he is the criminal monster who committed criminal acts; perhaps, even, there are two distinct and different men in question, or perhaps two different men in time – the first good-natured and peaceful, the second hardened, older, and labouring under the threat of a world plot. At the end of the first dialogue the interlocutors come to an impasse, but in an attempt to further the cause of truth Rousseau agrees to meet Jean-Jacques and the Frenchman agrees to read the books. The second dialogue is then devoted to the description of the man by Rousseau (and he turns out to be every bit as innocent and virtuous as one might have supposed), while the third dialogue turns around the Frenchman's reaction to his reading of the works.

No time is wasted in lining up the opposing forces in this quest for truth. At the outset of the first dialogue, interlocutor Rousseau describes an imagi-

---

1 Jean-Jacques Rousseau, *Œuvres complètes*, éd. Bernard Gagnebin et Marcel Raymond (Paris: Gallimard, Bibliothèque de la Pléiade, 1959), I, 656. All quotations from Rousseau's work will refer to the same edition, vols I–IV, and will appear in the text. I have modernized the spelling for the sake of clarity.

nary, ideal world which has all the characteristics of primitive nature and yet which integrates man into a happy society. In this world, which is at the same time very like our own and yet radically different (it is a world of harmony and peace), man would necessarily speak in a manner quite different from our own – speech, as the scriptor Rousseau has explained elsewhere, follows the moral vicissitudes of society in general (iv, 346). Indeed, in the ideal world the initiated recognize each other without the intrusion of mediated language. Within this imaginary realm, located outside the limits of time and space, communication stems from the *sign at its source*, which can never be feigned. When this sign does not emanate from the heart (a crucial term), it cannot reach the heart of another. But, on the other hand, when communication between the hearts does take place, there can be no mistaking it (i, 672). If the sign, as mediation, must become absent at the moment of presence (the moment when the two hearts, as it were, coincide), interlocutor Rousseau's description of the leap beyond language remains nevertheless anchored in the linguistic image of the sign. This 'language beyond language' is the word as presence, as plenitude, and contrasts with written language, which is always derivative, a pale and exterior representation. Hence books would have little place in such a society, and it would require the revelation of an important truth or the rectification of some grave error to stimulate the desire to write (i, 673).

Such of course, is the justification for the *Dialogues*, a work of deep negativity and anguish. And the strategy is clear. By evoking the mythic ideal in the opening pages – utopia is that society in which perfect communication is possible – the *Dialogues* propose to effect a reversal through the dialogual process and thus to occasion the return of the redemptive ideal within the self. Unable to dispel the malicious slander of his contemporaries in any other way, the author of the preface postulates a general hypothesis or fictional conjecture as the method by which he would attain truth, whether that of primitive man or that of the self. Thus giving his enemies every possible advantage (there is, it would seem, a world conspiracy against him), and to himself the severest of handicaps, scriptor Rousseau choses dialogue as the form best suited to dialectical argumentation. More important, he thematizes the presuppositions upon which the dialogue is based so that the work constantly questions its own paradoxical position: how can fabrication, fiction, lies, prove truth? What is the epistemological status of the method?

If Rousseau as scriptor has chosen the dialogue form in order to show, as he says, 'le pour et le contre,' that is, in order to apply a method of contraries to arrive at unity, it is because the dialogue form presupposes the possibility for communication through an intersubjective relationship which is outside or beyond it. Though dialogue, as language, is negativity, the external mediating vehicle which can never attain the inner self, it is at the same time, paradoxically, the only means by which man may express that ineffable sense of self. However, the *Dialogues* suggest that reading, as an act similar to, though different from, dialogue, may become the locus of an immanent utopia of the word. That is, access to authentic dialogue will not come through the progress of the reasoned dialogues themselves, but rather through a proper reading of those texts written by the fictive Jean-Jacques. Character Rousseau is a valid interlocutor because of his status as reader. He says of Jean-Jacques: 'il était pour moi le peintre de la nature et l'historien du cœur humain. Je reconnaissais dans ses écrits l'homme que je retrouvais en moi, et leur méditation m'apprenait à tirer de moi-même la jouissance et le bonheur que tous les autres vont chercher si loin d'eux' (I, 728). In the first dialogue the two interlocutors do not speak from the same position, and their conversation must remain only on the level of reason, for the Frenchman cannot engage in authentic dialogue until he has read. Interlocutor Rousseau reminds the Frenchman: 'Presque tout ce que vous m'avez dit dans cet entretien me prouve que vous n'y parliez pas de vous-même' (I, 771).

The reading the Frenchman gives to Jean-Jacques' works is problematic and is the subject of the entire third dialogue. Unlike interlocutor Rousseau, who is clearly Jean-Jacques' double, the Frenchman does not have this strange sense of familiarity with the author. His reading is explicitly the reading of the other, of all others. At the beginning of the third dialogue, the Frenchman quotes a series of fragments from Jean-Jacques' works in which Jean-Jacques vituperates against men of letters and passes in review doctors, kings, the rich, the great, the English, and women. Presenting the quintessence of Jean-Jacques' hostile attitude toward so many institutions of culture, the Frenchman unwittingly satirizes, or so it would seem, the extremely ambiguous role Jean-Jacques has chosen for himself. Then, lest we be taken in by this parody, the context of the Frenchman's reading is carefully prepared by a trip to the country so that his mind may be freed from the strictures of the society which surrounds him. His own method of reading, far from snapping out a fragment here and there, will be based on the continuous movement of the whole: 'en les achevant, j'examinais comme vous l'aviez désiré, dans quelles dispositions d'âme elles me mettaient et me laissaient' (I, 930). Placing himself in the same position as the author, and sounding his heart, the Frenchman concludes that he cannot but esteem the man of the works. He concludes further, upon a second reading, that Jean-Jacques is an inhabitant of the ideal world and, what is more, that there is an important link between the works. No longer is there any doubt in his mind; the model for this painter and apologist of nature was his own heart.

An important change has taken place in the Frenchman from the first to the third dialogue. Whereas in the first two dialogues he spoke only through the voice of public opinion, in the third he speaks from the heart. The proper reading, based on repetition and continuity, makes possible authentic dialogue between Rousseau and the Frenchman, who is now almost completely won over to the cause: 'Je crois J.J. innocent et vertueux, et cette croyance est telle au fond de mon âme qu'elle n'a pas besoin d'autre confirmation' (I, 945). Now the Frenchman's position is symmetrical to that of interlocutor Rousseau's at the beginning of the first dialogue: he has properly read the works but does not know the man. There remain only two small steps. The first is for the Frenchman to study Jean-Jacques the person (as interlocutor Rousseau has done), but this he refuses to do, declaring that any further proof would now be superfluous. He also refuses the second and last step: to publicly pronounce Jean-Jacques innocent and to set the voice of public opinion right once and for all. Thus at the end of the third dialogue Jean-Jacques has not been vindicated despite the transformation of the Frenchman through the act of reading, and one wonders whether this story does not couch a more general statement about the nature of reading and writing.

The voice of the author, as that of the reader, has been completely subsumed into the text of the *Dialogues*. As such, the work is an extremely complex commentary on the relationship between the author and his text, between the text and the reader, and on the problem of dialogue as writing. In attempting to create the conditions for a proper reading, something somehow goes amiss. At the very moment when unity between the interlocutors becomes possible, either because of a new internal feeling (in the case of the Frenchman) or because of a reinforced sense of inner plenitude (interlocutor Rousseau), the very slight difference between them (the unresolved final steps) is like a crevice through which may be glimpsed the infinity of distorted readings of the future. The problem of the reader has not been resolved. As a parting gesture, the Frenchman offers to become the guardian of the manuscript (which we are reading), to publish it one day in its authentic form, and to do everything in his power to reveal truth. However, as we turn the page to the epilogue, it is as though all the fears of the preface have been fulfilled. There scriptor Rousseau says: 'Si j'osais faire quelque prière à ceux entre les mains de qui tombera cet écrit, ce serait de vouloir bien le lire tout entier avant que d'en disposer et même avant que d'en parler à personne; mais très sûr d'avance que cette grâce ne me sera pas accordée, je me tais, et remets tout à la providence' (I, 659). If the dialogues, doomed thus from the outset, could not somehow realize the goal that they set forth (to move from negation to the positive assertion, to the silent communication of souls), in the supplemental epilogue scriptor Rousseau returns to the first-person 'je' and begins all over again to search for a proper reader. Who will read the *Dialogues*, he worries, and who will keep the manuscript safe from enemies for posterity? For a time it seems as though he will never be able to preserve the manuscript, and when he attempts to place a copy on the altar of the church of Notre Dame, only to discover that the gates are closed, even Heaven appears to have joined the conspiracy. His desperate situation seems irremediable when, suddenly, the vertigo of negativity culminates in a moment of reversal where Rousseau, as scriptor of the epilogue, passes from the clutches of public opinion to the apparent freedom of a peaceful, independent identity. The reversal comes about at the very moment when the 'je,' the scriptor, becomes his own reader in memory: 'Un passage de l'*Émile* que je me rappellai me fit rentrer en moi-même et m'y fit trouver ce que j'avais cherché vainement au dehors ... Ils auront beau faire un J.J. à leur mode, Rousseau restera toujours le même en dépit d'eux' (I, 985). Then, as if there never had been a work such as the *Dialogues*, J.J.'s next and last work begins: 'Me voici donc seul sur la terre, n'ayant plus de frère, de prochain, d'ami, de société que moi-même' (I, 995). It is here that the hermeneutic would seem to be fulfilled for Rousseau, for only as he becomes his own reader, his sole interlocutor, in the *Rêveries*, can the text be a unified whole unfolding as otherness. But if the obsession with the reader disappears only when Rousseau achieves the relationship of self-as-reader to text (as self), it is a position which is already shown to be untenable in the *Dialogues*.

Let us evoke the two approaches at work within the *Dialogues*: the first structural, the second genetic. The structure of the *Dialogues*, described explicitly in the preface, depends upon the functional relationship between the two interlocutors whose views at the beginning are antithetically opposed. Like the hypothesis of fictional conjecture, reasoned dialogue can have no ultimate significance unless grounded in a translinguistic guarantee: that is, the true origin to be revealed through reading. The genetic search (for the self revealed through the text) would pinpoint the source from which the structure is derived and locate the guarantor in truth as presence. And here precisely is the displacement in which we find Rousseau's most forceful and yet least explicit disruption of the hermeneutic, for the story of reading cannot be dissociated from the story of writing, which was of course the explicit theme of the *Essai sur l'origine des langues*.[2]

An indication that disruption of the hermeneutic comes through the interference of writing with reading occurs about three-quarters of the way through the first dialogue. Interlocutor Rousseau is discussing the behaviour of those involved in the conspiracy against Jean-Jacques, lamenting in particular their refusal to confront him (as in a dialogue) with the evidence. He states: 'Car il n'y a point de contradiction dans la vertu, et jamais pour punir un fourbe elle ne permettra de l'imiter' (I, 749). The Frenchman counters

---

2 See Jacques Derrida's decisive analysis of this text in *De la Grammatologie* (Paris: Editions de Minuit, 1967), 235–378.

immediately that Jean-Jacques would not agree with such a statement (at this point the Frenchman is still merely the spokesman for public opinion), and thereupon he quotes a sentence from one of Jean-Jacques' works: 'C'est en le trahissant qu'il faut punir un traître' (I, 749). He then asks interlocutor Rousseau how he would respond to such a maxim. Interlocutor Rousseau's answer comes not at the moral level, but rather at the level of the heart as absolute: 'Ce que votre cœur y répond lui-même,' he replies (I, 749).

Following a discussion of the moral implications of such a maxim, interlocutor Rousseau suddenly remarks, as a kind of afterthought, that he does not remember having read such a statement in Jean-Jacques' works. Then comes the following sequence:

R: Où donc a-t-il établi ce nouveau précepte si contraire à tous les autres?

F: Dans un vers d'une comédie.

R: Quand est-ce qu'il a fait jouer cette Comédie?

F: Jamais.

R: Où est-ce qu'il l'a fait imprimer?

F: Nulle part.

R: Ma foi je ne vous entends point.

F: C'est une espèce de farce qu'il écrivit jadis à la hâte et presque impromptu à la campagne dans un moment de gaîté, qu'il n'a pas même daigné corriger, et que nos Messieurs lui ont volée comme beaucoup d'autres choses qu'ils ajustent ensuite à leur façon pour l'édification publique. (I, 749–50)

What is striking about this passage is that, when asked for the co-ordinates of Jean-Jacques' play, the Frenchman responds with those that usually characterize traditional utopia – as being out of time and space. And this is where interlocutor Rousseau loses the meaning. Although clarification quickly follows – the play, written in a moment of gaiety, had been then stolen by the conspirators – such an explanation hardly accounts either for so gratuitous a theft or for the evasive and intriguing images evoked by the Frenchman. The context of the sentence reveals a situation of alleged injustice in which a young girl – fearing betrayal by her lover – angrily justifies the idea of intercepting a letter she believes to have been written by her lover to a rival. The passage, which thus obliquely refers to the problems (inseparable for scriptor Rousseau) of society, passion, and injustice,[3] locates the point of origin of the conspirators' immoral and highly false behaviour in this single sentence taken from a play by Jean-Jacques which was neither per-

---

3 In the *Essai sur l'origine des langues* and the *Discours sur l'origine de l'inégalité*, Rousseau shows the passage from nature to culture to be threefold: the birth of society was attended by the birth of language and passionate love.

formed nor printed because it had been taken away, erased. Whatever the moral justification for this sentence, so seemingly opposed to the virtuous principles of Jean-Jacques' other works, the sentence – thus obliterated at its inception – proves to be a true origin in more than one way. First, it accurately describes the hypothetical position of the conspirators, whose behaviour thereby testifies to a proper reading at the moral level. Second – and here is the surprise – it is a sentence from a play which was in fact written by scriptor Jean-Jacques Rousseau, entitled l'*Engagement téméraire*, a work published posthumously. Thus the sentence quoted by the Frenchman betrays a sudden slippage between the fiction of the dialogues – designed as negative metaphor to reveal truth as presence – and the literal reference[4] to a work of fiction which exists elsewhere (not nowhere). This slippage puts into question, from the very first dialogue, the ideal of reading to be elaborated throughout the rest of the work.

If the traitorous behaviour of the conspirators, which precludes neither lies nor trickery of any sort, stems from a correct moral reading of the sentence (within the context of moral corruption certain palliatives become necessary, even welcome, as scriptor Rousseau has shown elsewhere) the response of interlocutor Rousseau, with his instantaneous reference to the heart, suggests another equally proper reading. His response depends upon reversal from the negative (here the moral statement) to a positive which not only remains implicit but also requires the leap to another level (the heart as absolute). The two antithetically opposed readings (the one explicit, the other implicit) would seem to stand on equal footing in this passage, thus recapitulating the aporia of the entire first dialogue. However, the revelation of this sentence as a quotation (both absent from and now present in the works) cannot be neglected. The fiction that momentarily and paradoxically loses its fictive stance through reference to yet another fiction disrupts the process of understanding and shifts the referent, from the intersubjective relationship of the text to the reader, to an intertextual one. We may therefore ask whether the concern with reading and the obsession with the world plot are not variants on the theme of writing which had concerned Rousseau in his early anthropological works. The story of reading which is to authenticate the dialogue between the interlocutors is one more self-reflexive, and thus privileged, moment in the ongoing process of writing constantly preoccupied with its own origins.

Université de Montréal

---

4 See Paul de Man's intricate discussion of the problem of language and the referent for Rousseau: 'Theory of Metaphor in Rousseau's *Second Discours*,' *Studies in Romanticism* 12 (Spring 1973), 475–98.

O.J. MILLER

Reading as a Process of Reconstruction: A Critique of Recent Structuralist Formulations

One can trace the general 'accommodation' of poetics[1] to hermeneutics by comparing Tzvetan Todorov's characterization of interpretation in *Qu'est-ce que le structuralisme?* (1968)[2] with his reformulation of the same problem in a recent single volume *Poétique* (1973).[3] In the earlier volume, interpretation (or, as Todorov preferred to call it then, 'description') is seen as having serious limitations which are often unacknowledged by its practitioners. If interpretation has claims to some objectivity, it cannot satisfy its basic principle, which is faithfulness to someone else's text; 'Pour laisser la vie à l'œuvre, le texte descriptif doit mourir; s'il vit lui-même, c'est qu'il tue l'œuvre qu'il dit.'[4] Moreover the 'description' of particular facts about a specific text cannot constitute a science, and, Todorov concludes, 'si la description ne peut satisfaire à des critères scientifiques, elle perd sa raison d'être.'[5] In his more recent volume, Todorov's reservations about interpretation are much less categorical. Poetics and interpretation are now seen as two independent but complementary approaches to literary studies. Neither of the two activities is primary to the other; they are both 'secondary.' 'Une réflexion théorique sur la poétique qui n'est pas nourrie d'observations sur les œuvres existantes se révèle stérile et inopérante.'[6] But warns Todorov, this interpenetration, this constant movement between poetics and interpretation, should not prevent us from distinguishing clearly, at an abstract level, the differing objectives of both approaches. And in an even more recent publication,[7] French structuralists have shown themselves to be more aware of two distinct traditions of theories of discourse, which Todorov calls

1 Understood here specifically as 'structuralist poetics.'
2 'Poétique' in *Qu'est-ce que le structuralisme?*, ed. F. Wahl (Paris: Seuil, 1968), 97–166. In *Poétique de la prose*, Todorov attempts to distinguish between 'lecture,' 'commentaire,' 'description,' and 'interprétation.' See 'Comment lire' in *Poétique de la prose* (Paris: Seuil, 1971) 241–53.
3 *Qu'est-ce que le structuralisme? 2: Poétique*, Coll. Points, no. 45 (Paris: Seuil, 1968). Although the date of the original publication is retained for this single-volume edition, the actual text is a considerable reworking of the original one and appeared in 1973.
4 *Qu'est-ce que le structuralisme?* ed. F. Wahl (Paris: Seuil, 1968), 103
5 Ibid.
6 *Qu'est-ce que le structuralisme 2: Poétique*, Coll. Points, no 45 (Paris: Seuil, 1968), 21
7 See *Poétique*, 23 (1975), a whole issue devoted to 'Rhétorique et herméneutique.'

'rhetoric' and 'hermeneutics,' standing in opposition as a theory of 'production' to a theory of 'comprehension' and 'reception.' But hermeneutic theory envisaged by structuralists appears to be very different from that elaborated by the German phenomenologists. It remains to be seen whether the emergence of a type of 'cognitive rhetoric' preserving the 'facts' of immanence and linguistic basis so dear to French structuralists and semioticians can be reconciled with the German tradition rooted in phenomenology and concerned with the interaction of reader and textual poles.

The position taken in this paper is that the two approaches are not only complementary but interdependent; one approach cannot proceed without assuming the other. This situation may be stated in the form of two propositions.

A. Just as there can be no speech act without knowledge of the linguistic system, so there can be no reading process and interpretation without the assumption of a system of literary discourse. It follows that the articulation of this system, which is the concern of poetics, can only enrich the possibilities for interpretation. It is doubtful whether any hermeneutists would challenge this proposition, though in practice they appear to minimize its implications.

B. Since the articulation of the system of literary discourse can only be achieved through the medium of a text or texts, the reading process, and inevitably the interpretation, are the only means that will provide access to the elaboration of the system. Poetics hence implies, a priori, interpretation, just as hermeneutics as a theory of interpretation based on text-reader interaction paradoxically implies, a priori, if not an articulation, at least some sort of implicit knowledge of the system of literary discourse. It appears therefore that we are caught in a circle, though not a vicious one it is hoped, but one where we must make a choice and an assumption.

It is doubtful whether any fully committed formalist would accept the latter proposition. Access to and elaboration of the system of literary discourse do not imply for the formalist the need to interpret. In his recent study, 'La Lecture comme construction,'[8] Todorov suggests that the reconstruction of the fictional referent of narrative through the reading process involves two separate stages: 'understanding,' which is achieved through a process of signification, and 'interpretation,' which is achieved through a process of symbolization. To articulate the system one needs only to 'understand' the text, to be concerned in other words with that meaning which is immanent and signified by the text; it does not involve us in the process of symbolization where the reader's own world is engaged. This duality, signification/symbolization, is crucial to the structuralist argument that poetics

8 'La Lecture comme construction,' *Poétique* 24 (1975) 417–25

is founded on an objective and scientific analysis, the absence of which was discerned as the weakness in the interpretational approach to literary studies. As such, it bears closer scrutiny not so much in terms of whether the two processes can be distinguished at an abstract or theoretical level but rather whether, in the practical confrontation of reader and text, we can 'understand' without interpreting.

Before dealing with the distinction between signification and symbolization, Todorov devotes two important sections of his article to the nature of referential discourse and to what he calls 'narrative filters.' With respect to referential discourse, he makes four essential points. 1/ Not all statements that compose a narrative are referential; some are, some are not. 2/ Only referential statements allow the reader to construct an imaginary universe. 3/ Narrative statements are referential or they are not; there are no intermediary degrees. 4/ Referential statements lead to constructions of differing quality depending on their degree of generality or on the degree to which they evoke events perceptible to the senses.

While it is possible by and large to concur with these assertions, one cannot help feeling that they omit an important factor, namely the way referential statements function when inserted into a fictional narrative and are thereby subjected to various generic codes. To illustrate this point, one might cite an example sanctioned by Todorov himself in his study *Introduction à la littérature fantastique*.[9] A proverb such as 'all that glitters is not gold'[10] is presented as an example of pure allegory. In one sense this statement is referential and provides a mental reconstruction of gold glittering. But, as Todorov himself notes, the literal referential meaning passes almost unperceived since one reads the proverb at an allegorical level. In other words, the allegorical code inhibits the unfettered construction of the fictional referent ('gold glittering') and substitutes a conceptual world, or rather produces in the mind of the reader an abstract discourse ('appearances are deceptive'). Thus statements which we may identify discursively as being referential, may, when inserted in a text which is generically coded (in this case strongly allegorical), function in the same way as abstract discourse.

One might even go further and say that it is doubtful if any modern fictional text is entirely free of some kind of symbolic coding which undermines the free construction of the fictional referent. As Genette has pointed out with respect to Hemingway's most realistic novel, a referential statement such as 'he felt cold sweat run down his back' is translated without hesitation

---

9 *Introduction à la littérature fantastique* (Paris: Seuil, 1970)
10 The actual proverb cited by Todorov is 'tant va la cruche à l'eau qu'à la fin se casse.' I have substituted an English proverb which in no way alters the line of argument pursued.

by the reader as 'he was afraid.'[11] Or, as Seymour Chatman's application of Barthes' categories of cardinal functions, catalysts, indices, and informants to Joyce's story *Eveline* has shown, it is difficult if not impossible to avoid attributing to every segment of the story the term index, since any element may have a symbolic function.[12] To these remarks Todorov might well answer, as he has done with respect to allegory, that one must distinguish between symbolic coding which is explicit and that which is implicit. 'Il faut insister sur le fait qu'on ne peut parler d'allégorie à moins d'en trouver des indications explicites à l'intérieur du texte. Sinon, on passe à la simple interprétation du lecteur; et dès lors, il n'existerait pas de texte littéraire qui ne soit allégorique, car c'est le propre de la littérature d'être interprétée et réinterprétée par ses lecteurs, sans fin.'[13] But the explicit/implicit distinction merely returns us to the distinction between the two processes of signification and symbolization, which we will deal with presently.

Todorov's second section deals with 'narrative filters,' and again, by and large, there can be little quarrel with his discussion of how the various aspects of time, mode, and vision act as filters modifying the construction by the reader of the fictional referent. Yet an inevitable conclusion seems to flow from his remarks regarding the reading process: put simply, if time, mode, and vision act as filters which must be penetrated before we can begin the process of reconstruction and if it can be shown that these filters are factors in the interpretation of narrative, it follows that the reader cannot proceed to a level of signification without inevitably involving himself in a process of symbolization. One could of course argue that the filters are not operative until the process of signification has taken place. Such a position, however, seems untenable. Much more tenable, in our view, is the assertion that not only can no construction of a fictional referent take place without first passing through the narrative filters but also these filters are necessary agents in generating the interpretation of the narrative, at least of its modern form, the novel.

There seems to be a fundamental difference between a discussion of mode, time, or vision when the purpose is to describe the system of narrative discourse and a discussion of the same aspects when the intention is to consider the process of reconstructing the imaginary universe. In the first case we start from the proposition that the text generates both 'diegesis' and 'narration' in the sense that Genette uses these terms in *Figures III*.[14] Thus

11 *Figures III* (Paris: Seuil, 1972) 213
12 'New ways of analysing narrative structures,' *Language and Style*, 2 (1969) 3–36. Chatman uses the categories elaborated by Roland Barthes in his pioneering article, 'Introduction à l'analyse structurale des récits,' *Communications*, 8 (1966) 1–27. An English version of Barthes' article appears in *New Literary History*, 6 (Winter 1975) 237–72.
13 *Introduction à la littérature fantastique*, 79
14 *Figures III*, 71–6

we may discuss temporal questions of order, frequency, and duration or modal questions of distance and perspective as involving relationships between diegesis and text, and excluding questions of 'voice.' In the second case, we start from the proposition that the narrational process (or as Genette calls it, 'narration') generates both text and diegesis. Thus, in constructing the fictional referent, temporal and modal questions become factors of narrational strategies and essential elements of interpretation.

A series of brief examples may serve to substantiate these very general comments. Analeptic and proleptic segments in Katherine Mansfield's story 'The Daughters of the Late Colonel' are not simply anachronies of temporal order to be noted and categorized. Their situation in the text, the form they take, the interplay between the two categories are fundamental to the narrational strategy and interpretation of the story. The dominance of narrativized discourse or 'transposed' discourse (to use Genette's term) over reported discourse or 'immediate' discourse is not only a regulator of distance between text and diegesis in Camus' *L'Etranger* but also a function of the interpretation of the narrator/character and hence of the story he mediates. Finally the subtle modulation of inner and outer perspectives in Ring Lardner's story 'Haircut' is one of the central devices contributing to the interpretation of the story. It is hoped that these somewhat truncated illustrations substantiate the view that narrative filters, in modern fiction at least, are essential contributors to the interpretation of narrative.

Todorov's third section brings us to the heart of the problem. Here he proposes four stages involved in constructing the imaginary universe. Stage 1 is called the 'author's narrative.' Stage 2 is the 'imaginary universe evoked by the author.' To pass from stage 1 to stage 2 requires a process of signification. Stage 3 is the 'imaginary universe constructed by the reader.' To pass from stage 2 to stage 3 requires a process of symbolization. Stage 4 is the 'reader's narrative.'

Before dealing with the signification/symbolization distinction, some general comments are necessary regarding this four-tiered system describing the reading process. First, it is somewhat surprising to find the term 'author' appearing at state 2, and, unless we are to place Todorov in the Hirsch camp,[15] it is assumed that stage 2 should read: 'the imaginary universe

15 The position of E.D. Hirsch is well known in North American circles. In *Validity in Interpretation* (New Haven: Yale University Press, 1967), Hirsch maintains that the text preserves an 'original' meaning which is that intended by the author. In a more recent article, ('Three Dimensions of Hermeneutics,' *New Literary History*, 3 (Winter 1972) 245–61), Hirsch is less emphatic about authorial-intended meaning and now draws a distinction between 'original meaning' and 'anachronistic meaning' (or 'significance'). This distinction is not entirely clear to me and appears to approximate at times the signification/symbolization dichotomy developed by Todorov. It is doubtful however that Hirsch would consider that both 'original meaning' and 'anachronistic meaning' do not require an act of interpretation.

evoked by the narrative text.' It is assumed also that stage 2 refers not to what is inherent or immanent in the text per se but to the realization or actualization of what is immanent in the text within the reader's mind. In other words, it is the actualization by a real reader of an implicit reading position immanent in the text and open to semiological analysis. Secondly, it is somewhat difficult within a structuralist framework, except at a theoretical level, to envisage a distinction between stages 3 and 4, between the 'imaginary universe constructed by the reader' and his verbal or written transcription of this experience in the form of a 'reading.' Either one is obliged to contradict the structuralist position, based on Saussurian linguistics, and assert that thought precedes verbal expression, or to contend that the reader's narrative creates its own reality, a very unhappy notion for an interpreter of texts and one that Barthes has explored in *Critique et Vérité*.[16]

The critical distinction in terms of the structuralist argument however is the assertion that between stages 2 and 3 there are two distinct processes, signification and symbolization. It should be emphasized again that there can be little objection to this distinction at a theoretical level. It seems self-evident that the text signifies and in reconstructing the fictional universe the reader symbolizes. The real question, however, is whether in any practical manner the two processes can be distinguished. To answer this crucial question it is necessary to examine in greater detail the manner in which Todorov demonstrates that there *is* a clear difference between stages 2 and 3.

He argues, for instance, with reference to Constant's novel, *Adolphe*, that no reader doubts that Ellénore lives first with the Count de P. and subsequently leaves him to live with Adolphe. In other words, only a process of signification is involved. On the other hand, argues Todorov, there is no means to establish with the same certainty whether Adolphe is weak or simply sincere. Here, a process of symbolization is involved. He concludes therefore that Ellénore's exchange of lovers is signified by the text and 'understood,' whereas Adolphe's alleged weakness or sincerity is symbolized by other facts in the imaginary universe and hence 'interpreted.' But surely such a conclusion depends upon a nineteenth-century novelistic convention, namely that Adolphe reliably reports the facts. Such contracts between reader and text must surely vary with time. It can hardly be said that they are immanent features of the text. Does one, for instance, read Camus' novel *La Chute* in terms of the same novelistic conventions? A contemporary reader must surely read *Adolphe* in the light of *La Chute*, not to mention the multitude of stories related by unreliable narrators that populate fiction since the end of the last century. It is not certain that every contemporary reader

16 *Critique et vérité* (Paris: Seuil, 1966). Barthes attempts here to make a threefold distinction between 'science de la littérature,' 'critique,' and 'lecture.'

will 'understand' the signifying elements of the text in the same way as Todorov does.

Even if for the sake of argument one concedes that certain elements in the construction of the fictional referent are purely signified (such as Ellénore's exchange of lovers) and other elements are purely symbolized (such as Adolphe's alleged weakness or sincerity), it still seems that these two examples provide extremes of the text and that a greater part of the narrative segments cannot be construed in the same way as either purely signifying or purely symbolizing. To illustrate this point one might consider a passage which occurs early in the novel where the narrator-Adolphe comments on his early life. 'J'avais contracté dans mes conversations avec la femme qui la première avait développé mes idées une insurmontable aversion pour toutes les maximes communes et pour toutes les formules dogmatiques.'[17] From this segment of referential discourse, one presumably constructs, in terms of the process of signification, a mental representation of Adolphe's conversations with the woman and his gradual rejection of aphorisms. But throughout the novel the narrator has recourse to maxims and formulas as part of his narrative strategy. Consequently, my 'understanding' of the segment quoted is profoundly influenced by my recognition of this strategy. The manner in which I construct the segment is dependent upon my resolving a series of questions, the answers to which are hardly signified by the text. Is the alleged aversion to aphorisms an untruth told by the narrator about his past life? Is it an indicator of the difference between the narrator (the older man) and the character (the younger man), the character having an aversion to aphorisms, the narrator a fondness for them? Whatever the reader's final interpretation of this segment, it surely colours his reconstruction of the fictional referent. The words undoubtedly signify, but they automatically engage the reader in an interpretative process, especially since, nine lines earlier, the narrator has had recourse to one of his aphorisms.

It may be an oversimplification to attempt to resolve the issue by stating that where it is claimed that certain meanings are immanent, that the text is signifying and the reader 'understanding,' it is more correct to say that there is general reader agreement on interpreting that particular segment; and where it is claimed that a process of symbolization is involved and the reader is interpreting, there is merely disagreement in interpreting a particular segment. But such a resolution of the issue of symbolization/signification is better discussed in terms of the theoretical notions of 'determinacy' and 'indeterminacy' as elaborated by the hermeneutists[18] rather than within a structuralist framework.

17 *Adolphe* (Paris: Classiques Garnier, 1959) 25
18 See specifically Wolfgang Iser, 'Indeterminacy and the Reader's Response in Prose Fiction,' *Aspects of Narrative*, ed. J. Hillis Miller (New York: English Institute Essays), 1–45.

It is necessary now to take up another point raised by Todorov, namely the constraints imposed on the process of symbolization by the process of signification. These are of two kinds. The first are furnished by the text itself; the author (and here Todorov *does* use the term 'author') teaches us in a very short time how to interpret the events he evokes. The second series of constraints originate, according to Todorov, in the cultural context. The second point needs little comment; it accounts not only for individual interpretations of a particular narrative but also for varying interpretations throughout history. The first point, however, needs much closer examination. The contention here is that the text teaches the reader how to interpret the diegetic events. Without disagreeing wholly with this assertion, one must express certain reservations if it is being implied that the teaching process is signified by the text rather than an act of interpretation. On this point Todorov is somewhat unclear, though his analysis of *Adolphe* suggests that he indeed believes this process to be immanent in the text and thereby signified by it. The examples he quotes imply that the exegetic function communicated by the text is in direct correlation to the meta-exegetic function whereby the author initiates the reader into a system of interpretation that applies to the text. It appears somewhat dubious to assume automatically an homologous relationship between on one hand the narrational situation (involving the narrator and narratee) and on the other the author-reader relationship. An example chosen by Todorov himself from Constant's novel supports this view. Todorov assumes that the aphorisms in *Adolphe* indicate to the reader that individual actions are to be interpreted as a result of psychological laws contained in the aphorisms. While there is no doubt that this is part of the *narrator's* intention, it is possible to interpret the use of aphorisms as justifications of unjustifiable individual actions, in other words as part of the narrator's rhetoric or 'mauvaise foi.' Such a reading of *Adolphe* (and it cannot be considered as an intentionally perverse one) precludes accepting the interpretational process thematized in the novel in a meta-exegetic fashion, or to put it another way: in teaching the reader how *not* to interpret events, the process paradoxically teaches him how, indeed, to interpret. That Todorov's 'understanding' of the way aphorisms function in *Adolphe* is diametrically opposed to that suggested here is not of great consequence, providing we consider the matter a question of interpretation. What is important is the realization that the text does not signify its own interpretational process; it symbolizes it. To read a text 'auto-representationally' is still to interpret it.

The final section of Todorov's article deals precisely with the type of narrative where the process of constructing a fictional universe by a real reader is thematized in the text. Todorov notes that to some extent all fictional texts thematize this process. His choice of Stendhal's *Armance* to explicate in this way is justified on the basis that the process of construction is a major theme in this novel. One may perhaps question whether or not an 'auto-representational' reading of a literary work can be said to validate a critical or theoretical proposition about literature. However, if we accept the premise that it does, one might equally explicate in auto-representational terms, a novel where the process of reconstruction is of paramount importance – say Faulkner's *Absalom Absalom*.

In this novel, Shreve and Quentin set out not only to 'understand' what happened (to determine what events occurred and what they signified at the time of their occurrence) but to interpret what happened (to determine what these events symbolize in terms of themselves and their own present). When they have sifted through as many facts and versions of those facts as possible, they are still unable to 'understand' the events fully. Only in an act of imaginative interpretation do the events take on some meaning. If this interpretation of the novel has some validity, the Faulknerian text is telling us that the process of reconstruction by the reader is an integrative, holistic endeavour where to 'understand' is to interpret. Thus while it may be possible on the basis of a 'cognitive rhetoric' such as that outlined by Dan Sperber in a recent article in *Poétique*[19] to work out a logic that determines the 'sous-entendus' and 'lacunes' of particular narrative statements in a text, it is doubtful whether a hermeneutics, constructed on a sound linguistic basis and maintaining the concern for literary studies to be based on an examination of the immanent and signifying aspects of a text, can hope to explain the elaborate process whereby the human mind reconstructs an imaginary universe from a reading of the most innocent modern text. Here modern hermeneutics, founded on phenomenology, seems to offer a more profitable avenue of research, despite the obvious distaste such an approach might hold for those grounded in analytical philosophy or desirous of formulating a linguistic or discursive basis for literary studies.

University of Toronto

19 'Rudiments de rhétorique cognitive,' *Poétique* 23 (1975) 389–415

MICHAEL RIFFATERRE

The Reader's Perception of Narrative: Balzac's *Paix du ménage*

The present trend of studies on the narrative is towards an autonomous semiotics of the narrative, independent of the semiotics of the various forms which actualize narrative structures at the test surface,[1] and even more remote from the semantics of a particular tale, short story, or novel. This trend has an obvious drawback: at most it can yield a grammar of narrative possibilities and map out an abstract typology. This sort of grammar and typology cannot possibly explain more than the production of a text. Within that text it can describe the functions embodied in actors and their story, including the relationship between narrator and narratee, as opposed to the relationship between narration and reader.[2] But this approach cannot show how the functions are actualized at the surface of the text in its words; hence it must fail to explain the reader's perception of these, so that even though narrative analysis does give the rules of a text's grammar, or perhaps only parameters for developing such rules, it cannot explain the whole of the literary phenomenon, namely the interrelationship or interaction between text and reader.

Of course, it is perfectly possible to separate the two – the text as narrative and the text as literariness (that is, the text as an object of the reader's perception) – for the purpose of isolating problems, as long as we remember that the picture remains incomplete and cannot be interpreted without presupposition of the eliminated factor. But even such a methodology seems to rest upon a questionable postulate of Greimas's[3]: that the narrative at its

---

1 At the surface, that is, in its lexical, syntactic and stylistic features. See Claude Bremond, *Logique du récit* (Paris: Seuil, 1973) 46. The first part of the book convincingly exposes the shortcomings of this sort of typology. Propp initiated this approach; its most prominent proponent is now Greimas. On Bremond's own shortcomings see W.O. Hendricks, 'The Work and Play Structures of Narrative,' *Semiotica* 13 (1975) 281–328.

2 Gérard Genette, *Figures III* (Paris: Seuil, 1972) 265. On the 'reader's narrative' see Tzvetan Todorov, 'La Lecture comme construction,' *Poétique* 24 (1975) 417–25.

3 A.J. Greimas, *Sémantique structurale* (Paris: Larousse, 1966) 158–9: 'the semiotic level common to the various forms of narrative must be distinguished from the linguistic level and comes logically before the latter no matter what language is selected to actualize the former' (my translation). Greimas's most recent effort to reconcile textual surface structures and narrative structures does not abandon this postulate (Greimas, *Maupassant: la sémiotique du texte* [Paris: Seuil, 1976]).

immanent level is organized *before* its textual manifestations. From this postulate Greimas draws the conclusion that significance is not generated directly by the text but starts with the narrative structures. The supposition that the structures come before the actualization is no doubt logically true.[4]

Analysis therefore assumes that the text is the end result of a generative process. But *that* is irrelevant to a study of the narrative as an aspect of literature, for the text is, from the standpoint of text-reader dialectics, a starting point. It is with the text that the reader begins; it is to the text that he tries to adjust his own mythological or sociolectic input; it is upon the text that he builds his hermeneutic constructions. No abstract narrative typology can do justice to these reactions, because they are reactions to concrete linguistic forms. And unless analysis concerns itself with these concrete signs and their decoding by the reader, the uniqueness of each verbal work of art will remain unexplainable. I am not suggesting that we stop trying to find general rules, since there is no knowledge without such rules. I only propose that we seek general rules at another level. Instead of only looking for rules regulating narrative structures, I propose that we look for rules regulating the actualization of such structures in the text, that is, regulating the very performance of literature as communication. To the general conditions of communication, narrativity adds the constraints imposed by the succession of events it presupposes (suspense, teleology, with the outcome positively or negatively conforming to previsibility). However, these constraints are meaningless outside the meaning (literal or metaphorical) of the events and characters represented. For these latter are not beings or things, they are words already endowed with a pre-existent meaning. Communication will depend upon that meaning, and upon the semantic shifts – the catachresis of traditional rhetoric – resulting from equivalences posited by a narrative between representations of concepts separate in language. Nor is this all. Without actualization rules, there is no accounting for the text's ability to force the reader's attention towards its significance-carrying features (as opposed to its meaning as a 'story'), or for its ability to function as a set of constraints upon intepretation. Such rules must therefore explain how the reader retroactively recognizes details which must at first have seemed

---

4 But I am not sure it is genetically true. In the author's mind, surely (that is, in his language), verbal collocations, semantic fields and their lexical corollaries, the descriptive systems, as well as rhetorical tropes, precede and control the selection of narrative structures. Linguistic constraints must necessarily precede the modalities of discourse (of Saussure's *parole*). Of course, however correct this view of textual genesis may be, it is irrelevant to the present discussion, because anything going on in the author's mind is irrelevant so long as it does not show up in the text itself.

negligible or merely incidental, and how he interprets them as keys to the symbolism(s) of the text.[5]

My example is Balzac's *La Paix du ménage* (*Domestic Bliss*, or *A Truce in the Family*). It serves my purpose well because of its very brevity. The limited space[6] within which the plot must unfold gives the novelette an almost schematic quality, which brings to the fore the mechanically perfect interlocking of its episodes. The imbroglio is at once intricate and easily unravelled; it has 'a didactic clarity'[7] fascinating to connoisseurs, who rationalize it as a carryover of state techniques to the novel.[8]

According to the novelist's expressed intent, however, the true centre of interest should be moral: this is a *roman de mœurs*, a study of French mores in the heyday of the Napoleonic Empire, a dissolute era of open, feverish, pleasure-seeking, especially by the young women in pursuit of the Emperor's young heroes. The plot, rather in the vein of light comedy, works on the boomerang principle. A rake tries to seduce the wife of the man whose mistress he has already stolen from him; by his courtship he helps the wife win back her husband and loses his own mistress to a third party. The wife leads the debauchee on by seeming to accept a valuable diamond from him, whereas it is in fact her own jewel, recently 'lost' by her husband, secretly given to his mistress, who in turn gave it to her other lover, our own rake. Armed with this evidence, the wife forces her husband to confess his errors. Aside from the happy ending – which properly takes place in the bedroom – the whole series of events unrolls during a splendid ball given by a senator to celebrate one of Napoleon's victories. The husband has never had any intention of bringing his wife to the ball; she shows up unexpectedly, unescorted, to spy on him. She sits down all by herself in a spot that permits her to watch everything and be seen by everyone. She is beautiful, un-

---

5 On this identification of a narrative text's 'strategic points,' see Roland Barthes, 'Introduction à l'analyse structurale des récits,' *Communications* 8 (1966) 1–27, and Philippe Hamon, 'Clausules,' *Poétique* 24 (1975) 495–526. Balzac on these: 'aujourd'hui que toutes les combinaisons possibles paraissent épuisées ... l'auteur croit fermement que les détails seuls constituent désormais le mérite des ... romans' (now that all possible combinations seem to have been exhausted ... this writer firmly believes that henceforward the details alone will constitute the worth of novels) (quoted by Maurice Bardèche, *Balzac romancier*, [Paris: Plon, 1940] 202).

6 Some sixty pages long, thirty-five in the small print of the *Bibliothèque de la Pléiade*. I quote from the first volume of that edition (ed. M. Bouteron, Paris: Gallimard, 1951); translations are mine. *La Paix du ménage* was published in 1830, along with five other *Scenes of Private Life*.

7 The formula is from a contemporary's introduction to the collection, commissioned by Balzac himself (*Pléiade*, vol. 11, 164).

8 On the similarity to dramatic technique, see Herbert J. Hunt, *Balzac's Comédie humaine* (London: Athlone Press, 1964) 25. On the *Scenes* see Bardèche, *Balzac romancier*, 176–203. The dramatic schematization is a Balzac constant.

known, unattended; naturally the men get wicked ideas, the women become jealous, and the husband is seized with helpless frustration, convinced that she has come here to repay his unfaithfulness in kind.

She is literally the centre of attention. First, at the narrative level, she is the focus of the novel, being the object of all desires – desire to reconquer, or to possess, or at least to know. Secondly, at the descriptive level this focus coincides with the physical centre of the setting, the point of maximal light and maximal visibility or exposure, beneath a huge ornamental candelabrum. Common to all episodes of the story is the intent gaze of characters watching, ogling, spying – the would-be seducer stares at the wife, who is being observed by his mistress, by the husband, and by another witness, who is also eyeing the other two and who will exploit the jealousy of the mistress to his own advantage. Meanwhile the wife is watching her husband, thus closing the circle of gazes and desires. This is the mechanism of suspense and the motor of the reader's interest. These relationships can be readily translated into narrative structures. For instance, I might use the scheme of alternations between a creative and a destructive phase proposed by Bremond as the basic structure of narrativity.[9] We have here an exemplary case of equilibrium (presented by the circularity of desires) generating disequilibrium. The rake achieves this by acting to satisfy a new urge (his craving to possess the wife) in accordance with the function he embodies as a character (here, an automatic cancellation of the melioration process drives him to start a degradation process every time, as he abandons the one conquest in trying for another). Moreover, the novel's narrative dynamics can be epitomized by the perfect balance between the two basic processes, since the rake's self-destructive conduct corresponds, step by step, to the wife's improvement of her own lot. That these two processes are complementary is made obvious by the fact that she does not do much of anything; what her counterpart does negatively in his code becomes positive when translated into her code.

This combination is so simple it can apply to a number of texts. Hence it fails to account for the specificity of *La Paix du ménage*. At best it can lead us to an evaluation, very general and therefore of dubious usefulness, of the novel's achievement in striking a near-perfect equipoise between conflicting forces, thus creating an enjoyably high tension.

However, there is one textual feature pertinent to the uniqueness of this particular narrative. It is the link meshing the two unrelated traits into one and creating the almost mechanical interplay that weaves together actions and characters, and the story as moral lesson (or rather the parody of one). This feature is the formal constant at the surface of the text without which

9 Bremond, *Logique*, 162–73, 282–308 (amélioration and dégradation), on motivations, 187–8.

the structures outlined above would have no effect upon the reader, nor would they control his attention. This constant is the visual detail of the candelabrum, the one detail made mechanically conspicuous by repetition.[10] During each of the aforementioned episodes the candelabrum is alluded to, or described, in a relation of physical contiguity to the wife and naturally of grammatical contiguity to any word or periphrasis designating her. This constant continuity is overtly developed into a trope, since the stylistic structures make the candelabrum a metonym for the wife. In fact, this metonymy exactly corresponds to and formally represents the coincidence of narrative and descriptive focus.

The function of metonymy in the mimesis of reality and especially in literary realism was established long ago by Jakobson. Even the most unsophisticated reader, who may not know how to define the trope, is at least dimly aware of the importance that peripheral descriptions of things assume in a novel and of their use as periphrases to designate characters, their emotions, their state of mind, and especially their mental and moral development. What needs to be pointed out is that the text itself provides guidance to the reader in his interpreting of metonymies. At the very beginning of the novel (on its second page), the reader is confronted with an example of how a metonymy signifies, suggesting the way in which later metonymies will have to be deciphered. The metonymy at first looks like nothing more than a simile illustrating a point in a code amusingly borrowed from the language and stereotypes of a time when everybody saw everything from the viewpoint of the Emperor, master of all bodies and souls in France: 'les passions [avaient] des dénouements aussi rapides que les décisions du chef suprême de ces kolbacs, de ces dolmans et de ces aiguillettes qui plurent tant au beau sexe' (993: passions with denouements as abrupt as the decisions made by the supreme commander of these busbies, these dolmans, these shoulder knots so pleasing to the fair sex). Under the guise of a simile, however, the reader really gets a second reading, in figurative terms, of the moral law which has just been stated in abstract terms: 'hommes et femmes, tous se précipitaient dans le plaisir avec une intrépidité qui semblait présager la fin du monde ... L'engouement des femmes pour les militaires devint comme une frénésie' (992–993: men and women alike hurled themselves into pleasure with a boldness that seemed to presage the end of the world ... The women's infatuation with military men became a sort of frenzy).

The obvious, almost comical, substitution of military attire for hero as an

10 Repetition, of course, pertains here to the narrative structure. Otherwise, allusions to lavish, luxurious lighting are a descriptive commonplace in nineteenth-century French treatments of the ball or party theme (e.g., Balzac, *Sarrasine*, *Pléiade*, vol. 6, 79; Flaubert, *Madame Bovary*, Part I, chap. 8; the cliché 'éclairer a giorno'). The departure here is the fact that the light is *described* as a focus of attention, and in the text *is* such a focus.

object of desire instructs the reader of the text's basic postulate, that everything described must be a sign for something else. The thing described is three times meaningful: as a depiction anchoring the story in reality, as a reference to a paranoia shared by all actors, and as an indirect, symbolic representation or summation of what is going on next to the thing. In each case the metonymic link is established not merely by the physical contiguity of the words' referents, but also by a verbal contiguity, in terms of lexical collocations already established as stereotyped commonplaces. The semantics of a specific narrative are therefore developed under the constraints not just of language, as lexicon and grammar, or of reality, but also of a semiotic network.

This general rule applies to the candelabrum in a way pertinent to the narrative, because at each turning point in the unfolding of events the candelabrum-wife metonymy is given special status as a signifying complex and as an attention-getting or decoding-control device by the use of formal manipulations. The candelabrum's isolation underscores the centrality of the character, and its main physical feature, the light flowing from it so abundantly, is used as a code to heighten the tantalized curiosity or desire of the other characters (the first question about the wife addressed to the host is mistakenly understood as a question about the style and cost of the candelabrum[11]) and as a symbol of that curiosity or desire. That is, it works as motivation in the story and as a hermeneutic model for the reader. For instance, the wife as target is represented by her quality of riddle to be solved, a quality the reader cannot miss, for she is sitting right under the light and yet is depicted oxymoronically as one buried in darkness, shoved into a dark corner,[12] and the desire to solve the riddle, a metonym for desire, is couched in terms of lighting, like a pun: 'l'homme le plus déterminé à mettre en lumière notre plaintive inconnue [qui] a un peu l'air d'une élégie' (966: a man most determined to throw light upon our doleful mystery woman, who is something like an elegy incarnate).

I mentioned jealousy as the motor that sets the various characters going in unison, like clockwork, each one acting to keep the others from finding out who or what is worrying him or her: the jealousy suffered by husband and mistress is incapable of admitting who is causing it. The husband would rather murder than name the inconnue, that is, admit she is his wife; the mistress cannot bear even the mention of that woman. This block is again

11 *Paix*, 998
12 *Paix*, 996: 'enterrée dans l'obscurité malgré les bougies qui brillent au-dessus de sa tête ... repoussée de chaise en chaise par chaque nouvelle arrivée jusque dans les ténèbres de ce petit coin' (buried in darkness, despite the candles shining over her head ... shoved from chair to chair by each newcomer, into the shadows of this little corner) – a victim of the ladies' jealousy.

represented by the metonymy, which functions as a sign of displacement, of Freudian repression: 'Vous craignez de voir Martial aux pieds ... De qui? demanda la comtesse en affectant la surprise ... De ce candélabre, répondit le colonel en montrant la belle inconnue' (1009: You are afraid of seeing Martial kneeling before ... Whom? asked the countess, feigning surprise ... That candelabrum, the colonel answered, pointing out the beautiful unknown).

Since the candelabrum is literally substituted for the wife, the metonymy is transformed into a metaphor. This transformation is fully justified by the story, so that a surface form may be said to result from structure actualization. But the transformation itself in turn generates the principal episode and posits a code for the telling of the story. The nature of this code is the central factor that enables the reader to interpret the novel correctly. When the rake finally approaches the wife with an invitation to dance, he appears to be aiming at the candelabrum: 'Au moment où le maître des requêtes s'approchait en papillonnant du candélabre sous lequel la comtesse ... semblait ne vivre que des yeux' (1019: As the judge,[13] fluttering like a moth, drew nearer to the candelabrum under which the countess was sitting ... only her eyes, it seemed, alive). The reader cannot help noticing the moth image. In French it is more obtrusive, because the same word, *papillon*, is used for butterfly and night moth, and the verb derived from it (*papillonnant*, fluttering like a moth or a butterfly) connotes a mincing or zigzagging gait which is downright ludicrous in the context of a noun like *maître des requêtes*. The reader already knows from the story that the conduct of the rake is hardly judicial and that the information might now be discounted, but the text prevents such discount by the stylistic selection of his title, instead of, say, his name or a pronoun. The reader focuses perforce upon a verbal contrast between words tightly linked by predication, yet incompatible in their connotations. Hence, he perceives the seducer through a metaphor whose interpretation is regulated by the candelabrum. Indeed, the moth would have no textual significance and no contextual meaning if it were not read as a component of a composite sign, the flame and the moth, an image of love's fatally irresistible attraction ever since Petrarca. The metaphorization affects not only the seducer but the wife as well.

It is in the light of this compound sign that the reader will now see the story as a comedy of the follies people are driven to by love. The transformation of the most conspicuous metonymy in the novel directs his interpreta-

---

13 The seducer is indeed on the Bench. For the sake of simplicity, I translate a bit vaguely – using a term with similar social connotations in English – the prestigious title Maître des requêtes. This is a member of the Conseil d'Etat, France's highest administrative court, which considers claims of individuals against the State.

tion in two ways, both of which involve narrativity. First, the theme of the flame and the moth is readily understood as a code for the characters in conflict; the known outcome of the story subsumed by the theme portends what is going to happen to the seducer. The narrative thus succeeds in creating expectation or suspense without actually telling the reader that the snarer is indeed ensnared. The story is allowed to unfold without warning as to its outcome, at least within its own language. But the moth code constitutes a prolepsis.[14] Obviously an analysis made only at the level of narrative structures would miss the prolepsis entirely, for the prolepsis exists only at the semantic level, depending as it does upon the metaphorization. Secondly the metaphorization is not simply a deictic device showing the reader how to get ahead of the text, a device to create suspense – that basic component of narrative. The metaphorization is also a negative marker, since the theme belongs to a disillusioned or cynical version of the literary mimesis of love. As such a marker, it then regulates reading as interpretation (as distinguished from mere deciphering of a story), inasmuch as it modifies negatively every variant describing the characters' relationships. Thus the reader perceives the entire narrative as one formal unit of significance – many words expressing one message, repeatedly and through many variants. This message, this invariant, is of course the universal dupery, the cheatery of passion. The message might once again be perceived only haphazardly if the metaphorization here were not visibly derived from the same matrix as that which underlies Balzac's first moral pronouncement at the beginning of the novel. This pronouncement is the link between the two engines of interest – the plot's intricacy, and the stated moralistic intent: 'un trait de cette époque unique dans nos annales et qui la caractérise, fut une passion effrénée pour tout ce qui brillait' (993: a trait characteristic of this era unique in our annals ... was an unbridled passion for all that glittered).

'All that glitters' is the model for every single metonymy of beauty, passion, or simply desire, in the narrative: women, the switched diamond, most of all the candelabrum – as a light fixture, as woman, as desire. The stressed and reiterated metonymy, or perhaps I should say the candelabra code, the very selection of a code, makes for formal unity of the narrative and enables it to function as one sign. But what confers upon this sign its meaning is the repressed or cancelled component of the matrix sentence: indeed, all that glitters presupposes as a predicate the phrase 'is not gold.' The presupposition is all the more compelling because the whole sentence is a familiar proverb ('tout ce qui brille n'est pas or,' appearances are often

14 I borrow the word from Gérard Genette's terminology for the analysis of spatio-temporal diegesis: 'toute manœuvre narrative consistant à raconter ou évoquer d'avance un évènement ultérieur,' Genette, *Figures III*, 82.

deceptive[15]) – it cannot possibly escape the reader. Such is the model for love's deceptiveness, the looks that lie. The narrative therefore appears not just as a sequence of related functions but also as the textual expansion of one meaning, as a melodic variation or musical exercise on one semantic given. Here we can propose a rule that applies to this narrative, but its applicability will extend to texts other than narrative: the text is generated by expansion in the shape of a sequence of sentences making explicit an implicit (or censored) segment of a matrix sentence.[16] Again, one finds the link between the heuristic stage of the reading process, the decoding of traces left by structures at the surface of the text, and the hermeneutic stage. This link could not be established without consideration of the lexicon as a formal model for repetition. The narrative provides the sequence and the space. The repetition provides the comparability making possible the identification of comparable components as variants.[17] The very fact of the variation, the perception of the formal transformations, point to the significance.

The preceding observations on *Paix du ménage* can be rephrased in more general terms, as one of the rules which govern the decoding of the narrative as a unit of significance: in the lexical realization of a given set of variants of narrative invariants, at each point in the narration where a choice must be made between two equally possible events, that choice (and the resulting constraints upon the reader's interpretation) is regulated by the metaphorization of a marked metonymy. A metonymy is marked when it is singled out from among other descriptive features by stylistic overdetermination or simply by repetition (as in our novel).

A further conclusion is that the reading of literary texts is necessarily a structural reading: the text's forms are perceived not just as meaningful in context but as significant qua variants of a structure. The text makes this structural reading possible by providing, for each narrative focusing (or restricting of viewpoint),[18] a decoding model (like the busby and dolman indicating where the symbolism of metonymies lies or the candelabrum's functional tranformations). This model proposes in a condensed form the constant features which mark every component of the narrative segment derived from it. The task of formal analysis is to define the matrix for such a model, that is, to describe the coexistent narrative and thematic structures

---

15 The proverb is the same in English. So well entrenched is this truism in French that dictionary entries under *brillant* give the figurative antonym *solide* (glittering vs reliable or solid) before the literal one *terne* (dull, lustreless).
16 On the implicit or repressed matrix, see my 'Paragram and Significance,' *Semiotext(e)* (Fall 1974) 72–87.
17 Cf. A.J. Greimas, *Maupassant* (Paris: Seuil, 1976) 28–30 (see especially his contention that the concept of metonymy is inoperative in analysis).
18 On narrative focusing, Gérard Genette, *Figures III*, 206–24

which, in combination, distort descriptive systems so that the mimesis of reality becomes the symbolic representation of something else.

Anlysis must differentiate between discursive and diegetic levels, between the linguistic level of relationships not involving time and the level of the narration which is entirely and exclusively temporal. Greimas and his disciples regard the linguistic level as a deep structure of which the narrative would be the surface manifestation. Conversely, others, like Bremond, consider the narrative level a system which actualizes narrative structures and which is used as a figure (in the sense of rhetorical figures) for the representation of non-narrative verbal relationships. These form a temporalized discourse, which nonetheless remains exterior to the narrative proper.[19] I propose, instead, that far from being figures or the rhetorical implementation of narrative structures, far from being stylistic icing on the structural cake, the surface features of the text determine the two basic and inseparable components of the narrative: temporality and successivity.

Columbia University

19 A.J. Greimas, *Du sens* (Paris: Seuil, 1970) 135–55; C. Bremond, *Logique*, 88 ff

TIMOTHY J. REISS

Discursive Criticism and Epistemology

I wish to emphasize at the outset that the series of thoughts offered for consideration here should not really be considered as constituting a 'position paper,' for it cannot be said to offer a position. It could rather be regarded as part of research that may eventually lead towards a position – assuming that to be even desirable. On the one hand this paper is situated, in general, between a not inconsiderable amount of work on European discourses on the Renaissance and classicism (theatre, fiction, science, philosophy, 'grammar,' literary criticism) aiming at an epistemic analysis of the particular type of discourse that, by and large, remains our own, between this and on the other hand an awareness of the untenable nature of the epistemological claims of this discourse. More particularly, then, this paper is part of an attempt to find a more tenable epistemological position and to make it functional within the discourse of criticism. The present working paper lies between on the one hand an analysis of the concept of truth both implicit and explicit in the work of Frege and Peirce (in very different ways: the first giving birth eventually to logical atomism and modern analytical philosophy, the second producing a ternary semiotic that has yet to be exploited) and on the other an attempt to suggest a criticism that might make use of what has been discovered in other critical discourses, that of the philosophy of quantum mechanics for example. I insist, therefore, that the present statements, representing little more than a collection of ideas on the subject, compose a working paper, neither more nor less. As such, of course it is incomplete. To complete it here, however, would far exceed the bounds permissible.

The initial step is to explain the title. What I intend by the term 'discourse' can be approached through what is, at best, but a metaphor concerned with spatiality.[1] I take the Cartesian *cogito ergo sum* as the paradigm of this metaphor. Within this phrase is set up the image of an ideal self: perceiving, enunciating, and conceiving. The *cogito*, as simple thought, is put into a discursive relationship with the *sum* as simple being. Taken separately, these two elements of the paradigm are without meaning; the connecting *ergo* gives that meaning. The triple set provides the exemplary analysis whose

---

1 The second two paragraphs here are almost identical with the beginning of another essay, for reasons which are not hard to discover: 'Cartesian Discourse and Classical Ideology,' *Diacritics*, 6 (Winter 1976), 19–27.

projection is our own epistemological process: the place of simple thought, the space of mediation, the place of (concrete) existence.

I refer to the second as a 'space' rather than a 'place' because it is not conceived of as a definite entity/substance, as are the other two. It is taken as that area in which they are put into contact with one another, and where they are taken as explaining one another: the idealist will argue that thought can 'explain' being; the empiricist will argue that being 'explains' thought. Where the other two elements are 'substance' (in whatever specific sense of the term may be implied) the *ergo* is supposed as an indifferent, or transparent, mediator whose presence does not affect the 'real' nature of the other two. In a binary logic, the *cogito* and the *sum* may both stand as arguments, the *ergo* can only be a part of a function.[2]

Without the syntax provided by the function, however, the others make no sense. Indeed, we may say that they only 'exist' by virtue of the discursive *ergo*. The notion of a thought prior to syntax, or of known objects prior to it, is a matter of discourse: a particular elaboration of the discursive space thus performed as lying between them (see n. 2). Nonetheless, modern European discourses, analytico-referential as I call them, presuppose not only the division of thought and being but also the division of thought and 'its' expression. After the failure of logical atomism, with its picture (or model, to be more precise) theory of correspondence between logical and factual chains, analytical philosophy has inscribed this in its premises. Nonetheless I suggest that the original failure springs from the assumption of this difference, of this division.

At the outset of the *Tractatus*, Wittgenstein makes this assumption clear: 'the aim of the book is to set a limit to thought, or rather-not to thought, but to the expression of thoughts: for in order to be able to set a limit to thought, we should have to find both sides of the limit thinkable (i.e. we should have to be able to think what cannot be thought). It will therefore only be in language that the limit can be set, and what lies on the other side of the limit will

---

2 Only a triadic system such as that suggested by Peirce can render the three as precisely equivalent to one another and between themselves. In Peirce's system the sum will be the Object, the cognito Representamen, the ergo Interpretant – they are all, that is, seen as necessary parts of a discursive space with no one of them being ontologically privileged in relation to the others. This does not mean to deny that any form of knowledge is possible, rather that that of classical (or 'modern,' if one prefers) discourse is inadequate and distorted. On the other hand it proposes a quite different concept from that of the truth at which the disputes aroused by logical positivism seek to arrive. For these last still suppose a substantive division of a kind that results, for example, in arguments seeking to justify a claim of real relationship between theoretical concepts and concrete actuality. See, e.g. Raimo Tuomela, *Theoretical Concepts* (Vienna/New York: Springer-Verlag, 1973). Claims of this sort strike me as insoluble – as the incessant arguments pro and con indicate.

simply be nonsense.'[3] This 'nonsense,' argues Wittgenstein, is only so if we try to speak of it in language: it exists, but language can only 'show' it, language cannot express it as a content. There is, argues Wittgenstein, a totality of the world that exists in thought but which is inexpressible. Russell answers by affirming that to speak of the inexpressibility of this totality is to presuppose its existence, since it would be otherwise meaningless to speak of its 'inexpressibility.' He responds, then, that such a totality is a mere fiction, and all there is is the mass of atomic facts, which correspond to the mass of elementary (atomic) propositions.[4]

Russell's retort can be made concerning thought itself. That, too, must be a discursive fiction, for that, too, can only exist as a public concept insofar as it is expressed. If it be objected that such a view implies the neglect of the whole semantic process (the rendering in language of some other), the response can also readily be given. Unless we equate what Frege calls the *Vorstellung*, the individual's image of what appears exterior, with thought (but then we would have to allow that all animals think), we have to place thought as lying at the level of what Frege calls 'sense' (*Sinn*). Now sense is a matter of more-or-less abstract generality held in common by all those who share a given linguistic or other sign system. It must be so by definition, because otherwise all expression would be incomprehensible. However, sense, as Frege and others have pointed out, is already an expressive ordering of signs, and is not possible without this ordering: 'I do not deny that even without symbols the perception of a thing can gather about itself [*um sich sammeln*] a group of memory-images [*Erinnerungsbilder*]; but we could not pursue these further: a new perception would let these images sink into darkness and allow others to emerge. But if we produce the symbol of an idea which a perception has called to mind, we create in this way a firm, new focus about which ideas gather.'[5]

Since sense is public, it can be so only by communication: this means that sense is necessarily discursive, and ipso facto that this discourse is thought. The semantic process therefore exists in the actual production of propositions, and not in what those propositions might be intended to stand for. This notion of thought and discourse enables us to avoid two presuppositions of analytico-referential discourse that have led to the establishing of a particular ideology. For to ask what a given sign-system is an ordering of, what it stands for, depends on two prior assumptions: intentionality (*vouloir-dire*, which is to be discovered in the subject enunciating a given proposition) and

3 Ludwig Wittgenstein, *Tractatus Logico-Philosophicus*, trans. D. F. Pears and B. F. Mc-Guinness (London: Routledge & Kegan Paul, 1961), author's preface, 3

4 Ibid., introduction by Bertrand Russell, xxi–xxii

5 'On the Scientific Justification of a Conceptual Notation' (1882), in Gottlob Frege, *Conceptual Notation and Related Articles*, trans. and ed. T.W. Bynum (Oxford: Clarendon, 1972) 83–4

referential truth (to be discovered in the predicate of a proposition). To be able to ask about the meaning of a proposition in these terms supposes that these two assumptions have been occulted, because, if not, we could no longer ask the question in the same way. It would be apparent that meaning (as other) is formally produced by, and within, the discourse itself, and that its nature is the result of that formal production.

The notion of the inexpressible in Wittgenstein prevents the assimilation of thought to its expression and maintains the conception of language as the expression of something other. Only this notion permits Wittgenstein to affirm that 'the *truth* of the thoughts that are here set forth seems to [him] unassailable and definitive.'[6] The separation in question supposes, then, that there is a place (that of thought) independent of expression where the truth or falsity of expressed propositions can be judged. The concept of truth is essential to analytico-referential discourse. One might say that it is the one function conceived as absolutely essential to such discourse.

In the light of this, it is easy to see why classical scientific discourse formed the model for all discourses. While, for their truth, other discourses were obliged to suppose some other through thought, the discourses of the natural sciences, and they alone, are bound, on one side, by something that appears as genuinely and distinctly other. They appear bound by their reference to a series of facts – events, situations – whose order does not seem to be produced by discourse: at least once the Cartesian order of analysis is accepted. While this may not be the case as far as our knowledge of these series is concerned, it may be supposed (or, rather, it is supposed) to be so at the point of observation. That is, the situation dealt with by the discourses of the natural sciences is taken as beyond the control of discourse prior to the latter's elaboration, even though these discourses can be taken as existing prior to their inclusion of any particular situation. The types of event dealt with in other discourses could always be conceived as based in and as a product of the faculty for discursive production; they are not taken as 'bound' in this way. This, indeed, was Vico's objection to the classical ideal of knowledge as corresponding to the natural sciences, affirming that the only 'real' human knowledge is necessarily limited to that of our own systems.[7]

When we speak of an inductive system, we are apparently speaking of the

---

6 *Tractatus*, 6. It is apparent that quite different consideration is necessary as concerns the *Philosophical Investigations*.

7 *The New Science of Giambattista Vico*, revised translation of the third edition (1744), by T.G. Bergin and M.H. Fisch (Ithaca: Cornell University Press, 1968) 96, §331: 'the world of civil society has certainly been made by men, and ... its principles are therefore to be found within the modifications of our own human mind. Whoever reflects on this cannot but marvel that the philosophers should have bent all their energies to the study of the world of nature, which, since God made it, He alone knows; and that they should have neglected the study of the world of nations, or civil world, which, since men had made it, men could come to know.'

occulting – the repression – of the operative awareness of a particular ordering of the process of knowing. Galileo, Descartes, Bacon, were well aware, as their writings constantly make clear, that deductive scientific knowledge was an imposition of a logical conceptual order upon things otherwise unknowable, and that what we call 'phenomena' are but objects adjusted to a particular order of reason. Later, the natural sciences found it necessary to repress this consciousness, since otherwise no knowledge of real things could be presumed. In a sense, the claim of induction sought to satisfy this very grave problem. Its claim is that a reason is possible which takes its origin not in a conceptual a priori but rather in unmediated natural objects. It becomes necessary to demonstrate that perceptions have some identity with things (an impossible task, already assuming an immediate knowledge of things) and that these perceptions can somehow enter immediately into the reasoning process.

Later Cartesianism and empiricism undertook this task, and from Newton's *Opticks*, through Lavoisier's *Elementary Treatise*, right down to modern popularizers of science, such induction has been assumed as the only genuine basis for the scientific effort.[8] Indeed, Einstein's objection to quantum physics, 'God does not play with dice,' reflects this same attitude.[9] Yet this inductive method does no more than remove the awareness of manipulation.

Both Cassirer and Lévi-Strauss, among many others, have shown that the concept of an external nature can never refer to an unmediated nature. This concept is always the highly discriminated ground of our more particular knowledge, set for us by our past and present collectivity, in its language(s), conceptual habits, social customs, and so on. It is itself the result of a series of 'previous' deductions. One must therefore argue that knowledge, as a total accumulation of 'things known' at any given time and place, is the result of a constant dialectic between the ground made present as the result of innumerable past deductions (e.g. as nature) and the continuum of present deductions. This continuum is actually, as already suggested, the production of propositions in discourse. In this sense, the (be-)getting of knowledge is always deductive, and to speak of induction as the form of all true scientific knowledge – as the Enlightenment and the nineteenth century did, and as we

---

8 For a longer treatment of this matter, see my 'Espaces de la pensée discursive: le cas Galilée et la science classique,' *Revue de Synthèse*, 83–4 (juillet–déc. 1976).

9 Albert Einstein, in a letter of 7 Sept. 1944, to Max Born, in *Born-Einstein Letters*, (London: 1971), quoted by Ronald W. Clark, *Einstein: The Life and Times* (New York: Avon, 1972) 421: 'You believe in the God who plays dice, and I in complete law and order in a world which objectively exists, and which I, in a widely speculative way, am trying to capture. I firmly *believe*, but I hope that someone will discover a more realistic way, or rather a more tangible basis than it has been my lot to do.'

still tend to do – is only a means of hiding the fact that what we understand as objective truth is neither more nor less the result of an individual, or even collective, human choice (of the enunciator of any given scientific discourse) than was previous knowledge, scorned as scholastic or animistic.

There would seem to be no such thing as objective induction, as analytico-referential science understood it, and Peirce's idea of abduction, or retroduction, is possibly a more useful idea: in the sense of an hypothesis that may account for some of a series of evolving facts, itself part of an evolving semiotic; and 'facts' are understood as a communal and habitual experience of events, processes, situations. The emphasis on the supposed impersonality of induction was one of the many classical occultations which permitted the concealing of the personal origins of knowledge given as true, i.e. as an exact, objective description of things.

Having said all this, we must recognize that the discourse of the natural sciences was the first to recognize that this was not the way to deal with the 'power structure' of enunciation, that the idea of induction was getting in the way of its own ideal – the search for truth.

We may argue, with Peirce, for a constant relationship between fact/proposition relating to that of fact/action as a result of the first two (such that the relationship is his triadic one of object/representamen/interpretant), and that this produces the only practice of what we call truth, consisting in the stability of this relationship in regard to a given ground (phaneron). The truth it produces is not singular; it is not truth in opposition to falsehood. Rather it is a concept of truth as a stable mode of transformations: not of facts, not of propositions, not of activity, no matter what form the latter may take, but of the dynamic relation itself.[10]

It may be argued that the fact of science (objective, as it was taken to be) is not the same as the fact whose observation has been taken to be the job of the critic, literary or other. Literary language, Paul de Man has commented, 'is the only form of language free from the fallacy of unmediated expression,' that is, the only form of language whose text 'implicitly or explicitly signifies its own rhetorical mode and prefigures its own misunderstanding as the correlative of its rhetorical nature.'[11] The literary is thus taken as that exemplary use of language (= discourse) that makes functional the blindness of language itself, the fact that it hides what it claims to reveal: reference or intention, thing or concept. This places literary criticism in the peculiar position of being necessarily queried (as a pretended objective discourse,

---

10 See, Reiss, 'Peirce and Frege: In the Matter of Truth,' *Canadian Journal of Research in Semiotics*, (Winter 1976–7) 5–39.
11 Paul de Man, *Blindness and Insight: Essays in the Rhetoric of Contemporary Criticism* (New York: Oxford University Press, 1971) 17, 136.

saying something about something else) by the very discourse it wishes to explicate.

The contemporary outpouring of critical theory and practice is perhaps a result of this dilemma. It has often been accused, in certain manifestations, of being unnecessarily hermetic, of using a language which one critic calls 'Bulgarian' – presumably with unflattering and somewhat malicious intentions – of escaping into a region beyond comprehension. As for the last, that is a necessary result of its 'self-consciousness,' since the notion of 'comprehension' means precisely the ordering of a reality taken as objective both in regard to its ordering and in regard to the subject that does the ordering.

As for the first two, criticism finds itself today in a position similar to that of quantum mechanics some five decades ago. Having finally become aware that all discourse occurs, so to speak, in the space of the Cartesian ergo, which forms an artificial link between the thinking and the (thing) thought, it faces the difficulty of creating, of finding its own discourse capable of speaking within the space. The discourse sign-of-object from being overvalued is now being questioned not so much about its necessity – since everyday functioning is necessary – as about its mode of existence. Heisenberg's response to the positivo-materialist physicists' demand for a description of 'what actually happens' may well be adapted as the *devise* of contemporary criticism: 'The demand to "describe what happens" in the quantum-theoretical process between two successive observations is a contradiction *in adjecto*, since the word "describe" refers to the use of classical concepts, while these concepts cannot be applied in the space between the observations; they can only be applied at the points of observation.'[12]

This suggests that de Man is not altogether correct concerning the uniqueness of literary discourse and that the discourse of quantum mechanics in Heisenberg's analysis, for example, also accords with his analysis of the literary. It has long been pointed out that the scientific fact is, to the extent that it can be relationally known, a product of the discourse that envelops it. Furthermore, the uncertainty principle suggests that any fact is given as such only for the period covered by the stability of the triadic relationship object/proposition/(experimental) activity into which it can be inserted. Though the particular relationship at any given moment may be taken as an exact statement of that configuration at that moment, a change in any part of it will change the configuration without changing the 'precision' of the configuration. 'Truth,' then, lies in the repeatability of its transformations.

Since Peirce, and even more since the philosophical (and attempted

12 Werner Heisenberg, *Physics and Philosophy: The Revolution in Modern Science* (London: George Allen & Unwin, 1958) 127

logical[13]) elaborations of quantum mechanics, we are aware that sign-systems give us a 'truth' which consists in the ever-increased extension of their own relationships. The difficulty seems to be that, so stated, the truth they provide still tends to become the same Truth as the positivism that the modern embodiments of this sign-awareness in criticism – such as structuralism or the semiological practice – have so derided. While these embodiments lay a justifiable theoretical claim to self-consciousness (a psychologically tainted term suggesting a depth of self-ness that itself corresponds to the classical separation of thought and expression, for that notion of the self may well be taken as a metaphorical description of the discursive act itself), they do not include that self-consciousness in their actual practice. This practice, in that sense – and it is a major shortcoming – runs contrary to what are intended (and I would stress the word for the contradiction it underscores) to be its premises.

The dilemma seems to focus, first of all, on the concept of truth, and caught up in that of course are all the relationships in which sign systems are involved. Peirce would have it that this includes anything of concern to humans. In the long run, only the practice of discourse seems able to resolve the difficulty. All discourse practises upon what it claims to preach indifferently. Up to now this process has not shown itself capable, with a few exceptions, of escaping from the inflection of the linear, referential, binary logic of traditional empiricism. In theory, the enterprise that started in the late nineteenth century should have totally altered the nature, indeed the possibility, of such a concept as that of 'truth.' In practice the critical enterprises that claim to be its descendants merely tend to repeat the positivist or empiricist position (words used neutrally to indicate a particular type of discourse) that truth eventually lies in an exact description of a reality outside and independent of the discourse being used.

We are clearly not concerned here merely with the practice of criticism or of interpretation in isolation, but rather with the practice of all and any discourse. The dilemma, however, may be particular to the critical discourse insofar as this always takes an elaborated discourse as such as its object. The question here might be: in what sense can such an elaboration be the object of critical discourse? How far, and in what sense, can it be regarded as a separate entity having some truth value of its own? According to the discursive premise it cannot have any at all.

Indeed, such questions – and they are constantly asked – are the wrong ones. They correspond to a different discursive type: the classical one of analysis and referentiality. The concept of truth played the role, in that

13 I am thinking here of the attempts of C.F. von Weizsäcker to discover a ternary logic, a logic of the 'included third (middle).'

discourse, of a kind of measure of value. It was the most elementary discursive function. To questions of this kind we can use Heisenberg's answer. In the discourse of synchrony, a field, of triadicity, of dialogicism (to use just a few characteristic indices from a number of attempts at such discourses), the truth function is irrelevant. We do need, however, an operative function such that the discourse suggested by the theory may work in a form sufficiently stable to permit the elaboration of relationships that hold together, whatever the specificity of the discourse in question, and one which does not immediately falsify the theoretical premise (assuming, naturally, that we admit that premise, as I do). The idea of truth was a particular operative function for and within a particular type of discourse. It cannot perform in a different type.

Applied more specifically to literary criticism, we are no longer left with the possible opposition suggested here: text-oriented (fact) against reader-oriented (proposition), for example. We would have to consider a dynamic circuit composed of the discourse at trial, the critical discourse in process, and the interactive operation itself, which relationship would be constantly evolving because each of the elements would constantly be acting upon all of the others.

This is simple to say, considerably less easy to do. The result of such interplay is likely to be unreadable, or merely anarchic. This is partly because it does not seek, in any traditional sense, to adduce meaning, i.e. truth as opposed to falsehood; but also, quite simply, because we are used to the binary discourse of truth. This other discourse would seek rather to install process, to perform discourse as a constant order of transformations, to show that thought cannot merely fix information as knowledge but is necessarily a constant functioning of the operation of knowing, with knowing as the transformation of relations.

No doubt this is all very well. Still we cannot forget one very distinct and important attribute of the truth function: it was available to all, and once obtained it did not need changing; indeed, it could scarcely allow change by its very definition as truth. This social aspect of the function is exceedingly important, it is perhaps what most sustains it. If knowledge, however, is to be considered as merely a form of discursive practice, rather than as something grasped and then reproduced by a neutral discourse, there are a vast number of questions to be resolved: Can there be some single function (such as that of truth in binary discourse) that will simultaneously prescribe and describe our discursive practice as mediated expression? If so, can we nonetheless give it form, as a practice, in conjunction with a communicative (social, communal) exchange between a writer and a reader, a speaker and a listener? Can such a discursive mode function as a means of social exchange, or are we forced to use at least two forms of discourse, corresponding to the literary and the non-literary in de Man's sense? In fact, should speaking about interpretation not be its practice? How can you preach your practice and practise what you preach?

There is one space where the dilemma has been posed with particular acuity, because the discourse in question has been almost the very type of positivism. I refer again, of course, to that of physics. Its solution, if not necessarily transferable, is inviting. I am thinking of quantum mechanics. Here the use of the instrument/concepts known as the uncertainty principle and complementarity have included (and, one might say, ordered) the observer, inventor of discourse and experiment, within the experiment itself argued as a systematic imposition and creation of its own 'object' (series of repeatable relationships). This solution's significance for us, as it stands, is that it may be taken as a confrontation with that very discourse of science (though the solution tends to see itself as simply subsuming the discourse) that seems to form increasingly the ideal reference for much contemporary criticism, particularly that concerned with sign-theory, despite every urge to the contrary that one would suppose provided by its theoretical premises. At first glance, it also seems to answer, for its own discourse, many of the questions I have suggested above.

Université de Montréal

BRIAN T. FITCH

A Critique of Roland Barthes' Essay on Bataille's *Histoire de l'oeil*

The purpose of this brief paper is to present the results of a verification of Barthes' analysis of George Bataille's *Histoire de l'oeil*. I shall attempt to demonstrate the inadequacy of Barthes' essay, in the sense of its incompleteness, even within a purely Formalistic approach such as he himself considers to be the only one suitable in the case of this text. For this purpose I shall have recourse to two concepts that underly the writings of another French Formalist critic, Jean Ricardou: these are the concept of 'the generator of the text' and that of 'auto-representation.' In other words, the application of the Ricardolian hypothesis which I have already tested in previous studies of the French version of Beckett's trilogy[1] and Camus' novel *La Peste*,[2] and his short story 'Jonas,'[3] will serve to reveal the limitations of Barthes' treatment of this Bataille text.

It would be easy to consider the story or fiction of *Histoire de l'oeil* to be a mere pretext for an inventory of the various possibilities offered by eroticism. After all, all three editions of it published during Bataille's lifetime appeared under a pseudonym,[4] a procedure common to so many pornographic publications. What is clear is that here the fiction is not the essential: it is indeed a pretext for something else. Roland Barthes sees it as 'the story of an object,' and the object in question is, of course, the eye: 'How can an object have a story? No doubt it can pass from hand to hand (thereby occasioning insipid fictions like *The Story of My Pipe* or *Memoirs of an Armchair*); it can also pass *from image to image*, so that its story is that of a migration, the cycle of the *avatars* it traverses far from its original being, according to the tendency of a certain imagination which distorts yet does not

---

1 *Dimensions, structures et textualité dans la trilogie romanesque de Beckett* (Paris: Minard-Lettres Modernes, 1977)

2 'La Peste comme texte qui se désigne: analyse des procédés d'auto-représentation,' *La Revue des Lettres Modernes* Nos 479–83 [Série] *Albert Camus* 8 (1976) 53–71

3 '"Jonas" ou la production d'une étoile,' *La Revue des Lettres Modernes* Nos 351–65 [Série] *Albert Camus* 6 (1973) 51–65

4 Lord Auch, *Histoire de l'oeil*, 1st edn (Paris, 1928); 2nd edn (Burgos, 1941); 3rd edn (Séville, 1940); 4th edn, G. Bataille, *Histoire de l'oeil* (Paris: Pauvert, 1967).

discard it: this is the case with Bataille's book.'⁵ And Barthes goes on to say: *'Histoire de l'oeil* is, then, a metaphoric composition ... : one term, the Eye, is here *varied* through a certain number of substitutive objects which sustain with it the strict relation of affinitative objects (since they are globular) and yet dissimilar objects too (since they are variously named) ... The Eye seems, then, the matrix of a new trajectory of objects which are in a sense the different "stations" of the ocular metaphor.'⁶ But I shall claim that before it is the story of an object, *Histoire de l'oeil* is first of all and above all else the story of a word: 'oeil.' It is this word that generates the text, as we shall see; and that for which the fiction is a pretext is the text itself.

Although Barthes points out that the first variation from the eye to the egg, from 'l'oeil' to 'l'oeuf,' takes place on the level of both content (both objects being globular and white) and form (the two words having one sound in common and one different),⁷ he then goes on to ignore entirely all working out of the language of the text on the level of the *signifier*. This is the first important deficiency I see in his account of the text. For clearly the interrelationship of *signifiers* plays just as central a role in the generation of the text as the association of the *signifieds*. In fact, in their plural form, the two words '(les) yeux' and '(les) oeufs' have everything in common as far as their vowel sounds are concerned. The schema below shows in detail the various chains of signifiers together with the key textual references. There are two general points to be made here. One is that the principal elements in Barthes' 'metaphoric chain' are all accounted for in this schema: 'oeil'-'oeuf'-'soleil'-'couille.' This means that such a breakdown of the working-out of the text on the level of the signifier is exactly complementary to Barthes' own textual data. Or, to put it negatively, Barthes' analysis, while starting out in the right direction, stops short and fails to take this further dimension of the text into account. The second point to be noted is that the question raised by Barthes as to whether the metaphorical chain has a beginning and whether the metaphor entails what he calls 'a generative term'⁸ can now be answered affirmatively. And not because, in Barthes' words, 'l'oeil' predominates because it is the eye's story,⁹ but because the evidence produced by an analysis of the work of the signifier indisputably shows that the generator of the text is 'l'oeil,' whereas an examination of the

5 Roland Barthes, 'La métaphore de l'oeil,' in *Essais critiques* (Paris: Seuil, 1964) 238–45, first published in *Critique* in 1963 (cf. 238) [transl. B.T.F.]
6 Ibid. 239
7 Ibid.
8 Ibid. 241
9 Ibid.

metaphoric chain suggests, as Barthes rightly points out, a circular situation in which 'the paradigm does not *begin* anywhere.'[10]

Barthes' failure to take into account this dimension of the text is curious, to say the least. For on its very first page we read the following: '– Les assiettes, c'est fait pour s'asseoir, dit Simone. Paries-tu? Je m'assois dans l'assiette' (HO, 71).[11] Whereupon she proceeds to do just that. Here we have a play on words 'assiette' -(assieds)-'assois'/'asseoir,' functioning precisely therefore on the level of the signifier. The pun is no sooner pronounced by the character than it is acted upon and made flesh, so to speak, by being translated into an actual event in the fiction. Thus the fiction itself is generated by the play on and with words: a purely linguistic phenomenon. But what is remarkable here is that the agent of this linguistic generation of the fiction is the character herself. Her own actions are consciously determined by the structures of language, the common phonetic identity shared by two words. It is not that a real-life situation within the fiction provides the occasion for a pun, but quite the opposite: a pun provided the occasion for the fictive reality, the latter emerging directly from the former. From a traditional critical stance, one might say that the character thereby seeks to make reality coincide with language. However, the possibility of material reality being subordinated to and determined by language is manifestly absurd. For this to be possible, the world would have to be turned upside down. Now, the world upside down is, curiously, none other than fiction right side up. For each and every fictive universe is, of course, dependent upon the language which brings it into being. Thus, viewed from a contemporary critical perspective, the novelistic universe hereby reveals itself *for* and proclaims itself *as* what it is: a fiction. In other words, we have here an illustration of the manner in which the text contains within itself a reflection of the very process by which it has come to exist, the latter being, as it were, 'mis en abîme' in relation to the totality of the text to which it relates as the microcosm to the macrocosm.

This passage on the very first page of the work is not the only one which points to the text's own origins in the creative process. Indeed – and this is my second main criticism of Barthes' essay – it is because the text explicitly designates the manner of its own functioning that Barthes' analysis is, in a very real sense, redundant. That the *metaphoric* chain points to its own mechanism is clear enough even from the evocation of the bull's testicles quoted by Barthes where we read of them: 'les glandes, de la grosseur et de la

10 Ibid., italics are mine.
11 HO = *Histoire de l'oeil* (Paris: Pauvert, '10/18,' 1973). This is the revised version of the text first published in 1940.

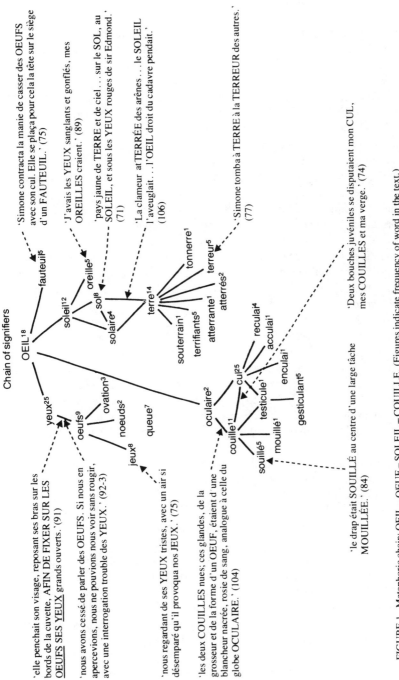

Chain of signifiers

'elle penchait son visage, reposant ses bras sur les bords de la cuvette, AFIN DE FIXER SUR LES OEUFS SES YEUX grands ouverts.' (91)

'nous avons cessé de parler des OEUFS. Si nous en apercevions, nous ne pouvions nous voir sans rougir, avec une interrogation trouble des YEUX.' (92-3)

'nous regardant de ses YEUX tristes, avec un air si désemparé qu'il provoqua nos JEUX.' (75)

'les deux COUILLES nues; ces glandes, de la grosseur et de la forme d'un OEUF, étaient d'une blancheur nacrée, rosie de sang, analogue à celle du globe OCULAIRE.' (104)

'Simone contracta la manie de casser des OEUFS avec son cul. Elle se plaça pour cela la tête sur le siège d'un FAUTEUIL.' (75)

'J'avais les YEUX sanglants et gonflés, mes OREILLES craient.' (89)

'pays jaune de TERRE et de ciel . . . sur le SOL, au SOLEIL, et sous les YEUX rouges de sir Edmond.' (71)

'La clameur at TERRÉE des arènes . . . le SOLEIL l'aveuglait . . . l'OEIL droit du cadavre pendait.' (106)

'Simone tomba à TERRE à la TERREUR des autres.' (77)

'Deux bouches juvéniles se disputaient mon CUL, mes COUILLES et ma verge.' (74)

'le drap était SOUILLÉ au centre d'une large tâche MOUILLÉE.' (84)

FIGURE 1   Metaphoric chain: OEIL – OEUF – SOLEIL – COUILLE. (Figures indicate frequency of word in the text.)

forme d'un oeuf, étaient d'une blancheur nacrée, rosie de sang, ANALOGUE À CELLE DU GLOBE OCULAIRE.'[12] However, this is also true of the working out of the *signifiers*: 'Simone me pria de la coucher sur des couvertures auprès du siège sur lequel elle penchait son visage, reposant ses bras sur les bords de la cuvette, AFIN de fixer sur les *oeufs* ses *yeux* grands ouverts' (HO, 91). Here it should be noted that the words 'oeufs' and 'yeux' are in italics in the text. Now this passage is even more remarkable and disconcerting when viewed from a traditional standpoint than the previous one quoted. For the pun only exists in the actual printed text itself and not within the fiction (since the pun is not verbalized by Simone), whereas the intentionality of the conjunction 'afin de' is directly and unequivocally attributed to the character Simone. Hence, the fictive character would have to be seen as somehow responsible not only for the fiction but also for the language of the text – even though she is not, of course, the narrator of this first-person narrative. In fact, the intentionality in question is that of the text which evolves, through the continual working out of language, towards its main objective: 'fixer sur les *oeufs* les *yeux*' – the bringing together both of the two words and the two objects.

It is not without significance that the fiction virtually begins with the 'jeu des oeufs' in the second chapter, which, in the fiction, leads to the 'jeu des yeux' while producing the text as text through the 'jeu *des* mots' arising precisely from a 'jeu *de* mots,' the words in question being none other than 'oeufs' and 'yeux.' Or, to translate the untranslatable; playing with eggs leads to playing with eyes through a process of playing with words. What better example of 'le texte comme jeu' or the playing out of language? The circularity of the text clearly extends beyond the circular metaphor Barthes draws our attention to.

Histoire de l'oeil repeatedly furnishes a commentary on its own workings, thereby revealing the principles underlying its own existence. And this fact is no less remarkable and worthy of note than the actual nature of its functioning, which is the intended subject of Barthes' essay. This self-commentary is nowhere more evident than in the following passage:

Et, comme je lui demandais à quoi lui faisait penser le mot uriner, elle me répondit *Buriner*, les yeux, avec un rasoir, quelque chose de rouge, le soleil. Et l'oeuf? Un oeil de veau, en raison de la couleur de la tête, et d'ailleurs le blanc d'oeuf était du blanc d'oeil, et le jaune la prunelle. La forme de l'oeil, à l'entendre, était celle de l'oeuf. Elle me demanda, quand nous sortirions, de casser des oeufs en l'air, au soleil, à coups de revolver. La chose me paraissait impossible, elle en discuta, me donnant de plaisantes

---

12 Within quotations from the text, capitals are my own, while italics correspond to italics in the original.

raisons. Elle JOUAIT GAIEMENT SUR LES MOTS, disant tantôt *casser un oeil*, tantôt *crever un oeuf*, tenant d'insoutenables raisonnements. (HO, 92)

The previously cited passages are all examples of the way the text throws up a reflection of itself. But they by no means exhaust the process of auto-representation. Equally remarkable and no doubt more original is the curious manner in which the fiction doubles up on itself to produce a metaphorical representation of itself:

Je l'embrassai longuement sur le front et les yeux ...
   L'IMMONDE BARREAU CÉDA APRÈS UN LONG EFFORT. JE L'ÉCARTAI DE TOUTES MES FORCES, OUVRANT L'ESPACE NÉCESSAIRE AU PASSAGE. Elle passa en effet, je la fis descendre, l'aidant D'UNE MAIN GLISSÉE À NU ENTRE SES JAMBES. Elle se blottit dans mes bras sur le sol et m'embrassa sur la bouche. Simone, à nos pieds, ... étreignit ses jambes, embrassant ses cuisses sur lesquelles tout d'abord elle s'était contentée de poser sa joue, mais ne pouvant contenir un frisson de joie, ELLE OUVRIT LE CORPS et, collant ses lèvres à la vulve, l'embrassa avidement. (HO, 95–6)

Thus one element of the fiction, an event, stands in a relationship of a metaphorical nature to another quite distinct event. The first two sentences of the second paragraph suggest a hidden meaning quite different from what they evoke, in the first instance, in the immediate context of the fiction: the image of sexual penetration. This other meaning ends up very shortly by manifesting itself explicitly on the level of the fiction, and the first passage thereby acquires retroactively the status of a metaphorical evocation of the later event. Here, then, the metaphor functions syntagmatically rather than in its usual paradigmatic fashion. And both of its terms figure as distinct and separate elements of the fictive universe, each serving to evoke a development in the unfolding of the plot.
   A few pages further on in the text, we find a further example of the same process. The narrator is in the park in front of the house in which Marcelle is being held prisoner: 'J'assurai mon REVOLVER dans ma poche et j'entrai: c'était un salon semblable à n'importe quel autre. Une lampe de poche me permit de PASSER DANS UNE ANTICHAMBRE, PUIS UN ESCALIER. Je ne distinguais rien, n'aboutissais à rien' (HO, 84). Note the importance of the 'revolver,' a phallic symbol par excellence, and the difficult entry he effects to enter the house. The rest of this passage is, to say the least, curious: 'J'étais d'ailleurs incapable de rien comprendre, envoûté; JE NE SUS MÊME PAS SUR LE MOMENT POURQUOI JE ME DÉCULOTTAI et continuai en chemise mon angoissante exploration. J'enlevai l'un après l'autre les vêtements et les mis sur une chaise, ne gardant que des chaussures' (HO, 84). It

should be remarked that he does not know why he undresses; but, by now, there is every reason to suspect that his 'distressing exploration' will end up assuming a sexual character and that the sexual symbolism will come to materialize explicitly with the unfolding of the fiction, which is what happens:

Je m'empressai de sortir; je sautai par la fenêtre et me cachai dans l'allée. Je m'étais à peine retourné qu'une femme nue se dressa dans l'embrasure de la fenêtre: elle sauta comme moi dans le parc et s'enfuit en courant dans la direction des buissons d'épines ... JE NE SAVAIS QUE FAIRE DU REVOLVER: je n'avais plus de poche sur moi. Je poursuivais cette femme que j'avais vue passer, comme si je voulais l'abattre ... NI DANS MON INTENTION, NI DANS MES GESTES, IL N'ÉTAIT RIEN DE SAISISSABLE.
Je m'arrêtai; j'étais arrivé au buisson où l'ombre avait disparu tout à l'heure. EXALTÉ, REVOLVER EN MAIN, je regardais autour de moi: mon corps à ce moment se déchira; UNE MAIN ENSALIVÉE AVAIT SAISI MA VERGE et la branlait ... les jambes nues d'une femme se collaient à mes jambes avec un soubresaut d'orgasme. Je n'eus que le temps de me tourner pour CRACHER MON FOUTRE à la figure de Simone; LE REVOLVER EN MAIN, j'étais parcouru d'un frisson d'une violence égale à celle de la bourrasque, mes dents claquaient, mes lèvres écumaient, les bras, les mains tordus, JE SERRAI CONVULSIVEMENT MON REVOLVER et, malgré moi, TROIS COUPS DE FEU TERRIFIANTS ET AVEUGLES PARTIRENT en direction du château. (HO, 85)

Already, in the first three sentences quoted, the sexual symbolism could hardly have been more obvious, painfully so in fact, as though the text, through its very clumsiness, were revealing its own workings. And if it is possible to see these first three sentences in a metaphorical relationship with the sexual activity at the end of the passage, why does the 'revolver' continue to manifest itself well after the orgasm it was earlier ostensibly and ostentatiously pointing to? The device clearly reveals itself as a doubling-up of the fiction whereby the story reproduces itself in the form of its own reflection.

The final passage I should like to quote at one and the same time illustrates the working out of the text both on the level of the signified and the signifier and constitutes an intratextual allegory, to use Todorov's term, of the process of writing:

Je marchais presque toute la nuit le long de la mer, mais sans m'éloigner beaucoup de X ... étant donné les DÉTOURS de la côte. Je voulais m'apaiser en marchant: mon DÉLIRE COMPOSAIT malgré moi des phantasmes de Simone, de Marcelle. Peu à peu, l'idée me vint de me TUER; prenant le revolver en main, j'ACHEVAI de PERDRE LE SENS DE MOTS comme espoir et désespoir. J'éprouvai par lassitude une nécessité de DONNER malgré tout QUELQUE SENS À MA VIE. Elle en aurait dans la mesure où je reconnaîtrais comme désirables un certain NOMbre d'événements. J'acceptai la hantise des NOMS: *Simone, Marcelle.* J'avais beau rire, je m'agitais en raison d'une COMPOSITION FANTASQUE où mes démarches les plus étranges se liaient sans finir avec les leurs. (HO, 79–80)

Thus, 'détours' produces 'délire,' 'tuer' *re*produces itself in the form of 'achever,' 'perdre son sens' gives rise to its exact reflection, hence its opposite: 'donner quelque sens,' 'nombre' reduces to 'noms' and, finally, 'composition fantasque' repeats 'délire composait' through a mere transposition of the parts of speech. More striking still is the parallelism in the evolution of the passage between fiction and writing whereby the precarious tension between *littéralité* and *littérarité* becomes inscribed in the text, each of the pairs of terms evoked above both referring to writing ('achever'/'sens des mots'/'hantise des noms') and contributing to the fiction ('tuer'/'donner quelque sens à ma vie'/'nombre d'événements'). As for the last sentence, it furnishes a commentary on the working out of language, which, as we have seen, constitutes the text: the fiction in which he 's'agite' as one of its protagonists and which comes into being through his agitation or activity as narrator is the product of a 'composition fantasque' which bears witness to the productivity of language consisting in 'des démarches les plus étranges' which 'se li(ent) sans finir avec les leurs.'

In conclusion, although I believe that literary works give out a message concerning their own production as texts (*littérarité*) while at the same time giving out a message constituted by the fiction (*littéralité*), the first tending to gain the upper hand in *Histoire de l'oeil*, I do not believe that these are the only messages a work emits. Contrary to Barthes' statement that Bataille's text confronts us with 'a signification without a signified,'[13] it does have a signified in the form of an implicit ontology that can be seen to emerge from the dimensions and structures of his whole novelistic corpus. Such an ontology, analogous to those I have analysed in the novels of Julien Green,[14] Georges Bernanos,[15] and Samuel Beckett,[16] is the third message the literary work gives out, and it makes the latter susceptible of the kind of analysis undertaken by the Geneva critics.

Now, to the extent that such an ontology is grounded solely in an analysis

13 Barthes, 241
14 'Temps, espace et immobilité chez Julien Green' in *Configuration critique de Julien Green* (Paris: Minard, 1966 = *La Revue des Lettres Modernes* Nos 130–3), 93–136
15 *Dimensions et structures chez Bernanos: Essai de méthode critique* (Paris: Minard, Lettres Modernes, 1969)
16 Fitch, *Dimensions, structures et textualité*

of the fictive universe as such, its existence is no less certain than that of the fictive universe itself nor is its status any more problematic, since the elaboration of such an ontology is a result of that very 'consistency-building' on the part of the reader (as analysed by Wolfgang Iser) upon which the fiction depends for its existence. It is then merely a kind of x-ray of the fictive universe revealing its underlying premises or ontological presuppositions: the world of the novel shifted onto a certain level of abstraction. However, it is precisely in as much as the implicit ontology goes beyond the fiction to encompass the formal structures of the works both on the level of the individual texts and on that of their interrelationship within the total novelistic corpus of a writer that the work's 'ontological message' may be reconciled with its 'formalistic message' (to use a convenient shorthand) and the data produced by each of these approaches to the text may be integrated. The problem of their integration, or rather of their co-ordination in a critical method including both types of analysis, is what preoccupies me at the present time. A refinement of the Geneva School approach, more systematized and more methodologically self-conscious (as attempted in my book on Bernanos), clearly gives a very pertinent account of one of the basic ways in which the reader/critic makes sense of the totality of the literary work; a Ricardolian-type analysis equally clearly, to my mind, goes some way towards accounting for the formal properties of the literary work.

The Ricardolian concepts of the generator of the text and auto-representation have, in my eyes, the status of hypotheses that need to be tested in relation to various novelistic texts, particularly those prior to the phenomenon of the French New Novel, which Ricardou himself has primarily addressed himself to. One of the main questions to be answered is whether these concepts have any applicability and pertinence for earlier periods of novelistic literature. My own tentative conclusions would be the following:

1 It is very possible that these concepts play a key role in the over-all formal coherence of a text.

2 I suspect that this type of analysis draws out what is common to all novelistic texts rather than what is specific to any particular text – particularly since the working-out of language on the level of the signifier, just like the permutations (on parts of speech, for example) that characterize Beckett's fiction, is governed and determined by the linguistic system of the language concerned.

3 One can see the same basic principle at work in the process of auto-representation and the working-out of the signifiers: that is the principle of 'dédoublement,' of doubling-up or duplication. For just as auto-representation consists of a double or reflection of the original, so phonetic or visual association between words consists of some basic common element

linking those words and is likewise a process of reproduction, but where the latter is accompanied by some modification (such as a change of consonant but a common vowel sound).

4 The analysis of the working-out of the signifiers represents, at the very least, one dimension of the formal properties of the text on the level of its smallest units. It should therefore prove to be complementary to the study of the larger elements of formal coherence.

University of Toronto

PART TWO

VERIFICATION OF HERMENEUTIC CRITICISM

CYRUS HAMLIN

Strategies of Reversal in Literary Narrative

For speculation turns not to itself,
Till it hath travell'd and is mirror'd there
Where it may see itself.   Shakespeare, *Troilus and Cressida* (III, iii, 109ff.)

This paper concerns an issue I consider central to any hermeneutics of literary narrative. It has to do with a sense of totality. How does any reader achieve through the act of reading an understanding of a literary work as a whole? As a starting point, I offer a convenient juxtaposition of models from recent critical theory: I.A. Richards's views concerning the plurality of meanings in poetry and Wolfgang Iser's concept of negativity as applied to the act of reading. Despite a basic agreement about interpretation, I perceive a point at issue between these theorists regarding the manner in which a sense of totality is achieved. In order to broaden the perspective on this issue, I then turn to the question of reversal as discussed in the context of German idealist theory, specifically in Hölderlin's comments on Sophoclean tragedy and Hegel's remarks in the Preface to his *Phenomenology of Spirit* concerning the language of conceptual thought. The tradition of literary narrative with which we are concerned must be broad enough to include both the concept of catastrophe in Attic tragedy and the concept of conversion in the New Testament. From examples of such traditions and theories appropriate to such works our own discussion may benefit with regard to the standpoint of the status of totality in modern hermeneutics.

I
The strategies of reversal I have in mind are directed primarily to the interaction between a text and its reader and the manner in which a critical understanding of the text also requires a measure of self-reflection by the reader in relation to the patterns and structures of statement established within the text. In this regard, a reader might argue as follows: 'I understand *what* I read because I recognize a reciprocal interrelationship between myself and the work, achieved through a complex, dialectical process of identification and differentiation. The meaning for me is achieved by me through this dynamic process of stimulus and response imposed upon me by the text.' This position may be clarified by I.A. Richards's concept of 'interinanimation' and Wolfgang Iser's concept of negativity.

In the recent collection of essays by Richards, published to celebrate his eightieth birthday, *Poetries. Their Media and Ends* (Mouton: The Hague, 1974), the term 'reversals' appears in the title of a piece discussing shifts of meaning in the use of words in popular ballads. The initial example is a radical shift of 'white' from associations of love to death in this anonymous fragment:

White was the sheet
That she spread for her lover,
White was the sheet;
And embroidered the cover.

But whiter the sheet
And the canopy grander
When he lay down to sleep
Where the hill-foxes wander. (59)

Richards refers to such shifts as 'inter-verbal interinanimations' (61), reintroducing a term he used as long ago as 1936 in his *The Philosophy of Rhetoric* to describe the essential metaphoric function of language in poetic discourse. The term was taken from John Donne's 'Exstasie,' apparently the only occurrence of it in all English literature, in a passage which has often served in Richards's writings as a model for the interaction of poems with their readers:

When love, with one another so
    Interinanimates two soules,
That abler soule, which thence doth flow,
    Defects of lonelinesse controules. (stz. 11)

Throughout his career as a critic, Richards has been concerned with the pluralities of function for words in poetry, caused by the complex interaction of forces within the contexts of discourse. What he opposed from the first was a simplistic notion of uniformity in usage (as in the technical terms of science), where one word would optimally be assigned to one meaning. He asserts, for instance, near the end of his argument in *The Philosophy of Rhetoric* (85): 'The full use of language ... [i.e. in poetry] takes its word, not as the repository of a single constant power but as a means by which the different powers it may exert in different situations are brought together and again *with an interinanimating apposition*' (italics mine). His book *How to Read a Page* (1943) was written in explicit opposition to such a ruthless reductionism applied to all of literature by the Chicago Great Books program, represented in particular by Mortimer Adler's *How to Read a Book*. More recently, in a lecture delivered at Victoria College, Toronto, in 1958, entitled

'The Future of Poetry,' Richards directed similar polemics against what he termed the 'vulgar packaging view' of meaning, where – to paraphrase his sardonic summary – the poet is assumed to 'wrap up' his poetic experience in a neat and elegant verbal package, which he then sells to us as a poem. 'We unwrap it, if we can, and enjoy the contents,' like children enjoying Christmas toys (reprinted in *So Much Nearer*, 174).

The act of reading, of understanding, of comprehending, is modelled for Richards on the 'interinanimation' of love rather than the unwrapping of a package. Correspondingly, in his later work (especially in *Speculative Instruments*, 1955) Richards developed an elaborate model for communication, borrowed and adapted from mathematical and linguistic communication theories. He offers two diagrammatic views of the model: a side view, which emphasizes complexities of transmission and the indeterminacy of both source and destination, and a frontal view, which distinguishes various functions involved in the activity of comprehending. (He lists seven: Indicating, Characterizing, Realizing, Valuing, Influencing, Controlling, and Purposing; see diagrams, appendix A.) Despite his stature as a critic, Richards's model has not received much attention, yet its implications for an implied hermeneutics are clear. In all his work Richards is concerned with the value of literature, not only for the experience of reading but above all as an instrument for education. Despite consistent emphasis on the pluralities of meaning in literary language and the diversity of forces involved in the act of comprehending, the essential philosophical-pedagogic conviction underlying this emphasis is never in doubt. The goal of reading is comprehension, just as the goal of education is wisdom; and the only valid criterion for measuring success in both endeavours is the degree of coherence, balance, integrity, or indeed – in Plato's sense – the ultimate justice achieved. Richards is committed, as a true Platonist, to the ultimate unity of the idea, and equally, as the spokesman of Coleridge's romanticism, to the self as a totality posited by the poetic imagination. Poetry endeavours – as Richards has often argued with conscious echoes from the *Biographia Literaria* – to reconcile opposing powers through a coalescence of the subject and the object, the knower and the known, the reader and the text. The unity of the poem and the totality of the comprehending mind thus become ideally one and the same. What the reader of the poem ultimately seeks is a reflective understanding of himself.

II

The concept of negativity is derived in general from the method of Hegel's philosophy, according to which the essential condition of man in history and society is that of estrangement or alienation. Human experience is therefore conditioned by a dialectic of opposing, fundamentally alien forces. Language, as the most sophisticated instrument of thought and knowledge, provides the most elaborate and comprehensive setting for this struggle. A hermeneutics of negativity thus provides a radically different outlook on the act of reading and the kind of knowledge which may thus be achieved. Wolfgang Iser, who approaches the hermeneutics of reading from the perspective of the aesthetics of reception (*Rezeptionsästhetik*) developed at the University of Constance, introduces the concept of negativity at the end of his forthcoming book, *The Act of Reading* (to be published in German by the Wilhelm Fink Verlag), as the most comprehensive criterion for the intersubjective relationship between reader and fictional text, through which the reader achieves an understanding of the text as a whole. (Iser would probably not accept these terms, as I think Richards would, burdened as they are with Platonic and Aristotelian associations – not to mention romantic idealist elaborations of the same. His preferred terminology is more neutral and more technical, as in the phrase: 'die Verdeutlichung der kommunikativen Struktur fiktionaler Texte,' which seems to be saying more or less the same thing.) In addition to Iser's forthcoming book, which he offered as a seminar to the Graduate Programme in Comparative Literature at the University of Toronto in the fall of 1974, the most recent volume in the series *Poetik und Hermeneutik*, vol. 6 (ed. by Harald Weinrich, München: Wilhelm Fink Verlag, 1975), is entitled *Positionen der Negativität*. This book contains a number of important contributions to the general question of negativity and hermeneutics, but unfortunately I was unable to secure a copy soon enough to do more than glance at it before preparing this paper.

Among various sources in contemporary theory from several different fields which have influenced Iser's views concerning the interaction between text and reader, two in particular deserve mention. The concept of indeterminacy, as applied to the structure of literary texts by the Polish phenomenologist Roman Ingarden, provided the basis for Iser's theory of interpretation in his essay of 1970, 'Die Appellstruktur der Texte. Unbestimmtheit als Wirkungsbedingung literarischer Prosa' (*Konstanzer Universitätsreden* 28). From R.D. Laing and the psychoanalytical theory of communication Iser adapts the notion of 'invisible experience' in interpersonal relations ('I do not know how you experience me, and you do not know how I experience you') to the interaction of text and reader, where the reader must construct his image of what is being said on the basis also of his sense of what is not said. Negativity thus emerges as a criterion of interaction for the text as a whole on the analogy of 'structured gaps' (*Leerstellen*) which occur throughout and of the principle of indeterminacy for the construction of the meaning.

A helpful application of the concept of negativity to a particular problem of interpretation was recently provided by Iser in his essay 'The Patterns of

Negativity in Beckett's Prose' (*Georgia Review* 29 [Fall 1975] 706–19). The behaviour of characters in Beckett's trilogy *Molloy, Malone Dies,* and *The Unnamable* is discussed as a sequence of self-projections in constantly changing situations which cause these projections to undercut themselves by exposing their fictional status. The result is a categorical denial of meaning through the unending rejection of fictions in such a way that the act of rejection itself becomes a structure of communication, whereby a sense of the self is retained ad infinitum within the finite limits of these fictions. Applying the same argument to the act of reading Beckett – whose work admittedly constitutes an extreme instance of negativity in fiction – Iser suggests that a corresponding dilemma occurs for any attempt to find a meaning. We always become painfully aware that the only meanings with which we emerge from our reading of the text are those which we ourselves project upon it and which the text quickly exposes as such projections. In the final meeting of his seminar on the hermeneutics of reading in Toronto in 1974, Professor Iser outlined in more general terms what he means by negativity as the result of criteria within a fictional text, conceived from a stance which is not given, in such a way that the reader is obliged to produce that stance through a process of self-alienation, attempting to formulate that which is unformulated. Our sense of the meaning is thus the product of a creative act, on our part as readers, fully as complex as the original creative act by which the text came to be written and, if I understand Iser correctly, achieved in dialectical opposition to, or in negative tension with, the text itself. Our sense of the 'truth' or the 'reality' of this meaning, traditional terms in criticism which Iser would clearly reject, is the result of a self-projection and is in the highest sense a fiction created by the act of reading. Meaning is the 'what-not,' the 'not-given' or 'no-thing' of the text, which may also qualify it as a valid reflection of our own identity, achieved through the act of self-alienation which occurs in the process of reading. This conclusion, paradoxically, may agree with the more traditional view of I.A. Richards concerning the status of the self in the act of comprehending (outlined above), but the role of the text in its interaction with the reader is clearly conceived in a radically opposite manner. I expect that for Iser's concept of negativity Richards could only be regarded as a positivist.

III

In his discussion of negativity Iser argues that the successful communication of the meaning as that which is not given depends upon a technique of reversal (*Wende*), whereby a dialectical sublation (*Aufhebung,* a Hegelian term) of what is said achieves the constitution of what is unsaid. My own view regarding the strategy of reversal in literary narrative, which may be in agreement with both Iser and Richards on the essentially dialectical nature of the reading process, can best be presented with reference to the complex plot of tragedy as defined in Aristotle's *Poetics* (chs 10 and 11), involving what he calls 'reversal' (*peripeteia*) and 'recognition' (*anagnorisis*). Traditionally, these concepts have been applied to the internal structure of drama, specifically to that climactic moment in the Sophoclean plot (looking to Aristotle's own favourite example, *Oedipus the King*) where the hero 'discovers' the truth about himself and his deeds and suffers as a direct and immediate consequence of this discovery a radical reversal of status, a change of fortune, a fall. There is no doubt where and how this occurs in *Oedipus the King*, indicated by the scream of the protagonist in response to the old shepherd's words revealing who he truly is. The completion of the tragic action is achieved through this moment of discovery and reversal. More recent discussions of Aristotle, however – and here I have particularly in mind the arguments of the late W.K. Wimsatt in his *Short History of Criticism* and in his essay directed against the edition of the *Poetics* with commentary by Gerald Else, 'Aristotle and Oedipus or Else' (reprinted in *Hateful Contraries*) – have acknowledged that Aristotle's concepts could also be applied to the affective dimension of tragedy, indicating the appropriate response of the audience to the moment of climax, involving an experience of recognition and reversal, not so much with regard to the truth about the hero (which is presumably known already), but rather concerning the ultimate significance of the tragic action as a whole, especially in its social and religious context. The legitimate measure of such reflective response, as critics of Greek tragedy have sometimes ignored, is the chorus, which in *Oedipus the King* presents the great hymn on the worthlessness of human existence in immediate response to the moment of catastrophe for the hero. Such a shift in Aristotle's argument from a theory of structure to an aesthetics of reception provides the possibility for a rehabilitation of the troubled concept of *katharsis*, not specifically in terms of a psychotherapy as Aristotle apparently intended, but with reference to the essential and complex interrelation between dramatic action and audience response which constitutes the meaning of tragedy. I find corroboration on this point in the important study by Hans Robert Jauss, 'Negativität und Identifikation. Versuch zur Theorie der ästhetischen Erfahrung' (in *Positionen der Negativität*, 263–339, esp. 300ff.), where katharsis is discussed as a 'communicative category in aesthetic experience.' Jauss's argument deserves more consideration than can be offered here, especially his theory of identification between hero and reader, which I find in some ways problematic.

My own point concerning strategies of reversal in narrative would be that here the somewhat facile distinction between verbal structure and the hermeneutics of reader response may be overcome. I would agree with the Aristotelian argument that reversal functions essentially as an aspect of plot, though it may also be (as Jauss argues) that it has equally to do with establishing norms of character. At the same time, however, the purpose of such a strategy is only fulfilled in the appropriate response of the reader, who according to the tenets of negativity must react to what is said or done within the work through a dialectical process of self-alienation, whereby alone a reflective awareness of the unspoken meaning as a whole is achieved. In this manner the moment of reversal is transformed into an act of discovery and recognition by the reader. To dramatize the kind of response I have in mind: the moment of reversal places the reader in a state of suspension or surprise through a radical disruption of continuity, requiring a reciprocal and opposite reaction, as if this gap in continuity were a direct call to the reader to be answered by his own act of recognition. The highest instances of such strategy in my experience occur in the dialectical method of Platonic dialogue and in the instances of conversion in the New Testament. The interlocutors of Socrates, who frequently offer so little resistance to his persuasion – such as Glaukon in the *Republic* or Phaedrus in the dialogue of that name – in fact serve to provide an example for the reader of the dialogue against which he can measure his own response. The education to philosophy which takes place within the dialogue thus provides an implied model for a corresponding reaction from Plato's reader. In the allegory of the cave, for instance, we are meant to identify as much as Socrates' own audience with the prisoner who breaks his chains in order to turn to the sunlight. Similarly, in the parables of Jesus from the gospel accounts – which seem so similar to the myths of Plato in their teaching method – the reader is clearly meant by the evangelist to feel himself directly addressed when the teacher ends his story with 'Truly, I say unto you' or 'Go, thou, and do likewise.' One of the finest moments of reversal in all literature, which may have profited from both Plato and the gospel narratives, occurs in the account of conversion in the *Confessions* of St Augustine. The author of the account, who also serves as the hero of his story, reports how he suddenly heard the voice calling to him in the garden: 'Take up and read! (*tolle, lege; tolle, lege;* viii, 12) As he responded then, turning to the passage in Paul's epistle to the Romans which revealed the truth of his conversion to him, so also, it seems to me, is the reader of the *Confessions* intended to respond with a measure of sympathetic understanding. Reading in the book about the Saint's reading in the Book is thus meant to achieve a sense of reciprocity as the basis for understanding. As one last instance of what I have in mind, taken from the modern lyric in a strictly secular context, I recall the powerful ending to Rilke's famous sonnet on the 'Archaic Torso of Apollo' (*Neue Gedichte anderer Teil*): 'Du musst dein Leben ändern.' The voice which speaks the poem – is it the poet addressing his reader only, or is it not also a voice for the eloquent silence of the statue as it spoke to the poet, inspiring his poem? – thus expresses in a moment of radical reversal what can be the only valid kind of response to the reading of the poem.

IV

The concept of reversal in narrative may be further clarified by comparison between two arguments from German idealist theory, which also provide unexpected insight, perhaps beyond anything intended by their authors, into the hermeneutics of reading. These are Hölderlin's 'Notes to Sophocles,' published in 1804 with his translations of *Oedipus the King* and *Antigone*, and Hegel's comments on the language of conceptual thought in the 'Preface' to his *Phenomenology of Spirit*, published in 1807. The former has generally been regarded, both by Hölderlin scholars and by theorists of tragedy, as a cryptic and extremely difficult argument based on a profound, if somewhat intuitive, insight into Sophoclean drama. The latter has been much discussed, particularly with reference to Hegel's dialectical method of argument, though never, to my knowledge, with reference to theories of discourse and hermeneutics. Both texts may be seen to address, though in totally separate contexts, a principle of dialectical interaction which is acknowledged to manifest itself within the verbal structure of discourse. In each instance, significantly, the moment of reversal crucial to understanding is defined with reference to rhythm as the overriding principle of sequential dynamics in discourse. It is my own surmise that this concept of rhythm, assuming that both Hölderlin and Hegel have essentially the same verbal phenomenon in mind, is crucial for defining the role of negativity in the reading process. That these two close friends, after having spent years together at the Tübingen Stift and in Frankfurt, may indeed have shared certain fundamental convictions about language can be argued, despite a lack of explicit documentary evidence, though time does not permit further elaboration at present. In order to be brief, and at the risk of an equal obscurity myself, I shall limit my remarks to the selected passages from the two texts appended to this essay.

In the two passages taken from the notes to *Oedipus the King*, Hölderlin refers to the drama as a rhythmic sequence of presentations (*Volstellungen*). What he has in mind by this is made apparent in the second paragraph of the second passage. The dramatic action proper is a sequence of discrete units which contrast and oppose each other in their juxtaposition: the dialogue with its internal conflict, the chorus as opposition to the dialogue, the various complications of formal interaction between these different parts. 'Everything is statement against statement,' says Hölderlin, 'which reciprocally sublates itself.' ('Alles ist Rede gegen Rede, die sich gegenseitig aufhebt.') Within this complex dialectical sequence, two moments are singled out as crucial for the tragic action and, above all, for comprehending that action.

The first of these is called the tragic 'transport' (described in the first passage): a moment in the rhythmic sequence which is empty and disconnected, like the caesura in metre. Hölderlin calls it the 'counter-rhythmic interruption' (*gegenrhythmische Unterbrechung*). Within this gap the two parts of the drama on either side are said to be placed against each other as opposing forces in balance. What Hölderlin has in mind by this is finally revealed to be the role of the blind seer Tiresias in both *Oedipus the King* and *Antigone*, who serves to interrupt the forward thrust of the action by revealing the will of the gods. The effect of these moments, if I understand Hölderlin correctly, is to turn the thrust of the drama back upon itself by establishing a separate, transcendent perspective upon it which must be integrated and resolved. The second moment which Hölderlin singles out, described in the second passage, clearly occurs at the climax of tragic catastrophe in both dramas, the supreme moment of peripeteia and anagnorisis in the Sophoclean complex plot. It is the moment of extreme opposition in the absolute conflict between god and hero, where – argues Hölderlin – the hero forgets both himself and the god, like a traitor, though clearly in a manner which is holy. In this moment of 'categorical reversal' (*kategorischer Umkehr*), at the uttermost limit of suffering, there is an absolute domination of time: the hero is completely absorbed and obsessed by the moment and the god is nothing but time; and both are 'unfaithful' (*untreu*). In this moment, time totally reverses itself, so that beginning and end are irreconcilable. The hero is completely caught up in this reversal and suffers the consequences of this contradiction. Tragic catastrophe is thus presented in quasi-metaphorical, quasi-metaphysical terms, admittedly very difficult to relate to the action proper of the respective dramas, so that above all the full significance of the event as political, existential, and religious revolution is emphasized in terms of the temporal or rhythmic process through which it is comprehended: by the hero in his agony of collapse, by the chorus in the horror of realization, and by the audience in the totality of katharsis.

In itself, Hölderlin's discussion of tragedy, despite apparent echoes of the Aristotelian concepts of peripeteia and anagnorisis, would not seem pertinent in any way to a hermeneutics of response. That Hölderlin nonetheless had such a concern in mind could be argued from his more general theory of poetic structure, particularly as outlined in his essay-fragment 'Über die Verfahrungsweise des poetischen Geistes.' No such elaboration can be offered here; yet a word may be said about the concept of the high point, or climax, of a poem. Within the dialectical sequence of the poetic discourse, such a moment constitutes simultaneously the extreme opposition and the complete union of the various elements which participate in the sequence, so that – as Hölderlin puts it – the Spirit (*Geist*) of the poem, the God of the myth, is manifested in its infinity: 'in diesem Punkte ist der Geist in seiner

Unendlichkeit fühlbar.' In this moment – which I take to be both a silence and a categorical reversal – the world of the poem is represented according to its particular structure and form: a world within the world, the voice of the eternal to the eternal ('als eigene Welt der Form nach, als Welt in der Welt, und so als Stimme des Ewigen zum Ewigen dargestellt'). This poetic world, this spirit, I submit, though itself unspoken, is represented thus through the dynamics of statement to the reader, who feels and comprehends it, just as the climactic moment in Sophoclean tragedy also manifests the ultimate truth of the drama to its audience.

V

Hegel's discussion of the act of comprehension through language, by contrast with Hölderlin's existential and religious concern with tragedy, focuses upon the narrowest particular as an instance in order to open up speculation as an abstract activity in and for itself. His well-known example of the 'speculative sentence' (*spekulativer Satz*) – which is clearly substituted in an implied polemic for the sentence of identity much discussed by Fichte and Schelling, namely 'I = I' – is: 'God is Being.' The first of the passages selected from the *Phenomenology* analyses the grammatical structure of this sentence in terms of the dialectical process involved in comprehending it. To do so, Hegel makes eloquent and intentional use of a fortuitous ambivalence in the term 'Subject,' as commentators have noted (most recently Jere Paul Surber, 'Hegel's Speculative Sentence,' *Hegel-Studien* 10 [1975] 211–30). On one hand the subject is merely the word which constitutes the substantive of the sentence, in accord with traditional grammatical terminology; yet on the other it is the consciousness which performs the act of speculation. As indicated in the complex statement of the passage, the process of understanding consists of two essential actions related to each other dialectically. First, the subject enters into the attributes of its predicate, literally loses itself, is destroyed (*geht zugrunde*). This content, to paraphrase the crucial statement, is thus indeed no longer the predicate of the subject, but is its substance, the essence (*Wesen*) and the concept (*Begriff*) of that which is being talked about. Second, as counterforce to this progression, the process of thought experiences what Hölderlin would call the categorical reversal and what is referred to by Hegel as a recoil (*Hemmung*) or counterthrust (*Gegenstoss*). An act of recognition occurs whereby the predicate, into which the subject has moved as its substance, is rediscovered to be the substance *of that subject*. The characteristic sublation of the dialectic is thus achieved, and the apparent loss of the subject into the predicate is corrected by its reestablishment as the *ground* of its substance. The activity of speculative thought is thus concluded and contained by the form of the statement as the conscious subject which is now known to itself. Hegel has here achieved, despite the convolutions of his own language, a description of the simplest possible statement as the dialectical process of thought toward reflective consciousness of itself. I submit, though Hegel may not have intended as much, that this is also the basic structure of the hermeneutics of reading, through which the reader comes to understand the text as he reads it.

Further clarification of this point, crucial to the argument of the entire *Phenomenology*, is provided by Hegel a page later in the second passage selected, where he offers the analogy of rhythm. The conflict between the form of a sentence and the unity of its concept, he argues, resembles the conflict between metre and accent in rhythm (by which I take it he means the interaction between the empty form of the metre, such as iambic pentameter, and the actual pattern of stressed and unstressed syllables by which that form is filled with the actual utterance that is made in any given line of verse). The rhythm, asserts Hegel, results from the vacillation and suspension (*die schwebende Mitte*) between these two and the unification of both. In a manner resembling such interaction, which achieves a harmony of unity and difference, the identity achieved in the form of a sentence between subject and predicate does not destroy their difference. The form sustains the differentiation of what it expresses, while its unity consists in the fact that the predicate expresses the substance into which the subject falls as a universal. The one is the pattern of stresses, 'the accent,' and the other its fading away. The concept of rhythm for Hegel therefore – as in a very different context for Hölderlin – contains the principle of reversal within itself as the crucial factor in the dialectical process of language. As stated in the third of the passages selected from Hegel's 'Preface,' the return of the concept into itself must be represented: 'dies Zurückgehen des Begriffs in sich muss *dargestellt* sein.'

VI

Any attempt to summarize by way of conclusion the various views assembled in this essay from Richards and Iser to Hölderlin and Hegel, with a brief excursus back to Aristotle, Plato, Sophocles, and the New Testament, is bound to appear an exercise in futility. Nonetheless a coherent and, I believe, crucial issue for the hermeneutics of reading has been pursued through all this discussion of reversals in literary narrative. At the risk of over-simplification, I offer the following three hypotheses concerning the way in which we achieve a sense of the totality of meaning through the act of reading a text. First, the interaction between a reader and a text which occurs in the act of reading must involve a dialectical relation between the particular, formal structure of what is expressed in the language of the text as a sequence of statements and some ultimate awareness of the meaning of the whole which is not expressed. Second, it is the primary purpose or intention of any literary work worth reading to communicate to its readers through the very limited, finite means of its verbal form some awareness of or insight into matters of an ultimate, unlimited significance. Third, strategies of reversal, as I have described them, constitute an essential technique in literary texts at all levels of narrative, from grammar and syntax to plot and character. Through this technique the essential dialectical relation is established with the reader as he reads and by its means the basically linear sequence of articulated moments in the process of reading, from line to line and from page to page, imposes simultaneously – perhaps in accord with what Richards called interinanimation or what Hölderlin and Hegel referred to more simply as rhythm, 'the rhythm of presentation' – a reflective or speculative awareness (in Hegel's sense) of the ultimate concerns of the text as a whole. These first two points seem axiomatic to me; the third reflects primarily the conviction underlying this essay.

To what extent would the various theories outlined above support these hypotheses? First of all, in the light of arguments from the idealists concerning the 'dialectical motion' of language (Hegel's phrase), the apparent opposition between I.A. Richards's concept of interinanimation and Wolfgang Iser's views on negativity may be resolved into a relative difference of emphasis on the essentially twofold process of the reading experience. The real issue, then, where the difference between the rival schools of structuralism and hermeneutics perhaps becomes truly irreconcilable, is the basic ambivalence and indeterminacy involved in the interaction between reader and text. On this point I can only offer what seems to be the consensus of the theoretical positions assembled here. The constitution of the meaning as a whole (if such a phrase is still acceptable) through the act of reading necessarily involves a sense of ultimate concern, which is open, indeterminate, boundless, and presumably unarticulated, yet which is only achieved by the reader through the dialectical process of comprehension involved in the reading of the text itself, which as verbal structure is by contrast fixed and determinate, closed and fully articulated. Simultaneously, however, and perhaps paradoxically, this process of opening up an awareness of such ultimate concerns involves equally a reflective turn of the mind back upon itself. The constitution of meaning in literature also requires an act of self-reflection and self-validation of the kind that Coleridge and Keats, with specific reference to the poetic act, called 'soul-making.' On this point I am a Hegelian, though in terms which I hope would also be acceptable to I.A. Richards, looking to that tradition of theory which we share from the romantics onward. What is communicated through the language of literature is not in any sense a content, as if contained in verbal wrappings according to what Richards called the vulgar packaging view. The meaning is established as the product of that complex dialectical process of sublation described by Hegel, where the subject (the mind of the reader) must first lose itself in the substance of its predicate (the verbal structure of the text being read), to be accompanied immediately by a categorical reversal, which re-establishes for the subject through self-reflection a sense of itself as the ground of that substance. What I understand is thus open, boundless, indeterminate, even infinite, and it is understood in and through myself as knower. At the same time the only instrument or medium for such under-standing, the necessary and sufficient means to such reflective insight, is the text itself, serving simultaneously as a mirror to the self and as a window ('a magic casement' in Keats's phrase) onto a vision of what Shelley termed the intense inane. I conclude with the passage from Shakespeare with which I began: 'speculation turns not to itself,/Till it hath travell'd and is mirror'd there/Where it may see itself.'

POSTSCRIPT

Two days after completing the final version of this paper I came across the following footnote in I.A. Richards's essay 'What Is Saying?' (1964) in *Poetries: Their Media and Ends*, 223, which I had overlooked:

converse is an interesting word in itself and in its relations with *convert*. The sense 'talk with' is relatively recent. Dr Johnson: 'to convey the thoughts reciprocally in talk.' The *-verse* element, means 'turning' this way or that. The religious sense of *conversion* looks back to Plato, *Republic*, vii, 518: 'The natural power to learn lives in the soul and is like an eye which might not be turned from the dark to the light without a turning round of the whole body ... of which there might be an art ... of turning the soul round most quickly and with the most effect.' That is what educa-tion, for Plato, was to be.

So also, I might add, was education to be for Richards. And how appropriate to find so suitable a term – more so, I think, than 'reversals' – to describe the kinds of turnabout in the act of reading literature which matter for the comprehending mind.

University of Toronto

74 / Cyrus Hamlin

APPENDIX A: COMMUNICATION DIAGRAMS BY I.A. RICHARDS.

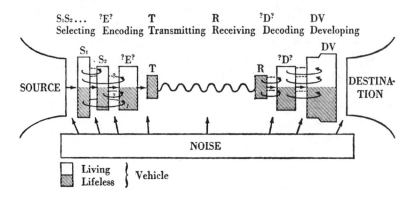

From 'The Future of Poetry,' *So Much Nearer. Essays Towards a World English* (New York: Harcourt, Brace and World, 1968) 158

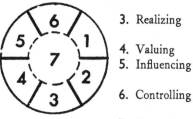

1. Points to, selects. . . .
2. Says something about, sorts. . . .
3. Comes alive to, wakes up to, presents. . . .
4. Cares about. . . .
5. Would change or keep as it is. . . .
6. Manages, directs, runs, administers itself. . . .
7. Seeks, pursues, tries, endeavours to be or to do. . . .

1. Indicating
2. Characterizing
3. Realizing
4. Valuing
5. Influencing
6. Controlling
7. Purposing

From 'Toward a Theory of Comprehending,' *Speculative Instruments* (London: Routledge and Kegan Paul, 1955) 26

APPENDIX B: EXTRACT FROM HÖLDERLIN

Der tragische *Transport* ist nämlich eigentlich leer, und der ungebundenste. Dadurch wird in der rhythmischen Aufeinanderfolge der Vorstellungen, worin der *Transport* sich darstellt, *das, was man im Silbenmaße Zäsur heißt*, das reine Wort, die gegenrhythmische Unterbrechung notwendig, um nämlich dem reißenden Wechsel der Vorstellungen, auf seinem Summum, so zu begegnen, daß alsdann nicht mehr der Wechsel der Vorstellung, sondern die Vorstellung selber erscheint.

Dadurch wird die Aufeinanderfolge des Kalkuls, und der Rhythmus geteilt, und bezieht sich, in seinen zweien Hälften, so aufeinander, daß sie, als gleichwiegend, erscheinen. Ist nun der Rhythmus der Vorstellungen so beschaffen, daß, in exzentrischer Rapidität, die *ersten* mehr durch die *folgenden* hingerissen sind, so muß die Zäsur oder die gegenrhythmische Unterbrechung *von vorne* liegen, so daß die erste Hälfte gleichsam gegen die zweite geschützt ist, und das Gleichgewicht wird, eben weil die zweite Hälfte ursprünglich rapider ist, und schwerer zu wiegen scheint, der entgegenwirkenden Zäsur wegen, mehr sich von hinten her gegen den Anfang neigen. Ist der Rhythmus der Vorstellungen so beschaffen, daß die *folgenden* mehr gedrungen sind von den *anfänglichen*, so wird die Zäsur mehr gegen das Ende liegen, weil es das Ende ist, was gegen den Anfang gleichsam geschützt werden muß, und das Gleichgewicht wird folglich sich mehr gegen das Ende neigen, weil die erste Hälfte sich länger dehnt, das Gleichgewicht folglich später vorkommt. So viel vom kalkulablen Gesetze.
Das erste nun der hier angedeuteten tragischen Gesetze ist das des Oedipus.
Die Antigonä gehet nach dem zweiten hier berührten.
In beiden Stücken machen die Zäsur die Reden des Tiresias aus.
Er tritt ein in den Gang des Schicksals, als Aufseher über die Naturmacht, die tragisch, den Menschen seiner Lebenssphäre, dem Mittelpunkte seines innern Lebens in eine andere Welt entrückt une in die exzentrische Sphäre der Toten reißt.
Friedrich Hölderlin, 'Anmerkungen zum Oedipus,' in *Werke und Briefe*, ed. F. Beißner and J. Schmidt (Insel Verlag, Frankfurt am Main, 1969) 2, 730–1

Die Darstellung des Tragischen beruht vorzüglich darauf, daß das Ungeheure, wie der Gott und Mensch sich paart, und grenzenlos die Naturmacht und des Menschen Innerstes im Zorn Eins wird, dadurch sich begreift, daß das grenzenlose Eineswerden durch grenzenloses Scheiden sich reiniget. Της φυσεως γραμματευς ην τον χαλαμον αποβεδχων εννουν.
Darum der immer widerstreitende Dialog, darum der Chor als Gegensatz gegen diesen. Darum das allzukeusche, allzumechanische und faktisch endigende Ineinandergreifen zwischen den verschiedenen Teilen, im Dialog, und zwischen dem Chor und Dialog und den großen Partien oder Dramaten, welche aus Chor und Dialog bestehen. Alles ist Rede gegen Rede, die sich gegenseitig aufhebt.
So in den Chören des Oedipus das Jammernde und Friedliche und Religiose, die fromme Lüge (*wenn ich Wahrsager bin, etc.*) und das Mitleid bis zur gänzlichen Erschöpfung gegen einen Dialog, der die Seele eben dieser Hörer zerreißen will, in seiner zornigen Empfindlichkeit; in dem Auftritten die schröcklichfeierlichen Formen, das Drama wie eines Ketzergerichtes, als Sprache für eine Welt, wo unter Pest und Sinnesverwirrung und allgemein entzündetem Wahrsagergeist, in müßiger Zeit, der Gott und der Mensch, damit der Weltlauf keine Lücke hat und *das Gedächtnis der Himmlischen nicht ausgehet, in der allvergessenden Form der*

Untreue sich mitteilt, denn göttliche Untreue is am besten zu behalten. In solchem Momente vergißt der Mensch sich und den Gott, und kehret, freilich heiliger Weise, wie ein Verräter sich um. – In der äußersten Grenze des Leidens bestehet nämlich nichts mehr, als die Bedingungen der Zeit oder des Raums. In dieser vergißt sich der Mensch, weil er ganz im Moment ist; der Gott, weil er nichts als Zeit ist; und beides ist untreu, die Zeit, weil sie in solchem Momente sich kategorisch wendet, und Anfang und Ende sich in ihr schlechterdings nicht reimen läßt; der Mensch, weil er in diesem Momente der kategorischen Umkehr folgen muß, hiermit im Folgenden schlechterdings nicht dem Anfänglichen gleichen kann. So stehet Hämon in der Antigonä. So Oedipus selbst in der Mitte der Tragödie von Oedipus.

Ibid. 735–6

Anders verhält es sich im begreifenden Denken. Indem der Begriff das eigene Selbst des Gegenstandes ist, das sich als *sein Werden* darstellt, ist es nicht ein ruhendes Subjekt, das unbewegt die Akzidenzen trägt, sondern der sich bewegende und seine Bestimmungen in sich zurücknehmende Begriff. In dieser Bewegung geht jenes ruhende Subjekt selbst zugrunde; es geht in die Unterschiede und den Inhalt ein und macht vielmehr die Bestimmtheit, d. h. den unterschiednen Inhalt wie die Bewegung desselben aus, statt ihr gegenüberstehen zu bleiben. Der feste Boden, den das Räsonnieren an dem ruhenden Subjekte hat, schwankt also, und nur diese Bewegung selbst wird der Gegenstand. Das Subjekt, das seinen Inhalt erfüllt, hört auf, über diesen hinauszugehen, und kann nicht noch andere Prädikate oder Akzidenzen haben. Die Zerstreutheit des Inhalts ist umgekehrt dadurch unter das Selbst gebunden; er ist nicht das Allgemeine, das frei vom Subjekte mehrern zukäme. Der Inhalt ist somit in der Tat nicht mehr Prädikat des Subjekts, sondern ist die Substanz, ist das Wesen und der Begriff dessen, wovon die Rede ist. Das vorstellende Denken, da seine Natur ist, an den Akzidenzen oder Prädikaten fortzulaufen und mit Recht, weil sie nicht mehr als Prädikate und Akzidenzen sind, über sie hinauszugehen, wird, indem das, was im Satze die Form eines Prädikats hat, die Substanz selbst ist, in seinem Fortlaufen gehemmt. Es erleidet, es so vorzustellen, einen Gegenstoß. Vom Subjekte anfangend, als ob dieses zum Grunde liegen bliebe, findet es, indem das Prädikat vielmehr die Substanz ist, das Subjekt zum Prädikat übergegangen und hiemit aufgehoben; und indem so das, was Prädikat zu sein scheint, zur ganzen und selbständigen Masse geworden, kann das Denken nicht frei herumirren, sondern ist durch diese Schwere aufgehalten.

George Wilhelm Friedrich Hegel, 'Vorrede,' *Phänomenologie des Geistes*, ed. Johannes Hoffmeister, 5. Aufl. (Leipzig: F. Meiner, 1949) 49–50

Dieser Konflikt der Form eines Satzes überhaupt und der sie zerstörenden Einheit des Begriffs ist dem ähnlich, der im Rhythmus zwischen dem Metrum und dem Akzente stattfindet. Der Rhythmus resultiert aus der schwebenden Mitte und Vereinigung beider. So soll auch im philosophischen Satze die Identität des Subjekts und Prädikats den Unterschied derselben, den die Form des Satzes ausdrückt, nicht vernichten, sondern ihre Einheit [soll] als eine Harmonie hervorgehen. Die Form des Satzes ist die Erscheinung des bestimmten Sinnes oder der Akzent, der seine Erfüllung unterscheidet; daß aber das Prädikat die Substanz ausdrückt und das Subjekt selbst ins Allgemeine fällt, ist die *Einheit*, worin jener Akzent verklingt.

Ibid. 51

Daß die Form des Satzes aufgehoben wird, muß nicht nur auf *unmittelbare* Weise geschehen, nicht durch den bloßen Inhalt des Satzes. Sondern diese entgegengesetzte Bewegung muß ausgesprochen werden; sie muß nicht nur jene innerliche Hemmung, sondern dies Zurückgehen des Begriffs in sich muß *dargestellt* sein. Diese Bewegung, welche das ausmacht, was sonst der Beweis leisten sollte, ist die dialektische Bewegung des Satzes selbst.

Ibid. 52–3

FÉLIX MARTÍNEZ BONATI

Hermeneutic Criticism and the Description of Form

This paper presents reflections on some of the things we do as critics or scholars of literature and on our tools and ends. Addressing myself to the general subject of the 1976 Toronto Colloquium of Comparative Literature, in which a part of the paper was read, I have limited my analysis to two ideal types of criticism, 'formalist' and 'hermeneutic,' endeavouring mainly to keep a clear notion of hermeneutic criticism as a central task of literary scholarship.

I define the ideal type of hermeneutic criticism in terms of (Husserlian) phenomenology and existentialism (including the so-called philosophy of life) and consider essential to this criticism the prevalence of natural language in its discourse and of conscious life in its frame of reference. Thus, I distinguish hermeneutic criticism from anthropological, sociological, or psychological interpretations with a reductive intent. The ideal type of formalist criticism I define through a concept of form as part (especially abstract part) of the literary object, and through the prevalence of defined ('technical') terminology in its discourse and of the medium of representation in its frame of reference.

As factual manifestations in the history of letters, hermeneutic and formalist impulses have merged from the beginning in Aristotle's *Poetics* in a variety of combinations, and only very recently have they strived for separation and purity of approach. The model of natural science and formalized language has since the nineteenth century elicited, by opposition, a self-affirmation of traditional, scarcely formalized 'interpretation' as the *other* science (Dilthey), but has finally in our century through phenomenology induced a (re)technification of the vocabulary, a self-awareness of concepts and ways (if not always of methods), while more recently a scientistic criticism of linguistic, semiotic (structuralist), or cybernetic inspiration has developed as 'formalism.'

Aristotle's *Poetics* presents a paradigm that illustrates the original conversion of hermeneutic and formalist approaches. Also, Cervantes' *Don Quixote* is used to illustrate the notion of the inexhaustibility of symbolic meaning by rational formulas and the use of formal description to enhance the perception of literary meaning. The point is that while formalism can be absorbed by hermeneutics, significance cannot be absorbed by formalism.

Traditional hermeneutic criticism in my view can and should develop technical terminology without losing its ground on natural language and the conscious experience of reading, i.e. it can and should absorb formalism as well as the insights of non-phenomenological approaches to the significance of literature (such as psychoanalytical, historical-sociological, and anthropological *reductions*). That it can is largely a matter of logical analysis; that it should is a matter of our desires for the life of our mind, of the things we want to do with literature.

It is generally accepted today that a radical diversity of goal and method separates criticism of existentialist-hermeneutic inspiration from formalist or structural criticism. This grounded, but not definitive, opposition takes place inside the field of the 'intrinsic approach' to the study of literature (Wellek-Warren) and relates to what has been equivocally called the immanent interpretation of the autonomous work of art. An equally radical opposition seems to confront two kinds of critical interpretations: the one that handles literature as ideological consciousness, or more generally as false consciousness, and the one that handles literature as a form of knowledge and therefore as a form of truth *and* of falsehood. In this paper I try to examine and circumscribe the methodological notion of what may be called hermeneutic criticism of literature. I argue that in the study of literature the concept of hermeneutic interpretation, viewed with consistency, becomes the concept of a certain kind of formal description. Hermeneutic criticism as defined here handles literature as knowledge, not merely as a symptom or manifestation (collective or individual) of a more or less unconscious life. Therefore, it is different from reductive interpretations as well as from some kinds of structuralist and formalist approaches. Nonetheless, certain conversions of these methods of interpretation seem not only possible but also tendentially necessary.

I

The label 'hermeneutic interpretation' for a certain kind of critical discourse does not sound well to the logical ear; however, it is used with good reason. Before we substitute for it 'hermeneutic criticism,' let us examine the conceptual field that emerges with this somewhat accidental designation.

In the expression 'hermeneutic interpretation' the word 'hermeneutic' obviously cannot carry the usual meaning of 'related to the art of interpretation,' since the expression then (equivalent to 'interpretation related to the art of interpretation') would be badly pleonastic or unnecessarily qualifying: if not all efforts, at least all sustained efforts, of interpretation are in some way related to a kind of art of interpretation. Hence, this primary meaning of hermeneutic should here be left aside. As the definiens of a kind of interpretation of literary texts, the hermeneutic character has to be understood, it seems to me, in a more recent sense, as partly derived from the concepts of understanding and truth in Vico's antirationalistic humanism and in Dilthey's theory of the human sciences (*Geisteswissenschaften*). In Dilthey's conception, understanding (*Verstehen*) of human expression is the basic mode of knowledge in the humanities, while the mere explanation (*Erklären*) of natural facts constitutes positive science. According to this view, we can understand the expressions and deeds of other men because we can in a sense relive the internal processes that led to the expressive action. The epistemological ground of understanding, thus, is consciously experienced life (*Erleben*). To this Diltheyan assertion of the basic function of life's self-consciousness and its reflection in 'historical' knowledge, we must add Heidegger's description of (human) existence. Heidegger defines existence as being intrinsically and necessarily interpretative, hermeneutical in a metaphorically extended sense, insofar as its being has to constitute itself always as a being situated in relations and structures of sense. Interpretation, so conceived, is not an occasional task but an inescapable business of human life. In such a contemporary philosophic context, art and literature tend to appear as the highest forms of knowledge of human life's condition and meaning, and as a power that affects – if minimally – the spiritual foundations of behaviour. A hermeneutic interpretation of literature, consequently, will be directed to the clarification of the existential content of poetic vision; it will not consider art in a merely formal manner as, say, a kind of immanent play or an absolutely autonomous construction of casual imagination, or a production of timeless beauty through harmonic form, or the like. This hermeneutic approach to literature might best be seen as developing with the stream of *Lebensphilosophie* and the existentialist branch of phenomenology (not so much, I think, with the analytical-descriptive branch of Ingarden and Husserl themselves).

Two characteristics of this view of literature must be made explicit here. The first is its orientation towards final qualities or the significance of totalities: the work of art is seen as the signifying product of a purposeful deed of the mind; human life and the world appear as its referents. The poem is taken as essentially articulated in a meaningful whole of experience, in opposition to the decomposing observation of abstracted objects that is exercised by an analytic intellectual interest. In this sense, for instance, Hans Lipps' position against formal logic in his *Untersuchungen zu einer hermeneutischen Logik* (1938) can be seen as a paradigmatic analogue: the abstract forms of traditional logic are reincorporated into the relatively concrete operations of verbal action and the performances of everyday existence – a field of inquiry including what J.L. Austin called 'speech acts.' The kind of apprehension of art involved in the hermeneutic approach can be seen emblematically rendered in Rilke's well-known poem 'Archaischer

Torso Apollos'; the epiphoneme that concludes the description of the sculpture and its effect on the viewer is, 'Du mußt dein Leben ändern': not a change of this or that aspect, but a metamorphosis of the contemplator's whole existence. (Let us note that the 'existential effect' of Rilke's poem is not the same as the one it asserts of the described sculpture; it suggests, rather, the pious acceptance of the forces of artistic revelation.) We may call this characteristic of pointing to the signifying totality and the finality of the work the 'existential' dimension of hermeneutic criticism.

The second trait of the concept of a hermeneutic interpretation to be stressed in our context may be called 'phenomenological.' The notion of phenomenology presents a certain difficulty. Generally it is true that phenomenology – and certainly Husserlian phenomenology – means the description of the given, and with it the reassertion of the given to our perception and to our intuition. The immediate presence of things – including their so-called relative, secondary, or subjective attributes, such as colour, aspect, expression – acquires hereby a status of substantiality and definitive objectivity. They are as 'real' as any properties of the world and cannot be declared merely apparent – as if they were not what they seem to be but were 'in reality' certain sets of not immediately given physico-physiological elements and relations. In the *Lebensphilosophie* this vindication of the validity of the concrete living experience of the world – against a physicalist reduction – has sometimes taken (in some of Ortega y Gasset's works, for instance) an extreme form: life, the 'dramatic' experience of being in the world, is the primordial reality ('la realidad primaria'); the models and the world-view of natural science are thus mere manifestations and products of certain theoretical and practical enterprises of life. We find this anti-Newtonian theme of Dilthey (or perhaps originally Goethe) stated explicitly in Heidegger. It constitutes a major countercurrent of modern 'scientific' culture. Husserl assumes this position through his 'principle of all principles' ('Das Prinzip aller Prinzipien,' *Ideen*, §24) that in a rough shorthand paraphrase we may state as 'what we see cannot be explained away.' This is the point of view I will tentatively assume in this paper, disregarding, for the sake of discussion, my reservations and doubts.

The difficulty with the notion of phenomenology I have in mind is the fact that in developing a method to secure the proper description of the given, Husserl introduces his own 'reductions.' They affect the suspension of the natural world-view, producing a retraction of the intellectual gaze, that concentrates now on the projecting structure of consciousness instead of naïvely taking in the projected object. The natural world-view becomes thus methodically alienated (a technique remotely reminiscent of the poetic 'de-familiarization' the Russian Formalists were studying in those years). There is then a general and a qualified or modified assertion of the given in Husserl's phenomenology, and it is the former type that belongs primarily to the hermeneutic trend I am trying to define. The second, a modified and obliquely reflective view, belongs rather to the formal-analytic phenomenology, as I will suggest again later. However, in the field of the interpretation of art, the approaches are congruent and eventually complementary.

I shall try to illustrate briefly the implications of this phenomenological trait of hermeneutic criticism. Let us assume that we are spectators of a play – not exactly the one written by Sophocles on the subject – in which the protagonist, a man of superior attributes, is told in a manner of divine prophecy that he will commit a terrible deed, so terrible that rather than accept his fate he defies the gods by fleeing the circumstances in which he thinks his presumed crime would have to take place. Subsequently, we see him unknowingly perform the fateful actions, discover his true identity and situation, and find himself precipitated into disgrace by this anagnorisis. We might well be moved by this spectacle to pity the hero and to fear the sheer possibility of such a destiny, to look in awe upon the power of fate, and to reflect humbly and ironically on the limits and illusions of human freedom. All these perceptions and responses – some of them totalizing and conclusive – which constitute a lived, conscious experience of the play, are immediately given in and with the play. But now somebody comes, cleverly and disdainfully telling us that what we have seen is not really the vain struggle of a certain marked individual against the superior power of cosmic will, that this story is a mask for 'deeper' events of a completely different nature which occur in ourselves as well as on stage while we, unaware of them, wrongly believe that we are contemplating a singular destiny of an obvious, though ambiguous, exemplary character. The real object of the representation would be the secret conflict of repressed desires belonging to the familial life of everyone, or the incestuous nature of power in a class-society, or the incompatibility of the notions of being earthborn and being born by parents, etc. Now, I do not submit that this is a fair allusion to Freudian, Marxist, and Lévi-Straussian interpretations of the Oedipus story. I simply want to illustrate a well-known and indeed very old gesture of the exegetic mind: that reinterpretative statement that negates the obvious meaning of the work, i.e. the consciously lived experience of the perfectly adequate spectator or reader. *Hidden* meanings (unconscious, ideological, archetypal, structural, etc.), no matter how relevant to the totality of existence, do not belong to hermeneutic interpretation in my definition unless the reader's basic experience of the work is enlarged by the interpretation in such a way as to let the hitherto hidden meanings appear on its horizon, the resulting aesthetic experience embracing both the first-given and the uncovered, previously hidden objects in a consistent whole of meaningful and conscious imaginary life. The second trait of the concept of hermeneutic interpretation, the phenomenological, is thus the assertion of the basic identity of the vision proposed by the interpretation and the vision experienced in the normal and even naïve reading of the work. Hermeneutic interpretation may expand and enrich the experience of the reader to great lengths, but it cannot result in negating the vision that originally inspires the reader and enlightens his conscious life (for example, as in Jaspers' sense of 'Existenzerhellung'), as if this vision were a quid pro quo, a mere disguise for another, entirely different meaning. This does not imply that psychoanalytic, Marxist, or structuralist reductions cannot be 'hermeneutic,' but that they can only be such if they can make the 'reduction' fit into the expanded overt experience. The enlargement of the field of consciousness might be the finality of hermeneutic interpretation. (One may consider, for instance, the possibility – or the impossibility – of introducing into the reading of Rilke's poem the ideology-critical interpretation of the sort given by Adorno in his *Jargon der Eigentlichkeit.*)

For the interpretation of modern narrative literature, this hermeneutic concept implies the basic reaffirmation of the individuality of the imagined persons, places, and events, i.e. it reaffirms the reader's experience of the fictitious situations and actions as being unique occurrences within the horizon of a temporality of historical character. Whatever exemplary, allegorical, or symbolic meaning may arise from the given imaginary actions, both straight reading and hermeneutic criticism will keep their individuality intact; the universal will not absorb the radiance of the singular. (I think that especially the 'reading' of fiction in the critical tradition of the English tongue tends to reach this interpretative goal.)

II

'Interpretation,' the second term of the expression hermeneutic interpretation also requires comment. One use of this word denotes the basic understanding of the primary meaning of a text, as opposed to the subsequent critical projection of this meaning into the universal context of literature, reality, and values. E.D. Hirsch's terminological distinction between meaning and significance, and the corresponding one between interpretation and criticism, points to this difference. Now, in this primary sense, there is only one kind of interpretation, the one that leads to the initial and, in a sense, full understanding of a text. This interpretation or understanding is the antecedent both to hermeneutic and to 'formal' criticism, although it certainly contains an undeveloped, precursory grasp of the corresponding subjects of both. This is eminently true of the generic keys of the reading and of the work's 'vision.' Even the full description of a sound pattern – including, say, intonational curves, emphasis, and the like – presupposes the interpretation of the basic meaning. In fact, our general subject – formalist and hermeneutic criticism – confronts two kinds of commentary that can only arise beyond the more or less accomplished critical task of philological hermeneutics. However, both formalist and hermeneutic approaches do modify the memory of the basic reading or influence the rereading in the classic path of the 'circle of interpretation.'

III

I take 'formal' criticism to be the description and discovery of parts of the literary work, of the relations between these parts, and of these parts to the whole. There are, in Husserl's sense (*Logische Untersuchungen*, III), both independent ('selbständige') and dependent ('unselbständige') parts, this delineation being in consonance with Aristotelian and neo-Aristotelian notions. Parts are, for instance, metrical patterns, lexical elements, syntactical constructions, 'figures of speech,' images, motifs, 'scenic' passages, 'panoramic' summaries, characters, 'story' ('fable'), 'plot' ('sujet'), episodes, genre, archetypes. Parts are generated by severance (chapters, passages, expressions, etc.) or by abstraction (patterns, style or the particular manner of discourse, type of world-view, fable and sujet, characters, etc.). 'Forms,' in the usual narrow sense, are dependent, abstracted parts, and are often hidden – as, for instance, a simple pattern in a rich surface.

Let us note that each kind of part is separately considered in the *Poetics*. Aristotle, implicitly but obviously, distinguishes the two Husserlian principles of partition: parts by abstraction are 'the six parts of tragedy': myth (plot), character, diction, thought, spectacle, and music; parts by severance are prologue, episode, exodus, and song of the chorus (*Poetics*, 12).

IV

It is easier, I think, to find instances of mixed formal-hermeneutical criticism than to find pure hermeneutical interpretation or pure formal description. Some of Roman Jakobson's analyses of poems might be strictly formalistic, or almost so. On the other hand Heidegger's exegeses of Hölderlin's or Rilke's poems point almost exclusively to the visionary content and tend to be conceptual paraphrases of a ciphered metaphysical revelation. It is well beyond discussion that a decisive enlargement of our knowledge of literature has been brought about by these authors. Considered just as interpretations of single literary works, however, these two types of criticism may seem, when taken separately, insufficient. They do not necessarily bring us back to a heightened awareness of the gift of poetry nor comprehend or circumscribe the poem conceptually in its full being. A radical exclusivity of these approaches was presumably indispensable for their emergence; however, when applied with equal exclusivity they lack the control and orientation which would be provided by utilizing the corresponding other side. Some accurate criticism of Jakobson's descriptions has been in fact based on his neglect of the difference between aesthetically effective and perceptually irrelevant patterns – a neglect that may be derived precisely from the disregard of the final existential effect and significance of the poem. Heidegger's reading on the other hand seems to overburden the poem's vision with a far too general, and only derivatively related, philosophic analysis of poetic as well as extrapoetic openness to being. A substantial consideration of poetic form should lead to a more exact sounding of the particularity and sharpness of the poem's own hermeneutic of existence.

v

While formalist criticism crystallizes in descriptive assertions of a conceptually precise and terminologically defined meaning, hermeneutic interpretation relies more on the words of ordinary language and on the traditional vocabulary of philosophy, and tends to end by suggesting the superiority of an enriched silence (since, among other things, the given is individual and 'individuum est ineffabile') and the renewed reception of the poetic text (cf. M. Heidegger: *Erläuterungen zu Hölderlins Dichtung*, 'Vorwort'). The epistemological ground (the mode of experience of the object) of hermeneutic interpretation of poetry is the same as that of impressionistic utterances and the interjections of enthusiasm. It is, as Emil Staiger says, the 'feeling' of the lover of poems ('Die Kunst der Interpretation').

While hermeneutic interpretation focuses naturally on the represented objects – persons, places, events (including verbal events), the stream of life – formalist description focuses unnaturally (in the Husserlian sense in which the phenomenological reductions produce an unnatural disposition to the world) on the representation itself – persons as characters, places as settings, events as motifs, the stream of life as the network of *signifiants* and *signifiés*. Hermeneutic criticism deals ultimately with literarily represented life, formalist criticism with literary representation. (Being a possibility of life, literary representation can, of course, occasionally become a literarily represented object, and thus a subject of purely hermeneutic discourse.)

Much of structuralist criticism is an analysis of the representation itself, which is brought to objectivity through a methodical negation of what is represented. Jakobson's conception of poetic discourse ('Linguistics and Poetics') as that which is devoid of referent and is essentially pointing back to itself – a statement that does not make good sense unless taken as a useful methodological violence – synthesizes this turn away from imaginary vision and into the opaque thingness of language. Literature comes to be seen as a non-representative art, a texture of a particular material – language, discourse – whose complex internal relations have to be shown in the plurality of its levels of meaning (as, for instance, in R. Barthes' 'codes'). The world of literary imagination, ultimately our world, with its values, tends to disappear in this criticism. Undoubtedly, rendering the text opaque, i.e. turning the material or medium of poetry into the object of criticism, constitutes an epochal discovery of contemporary aesthetic reflection that runs parallel, not only to Husserl's transcendental reductions, but also to literature's own self-ironization and the breaking of its straight mimetic function (a deed that has precursors such as Cervantes). But clearly the price of this discovery is one-sidedness. The extension of the concepts of language to cover all reality and to envision discourse as the substance of the universe is an admirable catachrestical tour de force that seems to unite structuralist and Heideggerian perspectives and thus formal and hermeneutical approaches. I suspect, however, that it only leads to the reinforcement of the evidence of the difference between what we ordinarily call the whole of life and reality and what we ordinarily call language (understanding language as a part of that larger being). And so, the relation of one to the other, i.e. the phenomenon of reference and representation, reappears anew.

The text of a piece of hermeneutic criticism, we may conclude, will point back to the text of the interpreted work, indicating an enriched rereading of it, and will tend to subordinate itself to the poetic text and keep it transparent, that is, mimetic. Formalist critical texts confront the literary text as their opaque object, or decompose (Barthes) and alter it. Reductive interpretations substitute another final text for the poetic text.

VI

In the context of our present considerations, it may be said that the prototype of literary criticism, Aristotle's *Poetics*, is clearly a synthesis of formalist and hermeneutic insights, though in such a way that formal features are consistently seen as subordinated to the (hermeneutically understandable) ends of the work of art. Aristotle distinguishes two major total qualities or values of the work of art for life. One, proper to all art insofar as it is 'imitation,' is to provide knowledge by comparison and idealization (or better, ideation) – this is the 'philosophic' value of verisimilitude. The other is the specific ultimate emotional effect attached to each kind or genre – purification through pity and fear, in the case of tragedy, a certain laughter in the case of comedy.

Knowledge and catharsis are not counted by Aristotle as 'parts' of tragedy but as ends. Now the generic determination of the parts, intrinsically and in relation to each other, i.e. the form of the work, is derived from the anticipated goals of verisimilitude and cathartic effect; form, according to Aristotle, serves these ends and is subjected to being adequate to them. The only limitation to this functionality of form, in the text of the *Poetics*, is probably the imperative of beauty in proper magnitude and proportion. It seems to be Aristotle's view that suitable form *produces* the ends for the spectator, although the ends, as final causes, are anticipated by the artist and so, in the perspective of the maker, produce the form.

The *Poetics* does not indicate whether the individually qualified ends of a given work can be conceptually abstracted from it and so 'at hand' independently from the corresponding work. It seems reasonable to understand that, according to Aristotle, the philosophic virtues of art can also be attained by philosophy itself. The generic emotional-ethical power, on the contrary, does not seem to be thought of by the philosopher as attainable by other than poetic means.

VII

Not only the historical prototype but also the permanent paradigm of criticism is a synthesis of formalist analysis and hermeneutic interpretation. Although the theory of poetry has sometimes taken the role of asserting a mere external conjunction of a profitable (philosophic and moral) content and a delightful (artistic) coating, as in Horace's repeated formula, and although there might well be an art of literature in which form is an external rhetorical strategy to convey a certain autonomous content, modern critics have tended to insist on the inextricable unity of content and form in the highest manifestations of poetry, that is, in the inexpressibility of the given content by any other than the given form, and consequently in the character of necessity and unlimited relevance that belongs to the determinant, unique form. The contemporary idea of art and literature tends in fact to negate the distinction of form and content. However, at least one version of the distinction survives: the concrete whole of each work of art (the 'sensual' form in which the distinction of form and matter – or 'substance' – is suspended) is seen as the unique carrier of a single meaning (or as the unique releaser of a single effect) that originates, articulates, and precariously transcends the bulk of the work. Rather than as independent wisdom enclosed in a rhetorical shrine, content appears now as the functionally rendered and generating *telos* of an intuitively given organization – a notion that underlies many a work of criticism to this very day and obviously represents a transfer to the singularity of the individual work of Aristotle's structural concept of the genre.

If the content of a literary work of art could be attained independently from the given artistic form, literary form and art would be indeed casual and external, unnecessary to the existential visions and responses that are an essential part of what makes literary works estimable. Literature would be in that case an inferior decorative art, an 'ancillary' (Alfonso Reyes) technique – at best illustration, allegory, didacticism; at worst propaganda of a previously given content, secured independently from art. In addition, criticism would dissolve into a rhetoric or didacticism of form on one hand and a philosophy of content on the other. No intrinsic coherence would bind such formal and hermeneutic approaches (except if it were possible, as some transformational structuralists programmatically pretend, to deduce strictly the complete text of the work from a generating deep structure of conceptual nature – an elementary system, or taxonomy, of meaning).

This is the condition to which, according to Hegel's lectures on the philosophy of art, art (and aesthetic criticism) must fall when reason and philosophy reach the stage of completely possessing and being able to express conceptually the universe: no content would then any longer necessitate a form other than the concept, and no artistic form could then carry a content inextricable from it. Art would have become irrelevant for the highest goals of the spirit. This historical degradation of the function of art posited by Hegel continues to be implied, unexpressed, and often unsuspected in some Marxist criticism, as well as in structuralist criticism of cybernetic inspiration.

However, both in and after Hegel's time, literature's self-consciousness has tended to stress its symbolic or visionary (not merely allegorical) character, i.e. its pretension of carrying a truth unattainable by conceptual, rational means. This theoretical function of literature, or 'symbolic art,' was precisely what Hegel considered to be the already-surpassed, primitive phase of the preconceptual, prerational (not metarational, as modern symbolism understands itself) attempt at discovering the divine mind. Whether it is more sensible to call it the modern ideology of artistry and of criticism, or simply the right apprehension of the function of artistic imagination, artists and critics in our time have very often claimed that the given form of the work of art is essential to, and inseparable from, the experienced content, that art provides a vision unattainable by other means (and superior to other kinds of knowledge), and that criticism has to consider form if it is to account for content. 'Technique as discovery' (Mark Shorer) is one among many contemporary versions of this aesthetic notion and critical paradigm. This claim for the unique theoretical (intuitive and expressive) function of art has distinguished Crocean aesthetics as well as Vosslerian and Spitzerian stylistics. Their criticism (prone to a psychologistic apprehension of expression) has been an effort to show the reciprocity of form (diction, style) and personal vision. Emil Staiger's and W. Kayser's criticisms have been based on the assumption of the necessity of the inseparability of the given form and content and have articulated formal analyses in the interpretative synthesis. A comparable design inspires Jean Rousset's *Forme et signification* and many other contemporary critical works. As for archetypal criticism in Northrop Frye's conception, I think it might be seen as a model of formal-hermeneutic interpretation: archetypal images and structures are brought into the basic fictional world of the work, expanding and articulating it and illuminating its more profound significance.

The assertion of the theoretical, visionary function of art has also received a remarkable emphasis from the Heideggerian contributions to a modified understanding of truth and knowledge, especially through the notion of the revelatory power of mood (*Stimmung*). That the experience of art is, in a marked sense, tonal is already an Aristotelian insight, even if it cannot be said that a theoretical power is explicitly accorded to mood in the *Poetics*. Mood is determined and objectified, if not created, by formal features (such as imagery and rhythm), and thus this revelatory power of art is clearly bound to the generic or stylistic form of the work. Incidentally, to put Aristotelian thoughts in the context of existential-hermeneutic philosophy is probably not such a violent connection as it may seem at first. Hans-Georg Gadamer insists on the basic identity of Aristotle's concept of a practical knowledge as distinct from a theoretical one, the Roman notion of *sensus communis*, and the foundations of Vico's defence of the humanistic tradition and 'rhetorical' truth against modern science's notion of method. From this tradition Gadamer derives his own view of art as a mode of knowledge and truth (*Wahrheit und Methode*, I, 1, ß, and *passim*).

To put it in a final simplification: if the existential content of a work of art can be expressed in conceptual terms, then art is only one way among others of conveying certain truths or information, and criticism is only a science of rhetoric of didactically forceful and pleasurable forms. The study of art divides, following this assumption, into such rhetorical criticism and into a philosophic recognition of contained 'thought.' On the other hand if the existential content of a work of art cannot be stated in conceptual terms, then it cannot be defined, described, or even properly named. Art is then a privileged way of knowledge, and criticism is both a directly impossible science and a possible science of the way, i.e. the *forms*, through which that conceptually unformulable knowledge is attained. Thus, the study of form becomes the indirect and only possible study of nameless content.

If it is true – as I believe it is – that descriptions of form are the only critical method for conceptually pointing to existential content, that does not mean that all descriptions of form accomplish this task. In fact, there is narrow 'formalistic' criticism, i.e. a criticism that – its fruitfulness notwithstanding – does not lead to a more articulated vision of the existential significance of art. Indeed, precisely this kind of formalism often goes hand in hand with a reduction of content to a disposable thought that can be expressed by conceptual formulas. Art becomes for this criticism a system of forms to convey a separable content. I will exemplify this kind of unintegrated interpretation by mentioning some of the critical views of Cervantes' *Don Quixote*. I will try to suggest, referring to the same novel, how a description of form may lead to an expanded, more articulated vision of metarational content. The form of a literary work can be seen as the very complex structure of a gesture of communication that points to the world shared by author and reader and purports to reveal its unnamable sense. (However, a distinction must be observed here: a short formulation of a work's meaning in conceptual terms – a definition of its theme – may be intended not as an identification of the content of the work but simply as the description of one of its forms – one of the possible allegorical projections of its world, i.e. one of the lines of significance that can be found in the symbol by an abstractive operation. Such a definition does not pretend to exhaust the sense of the symbol but merely points to it and aids in the recognition of it.)

What seems to be the corresponding inverted mistake is perhaps an innovation of our days: the rhetorical-stylistic reduction of conceptual discourses (philosophic, scientific, ideological) as if they had no content independent from the concrete form of their communication. It seems obvious to me that there are 'bodies of knowledge,' sciences, and doctrines, accessible and operative through an unlimited number of different forms of expression. A textbook of geometry is able to render accurately Euclidian insights in a form different from the original. Systematic expositions of scientific or philosophic disciplines may not completely exhaust the theoretical contents of the original contributions but may reasonably approach that goal. On the contrary, a systematic exposition of the world-view of literature, if at all sensible as an enterprise, will never displace the singular works, will never aim at procuring the full contents of the literary works. A radical difference separates a treatise of quantum physics or a survey of existentialist philosophy from 'systematic' overviews such as the *Anatomy of Criticism*, Bachelard's exploration of the universe of images, or the recent *L'Univers du roman* by Bourneuf and Ouellet, since these works of criticism describe systems of literary forms, in the sense I have defined, not of literary contents. To confound these diverse kinds of intellectual enterprises in a panrhetorical reduction of discourse is, to use the words of Bertrand Russell, 'a disservice to thought.'

A note also on 'metarational' contents of knowledge: we may preferably understand this term as relative to the historically given possibilities of contemporary conceptual discourse. In order to sustain the distinctions we have been working out, we do not have to claim that there are contents of knowledge that are essentially unattainable by rationality. Nor do we have to decide on the other hand whether John Searle is right in asserting his 'principle of expressibility,' according to which 'whatever can be meant can be said' (*Speech Acts*, 1.5 and 4.5). I suspect there is some difficulty in defining 'to mean' without turning the sentence into a pointlessly tautological one. Searle's principle corresponds, it seems to me, to the idealist notion of the universality of reason ('Universalität der Vernunft'). However, Searle includes showing in his notion of linguistic reference and expressibility of meaning; and showing obviously cannot be counted as a rational, conceptual reference.

VIII

Let us look for a moment through the conceptual frame we have been developing to one of the most characteristic structuralist topics: the interpretation of the literary work of art as the multiple repetition, in a succession of changing forms, of one and the same meaning. Jakobson's idea of the poem is precisely that of a discourse that projects over its syntagmatic axis elements of a single linguistic paradigm, i.e. a discourse that essentially repeats (and expands), by successive actualization of different elements of the same paradigm, the meaning that defines that paradigm (a view that recalls some of Riffaterre's analyses). The repetitive succession of elements is often seen in structuralist criticism as implying a variation of 'codes' (subcodes, more properly). The connotations would change while the denotation remained identical. Lévi-Strauss's explanation of the meaning of myth implies not only that different versions of the same myth are equivalent in meaning as long as their narrative units correspond to the same set of paradigms, but also that each version is intrinsically redundant and deploys in the form of a developing story a static conceptual incompatibility whose illusory conciliation the myth creates. A.J. Greimas has elaborated this notion into a semiotic theory of narrative, indicating a system of transformations that would generate the narrative starting from the achronic elementary structure of sense. He thereby introduces a dynamic moment into the meaning of the *récit*: the performance, by the order of succession of the story, of a conceptual mediation or negation that, in the deep structure, opposes the final state of affairs to the initial one. Nonetheless, the *récit* remains for Greimas enclosed in the achronic conceptual structure that is to be understood as the sense or meaning of the narrative. The meaning of a narrative discourse thus appears as a conceptualized world-view – as if the meaning of an unheard sentence were that of a previously conceived word.

Several points of this structuralist conception clearly contrast with the hermeneutic one. Obviously, the reader's experiences of the irreversible time of the story are not compatible with the structuralist reduction. Moreover, the concrete form of the literary work, i.e. the singularity of its shape and determination, appears in it as, if not completely irrelevant, at least not relevant for the production of the meaning of the work. The rhetorical or stylistic differences of different versions of a story must be consequently regarded as merely artistic and not pertinent to their sense. We recognize here the old notion of a deep content that can be expressed by a virtual myriad of more or less pleasant forms. However, the structuralist's ultimate content is, most characteristically, not a 'thesis,' a 'truth,' or a sentence (some structuralist studies, of course, do postulate a sentence as a transformed kernel of a poem), but a taxonomy, a semantic frame for discourses, a *langue* rather than a *parole*, a 'semantic micro-universe,' not a singular action of the mind.

It is true, I believe, that no expressive action, no storytelling, can occur without implying and actualizing the achronic (or synchronic) space of the corresponding expressive system, so that no story can develop outside a 'semantic micro-universe.' The difficulty for this structuralist view of the meaning of narratives arises from the obvious possibility that an unlimited number of stories can be produced inside the frame of the same narrative grammar and the same semantic units. Are they all going to have the same sense? Do all sentences of a given language say the same thing? In a certain way, in a limited sense of 'sense' (such as the manifestation of a particular cultural modality of the human mind), yes. But when we experience literature as meaningful and speak of the sense or content of this or that work, we use the word 'sense' with a richer connotation. A hermeneutic interpretation will not disregard any lived semantic dimension of the experienced poem.

The theoretical possibility of a strict deduction of the text of a literary work from a conceptual kernel of sense (this being the ideal of some of the formalist descriptions upon which we are commenting) rests, among other things, on the validity of the assumption of the universality of reason, i.e. the possibility of a translation of all contents of experience into sets of conceptual units, or semes. This amounts to the assumption of the possibility of constructing the strict equivalence of the world known 'by description' and the world known 'by acquaintance,' in Russell's terms. This would imply a strong formulation of 'the principle of expressibility': all that can be meant can be conceptually identified, so that whoever learns the definition will not gain new knowledge by a direct experience (perceptual or imaginary) of the object. The weaker version, which accepts showing as part of the definition, will not be sufficient as a hypothesis for the thesis of the deducibility of literary texts from conceptual kernels: the exhaustive reduction of all possible content to universal semes is the prerequisite of the deducibility of any literary content. Thus, the connection of semes to other semes would be indistinguishable from the corresponding complex of experience and the conceptual frame of language indistinguishable from the universe. Such a language would be not more and not less of a prison than the universe itself. The whole content of human experience (sensitive, emotional, perceptual, volitional, etc.) would have to be totally formalized, the 'world' converted into language, the substance of content translated incessantly into form. This goes beyond the accomplishment of natural languages, which merely point to the substance of experience through the form of their contents and merely create the order for the presence of things. It would be necessary to reduce 'the things of life' incessantly to named sets of named forms, i.e. to create the universal mathematics, the *mathesis universalis*. That is one of the thinkable conditions under which a computer could generate a work of literature from its 'deep meaning,' or, inversely, read it *with complete understanding.* Would such a cybernetic success invalidate the distinction of hermeneutic and formalist criticism, of understanding and explanation, of man and machine?

Envisaging this task, one sees the abyss separating our world from our language. And because the accomplishment of universal formalization seems as remote as is the conclusion of all science, we have to continue discussing literature – as well as other things – on the basis of conceptual insufficiency and of the community of undefined, lived experiences, to which we merely point. That is why we deal more fruitfully with imaginary objects than with semes, with a fictional world than with a 'text.' Lullus' *ars magna*, Descartes' or Leibniz' *mathesis* and *characteristica universalis* do not seem a reality yet. Rather, we may have to take, alas, the way of Hesse's *Glasperlenspiel*. (Such is the historical and theoretical magnitude of the questions involved in our methodological alternatives.)

IX

The interpretations of Cervantes' *Quixote*, like those of many other works, provide some good examples of criticism divided into a conceptual semi-philosophy of content and a formalist catalogue of rhetorical parts. Some formulable 'universal truth,' well known independently from Cervantes' creation (say, that human life is essentially determined by 'the eternal conflict of idealism and materialism,' as H. Hatzfeld stated long ago in his influential study *Don Quixote als Wortkunstwerk*, 1927), is supposed to be the theme expressed by the fictional world of the novel. Thus, Don Quixote would incarnate idealism, Sancho and the world at large, materialism. However, this novel, we are subsequently told, is not abstract allegory, since the characters, places, and events have – beyond their conceptual kernel – all the concrete fullness of life (a property usually seen as a basic artistic quality, emphatically postulated and rarely discussed). The literary forms through which the content is said to be expressed – motifs, stylistic devices, techniques of representation, action, dialogue, etc. – are catalogued and more or less consistently related to the stated content as its various particularizations. Ideally, I suppose, the conceptual content or theme would be seen as generating (structurally, if not psychologically) the parts of the work – ambiguously conceived both as images of concrete life (lived in the straight reading) and as technical forms and elements of literature (analytically abstracted by formal reflection). This kind of assumed content cannot be seen in an Aristotelian manner as being the end inaugurally and solely produced by the form of the work.

There is something obviously unsatisfactory about this kind of interpretation. First, the images and forms of the work mostly reject, so to speak, the transformational regress to the pretended conceptual origin, overwhelmingly surpass the limits of such a meaning, and do not fit in any sufficient measure into the formula, precisely because they do not constitute a mere allegory. Clearly, the invalidation of such an interpretative thesis would result from the attempt to translate all or most concrete deeds of the heroes into examples of concepts. Thus, John J. Allen, in an attentive study of Don Quixote's behaviour (*Don Quixote: Hero or Fool?* 1969) has shown some traditional generalizations of this kind to be false. Secondly, the enunciated content appears to be either a truism or a non-illuminating topic of popular edification, a 'message' blatantly disproportionate to the felt significance of the work.

However, the contention is that the existential content of the work cannot be properly interpreted in this conceptual-allegorical way, no matter how refined the conceptual formula, within the present limits of language. Among other things, like the comedy of a laughable case, the allegory of the incongruence of systematically idealizing imagination and reality, etc., the book, we see, is a symbol in the Goethean-Hegelian sense and cannot be rationally exhausted in the terms of contemporary discourse. I assume that we are still in this respect the contemporaries of Cervantes.

x

A hint of the metarational nature of the book's visionary content as well as the insurmountably contradictory character of any perceptive attempt at its definition can be obtained by putting together some of the most remarkable interpretations of the central character. They are logically and even imaginatively irreconcilable. A superinterpreter (just vaguely Riffaterrian) would be confronted with a laughable fool who is an existential hero (A. Castro) of religious dimensions (M. Unamuno); possessed, however, by the demon of abstract (wrong) idealism (Lukács), or rather by the eternal ideal of justice; obscured by a false kind of literary imagination but nonetheless performing a heroic deed of imagination (romantics); led astray by the anachronistic projection of the past and poetic world of heroic times into the prose of civilized (*bürgerliche*) society (Hegel and similarly Ortega), but announcing a coming new order of things (some Marxist critics). And so on. What emerges is, among other things, an archetypal blend of the *miles gloriosus* and Jesus Christ. Each one of these views of Don Quixote is right insofar as it can be somehow projected into the book; each is wrong to the degree that it leaves untouched most of the substance of the character. If we could press all of them together, the compound might be supposed right, but would never be seen to be so, because the price of such inconsistency is the unthinkability of the proposed notion, i.e. the blindness of the interpretation.

The ambiguity or ambivalence of Cervantes' vision or 'message' has become a major topic of the pertinent criticism. With it has come awareness of the elusive character of the 'philosophy' or existential content of the work, the inappropriateness of expecting from the book a conceptual statement. (Twentieth-century criticism – especially, of course, the 'new critic' – has repeatedly taught a positive view of the ambiguity of literary discourse, in my view another manifestation of the same essential metarationality of literary experience we have been considering.)

The form of the book can in principle be unambiguously and coherently described, even if we admit that the factual difficulty of doing so might be insurmountable. The presence of form arises from the operation of applying methodological concepts; thus, it seems naturally and appropriately exhausted by conceptual description. Let me now suggest the kind of formal study I have in mind as an indirect reference to existential content. From the variety of possible formal approaches to the text I will distinguish some elementary and macroscopic patterns, such as a repeated scenic paradigm and the archetypal parable of the voyage, and simplify them to the extreme.

XI

One essential inadequacy of an exegesis of content in terms of a conceptual statement (in addition to the insufficiency of the conceptualization of artistic vision) derives from the difference in kind between the intellectual experiences that correspond to rational discourse on one hand and novelistic vision on the other. They are radically diverse operations of knowledge and totally different games of the mind (one pointing to abstract order, the other to concrete immediate presence), and their results could be at most congruent or symmetric but by nature never identical or equivalent: the difference is between knowing all there is to know about an experience and living it. When rational discourse is grounded on the imaginary field or reading intuition and bound to it by a deictic relation (a sort of 'Deixis am Phantasma,' in K. Bühler's terms), a community of identical object and goal unites criticism and 'contemplation' (or, as it is said nowadays, 'consumption'). The experience of narrative content is inseparable from the movement of reading, i.e. the temporal experience of a developing complex image, given through a progressively richer medium of subjective (emotional, ethical) attitudes. Let us consider three patterns of such movements in *Quixote* – movements of live reading that obviously contain the themes, mentioned above, of the interpretative tradition, in a way that goes beyond unequivocal allegory.

The first is the cyclical movement of each of the various 'adventures' of Don Quixote that constitute the variations on the same paradigm: pulling Sancho with him by the force of his conviction about the way things are and should be, Don Quixote arrives in a certain situation that he misinterprets in terms of the world of chivalric romance. His subsequent actions end with the corresponding failure (or with an equivocal success). The conflict of his view of the situation and the situation as it turns out to be (i.e. the conflict of the imagination of romance and comic-realistic imagination) is resolved by Don Quixote maintaining his view of things and hypothesizing an extraneous (magic) alteration of the 'real' situation. As his world-view remains untouched, his mission continues. This is a mocking view of the power of infantile imagination upon a dignified adult, a kind of humorous ironic picture of the bondage of reason by the systematic forms of unempirical imagination and, more remotely, by doctrinal thought or ideology. No doubt, this form is considerably allegorical. However, it is also, as such, ambiguous, since it suggests at the same time the pathetic greatness of enduring heroic will.

Secondly, there is, mainly by means of the episodes and interpolated stories in which the protagonist is not Don Quixote, the broader movement of the book as a whole through the diverse regions of imagination – pastoral, picaresque, 'Italian' love intrigue, Byzantine peripeteias, etc. – in which a metasymbolic relativization of literary imagination and its principles takes place. This constitutes an exploration of limits that circles back to comic-realism and also shakes the foundations of realistic imagination. The projection of the shadow of 'mere literature' into the image of life pushes the disillusion of human knowledge to the limits of the uncanny. This central motif of Spanish Baroque deepens here beyond the historical period into a still unlimited actuality.

Finally, there is the archetypal movement of the quest of Don Quixote, which turns out to be a quest for knowledge and self-knowledge, an 'education process' (Menéndez y Pelayo), but a very strange one since there are two myths in the story: the comic myth of a hero who loses his sanity and the domestic wisdom of the home until, after many a day, he recovers both, and the rather tragic or pathetic myth of the hero who sets out to bring justice to the corrupt world but is defeated and reduced. So the hero's fall is the hero's salvation, and the hero's salvation is the hero's fall. The reader is brought to this ambiguous final peripeteia (which magnifies the same duplicity of meaning found in the cycle of each adventure) and is thus led to sustain a contradictory mouvement of vision and the emotional conflict of empathy and irony towards this 'exemplary' destiny. In this logically insoluble posture, the reader can only maintain, deep in his own self and for a time, the pulsation of life's ambivalent and unformulated imperatives.

I would like to emphasize that I believe the joy of reading Cervantes' *Quixote* is fundamentally, at the elementary level, that of play, and not that of knowledge. It emanates from the imaginary plenitude obtained by a comic subject. A hilarious situation is displayed in the seeming infinitude of new and ever more complex versions. The image, sustained by a network of motifs and meanings modified slightly in each successive scene, impresses us as inexhaustible and as consistent as life and effects the presence of the characters as individuals. But the basic comedy – the mad incongruence between the elderly, impotent, introverted small village dreamer with his rustical attendant, and the (in itself incongruous) world-historical mission they assume – contains the germs of the ambiguous allegory that develops into an inexhaustible symbol. Thus, the inferior and laughable outsiders become the carriers of the highest dreams of humanity, incarnate kindness, and rectitude. The position of the little heroes and the big world reverses constantly. The mad enterprise lets the ideals of a literary tradition regain the breath of life, break down, and arise weakly again and again. The ambivalent exploit is rewarded by fame, attention, and admiration – of the ridiculous art. While Don Quixote and Sancho slowly learn to look through the vanity of worldly greatness, we learn to see and feel more profoundly the ethical complexity of life, and the questionability of the ways we constitute it through imagination.

These precariously suggested descriptions of structures are not conceptual translations of the visionary content of the book, nor are they intended to replace the work's vision. They can only be instrumental in providing a more attentive experience of this poetic image of the world. Moreover, they try to intensify the awareness of the dynamics and movement of the literary experience. I think this may touch that dimension of literature that is 'rhetorical' in W. Booth's sense and that is also present in S. Fish's model of 'self-consuming artifacts,' although the descriptions of form I have suggested (similar to the Aristotelian description of tragedy) only point to a response of reflection, an ambiguous effect, and not to an unequivocal inducement to action.

XII

The key to as well as the controlling instance of hermeneutic criticism appears to be a methodologically uncontrolled experience: 'straight,' 'normal' reading. Although this presents an often discussed and very difficult problem that emerges thematically in the critical works of W. Iser and H.R. Jauss, one that I have not examined fully, let me at least suggest that the objection of 'subjectivism' to this epistemological foundation should not be pronounced too soon. The reading of literature as art (in opposition to methodical, critical 'readings') is a traditional institution constituted by specific, although currently for the most part inexplicit rules; it is not merely determined by indefinable 'tact' and 'taste' and traditional 'prejudices' (as Gadamer indicates) or by an instinctive drive towards superior life. Certainly, for the reading of each work, a creative singular projection of generic keys (since each work is both genre-determined and *sui generis*), as well as the sense of the singular, must complement the general attitudes of the literature-reading operation. However, creative subjectivity is naturally controlled by the institutional structure of literature. This, of course, does not imply a critical or reflective awareness of the constitutive rules and generic keys on the part of the reader (nor of the author), just as the ability to speak does not imply a theoretical knowledge of grammar or of the rules of speech acts. These rules of intellectual behaviour organize each reading as a meaningful act of cultured life that is institutionally conclusive (and so may have or fail to have 'closure' in B. Herrnstein Smith's sense) and that, if successful, ends in the production of a totality of vision and an acutely determined mood. The reader's gratification – be it a greater or a lesser one – because of the institutional form of the experience is in any case complete. A certain ecstatic suspension of the continuity of the current of life is a manifestation of the same behavioural structure that obviously gives its relative validity in principle to the praxis of equivocally named 'immanent interpretation.' By the mere performance of straight and successfully tactful reading, the vision and the symbolic meaning of the work, if it contains any, are open to the reader. There he stands, in the unlimited opening of the work and, if the work is true to life (and not an 'inauthentic' concealing image), in the truth of life. He stands imaginatively beyond literary forms and beyond language (in the ordinary sense of the word) in the substance upon which language and literature rest.

This initially (and finally) articulated, structured transparency of vision is indeed, as we said, the epistemological ground of hermeneutic interpretation. It is the basic adequacy of this vision that validates it. However, in the typical circular manner, the proper form-describing interpretation – through briefly rendering the work opaque – expands, clarifies, and, to an uncertain extent, rearticulates and modifies the vision.

I have stated that a coherent and communicable interpretation of the existential content of a literary work which does not preclude the metarationality and complexity of meaning can be only indirect: it has to be mainly a description of the form (structural, archetypal, generic, stylistic) that sustains the lived image and thus can lead the reader closer to it. The hermeneutic descriptions of form have initially to follow the orientation of the precursory experience of 'naïve' reading (which in the case of works of unusual type or remote origin, of course, has itself to be reflexively constructed). They become a kind of *showing* of the proper vision and the symbolic meaning, a kind of 'ostensive definition' (B. Russell) or a gesture of 'deictic' (*deiktisch*, K. Bühler) reference towards that which is irreducible to concepts.

The final content of literature is not language in the ordinary sense, neither *langue* nor *parole*. That is why discourse, although it seems to – and to a certain fundamental point does – produce language, cannot absorb or reabsorb it. Although there is a formalistic criticism that deliberately encloses itself in the limits of language, there is no prison of language. The bricks of language (to continue with this Nietzschean metaphor recalled by F. Jameson) are transitive; they put us constantly back outside, beyond themselves; they are a means to our self-transcendency. They are made by man to perform precisely this. We are always eminently outside, in the open. The problem of criticism is precisely the inverse: to make the transparency of vision opaque enough to handle and to communicate, to construct the instantly fading transit-houses of discourse that throw us out again into vision – an expanded one, a shared one.

University of Illinois at Chicago Circle

WOLFGANG ISER

Narrative Strategies as a Means of Communication

The following talk is based on a proposition I cannot specify here but for which I have given supporting evidence somewhere else.[1] The proposition refers to the relation of the literary text to the world in which it was produced. To put it briefly, a literary text draws from two different systems which exist outside the text itself: the system of its historical situation and social norms and the system of previous literatures and literary norms. The elements selected and encapsulated in the text are called the repertoire. These elements are, of course, selected and rearranged within the literary text itself according to the particular intention of that text. And the specific effects of this rearrangement of the elements of the repertoire vary according to the particular work under consideration.

There is, however, a need for some sort of guidance for the reader, some reference points, which in their residual familiarity provide a background through which the new system presented in the literary work can be approached and against which it can be measured. To put it again very briefly, the novel's concern with historical and social norms helps to establish an immediate link with the empirical reality familiar to its readers, and the presentation of this material serves to involve the reader in the world of the novel and so to help him to understand it and ultimately his own world more clearly. But these norms or conventions lose their social regulatory function once they enter the domain of the novel, and they may thus be subject to discussion and investigation. The material selected from previous literature is also placed in a new context and is subject to a similar depragmatization. The recurrence of these elements, too, provides a framework for new rearrangements in the novel at hand and guides the reader in part through the recall of his reactions to the material to which allusion is made. The reader is thus called upon to establish a system of equivalences out of the selected elements of the repertoire, a system I shall call the aesthetic object of the text. This is the proposition from which I intend to start focusing attention on the specific structure underlying that process of rearrangement within the text which ultimately prestructures the aesthetic object the reader is given to produce.

1 Wolfgang Iser, 'The Reality of Fiction: A Functionalist Approach to Literature,' *New Literary History* 7 (1975–6) 7–38

THE TASK OF STRATEGIES

The selection of social norms and literary allusions sets the work in a referential context within which its system of equivalences must be actualized. The function of the strategies is to organize this actualization, and they do so in a variety of ways. Not only do they condition the links between the different elements of the repertoire, thus helping to lay the foundations for the production of equivalences, but they also provide a meeting-point between the repertoire and the producer of those equivalences, namely the reader himself. In other words the strategies organize both the material of the text and the conditions under which that material is to be communicated. They cannot therefore be equated exclusively with 'representation' or with 'effect,' but in fact come into operation at a point before these terms are or can be relevant. They encompass the immanent structure of the text and the acts of comprehension thereby triggered off in the reader.

The organizational importance of these strategies becomes all too evident the moment they are dispensed with. This happens, for instance, when plays or novels are summarized or poems paraphrased. The text is practically disembodied, being reduced to content at the expense of effect. The strategies of the text are replaced by a personal organization, and more often than not we are left with a peculiar 'story' that is purely denotative, in no way connotative, and therefore totally without impact.

Now as the equivalence system of the text arises out of the combination of its elements, and as the reader himself must actually produce this system, it follows that the strategies can only offer the reader possibilities of organization. Total organization would mean there was nothing left for the reader to do, and furthermore that the combination of elements together with their comprehension could be defined in a total manner. Such total combination and comprehension may be possible in scientific texts, but not in literature, where the text does not reproduce facts, but at best uses such facts to stimulate the imagination of the reader. Indeed, if a literary text does organize its elements in too overt a manner, the chances are that we as readers will either reject the book out of boredom or resent the attempt to render us completely passive.

The strategies can generally be discerned through the techniques employed in the text, whether narrative or poetic. One need only think of the panoply of narrative techniques available to the novelist or the dialectical pattern employed by the sonneteer. However, our concern here is not with the techniques themselves but with the structure underlying them. What is this structure? The question is rather complex. One must bear in mind not only that the strategies organize the references of the repertoire together with the possibilities for their comprehension but also that they have to fulfill the function of what the speech act model calls the 'accepted procedures.'

These procedures incorporate all those rules and processes that must be common to speaker and listener if the speech act is to succeed. But in a fictional text, which by its very nature must call into question the validity of familiar norms, how can this 'common ground' be established in order for the communication to be 'successful'? After all, the ultimate function of the strategies is to *defamiliarize* the familiar.

THE OLD ANSWER: DEVIATION

The problem posed by this generally accepted function of the strategies has led to the structuralist model of deviation. We cannot enter here into the diffuse and often barren discussion of the 'poeticity' of a text through deviation, but it is important for us to bear in mind the limitations of the deviationist model if we are to transcend it in our search for the structure underlying the strategies. Deviation as a central condition of 'poeticity' has long since been denigrated as 'deviationist talk,'[2] but as an explanatory hypothesis it still lingers on, as can be seen even from the work of Lotman.

The deviationist model was given its classic outline by Mukařovský in his 1940 essay 'Standard Language and Poetic Language': 'The violation of the norm of the standard, its systematic violation, is what makes possible the poetic utilization of language; without this possibility there would be no poetry.'[3] Leaving aside the many criticisms already levelled against this idea, we can see here the fundamental implication of the deviationist theory together with its most powerful argument which has retained its cogency, at least up until Lotman. Put explicitly, it is that a violation of the standard possesses 'poetic quality' in so far as the standard is always evoked by the violation, so that it is not the violation as such but the relation it establishes which becomes a condition of 'poetic quality.' Mukařovský does allude to this situation in his essay: 'The background which we perceive behind the work of poetry as consisting of the unforegrounded components resisting foregrounding is thus dual: the norm of the standard language and the traditional esthetic canon. Both backgrounds are always potentially present, though one of them will predominate in the concrete case.'[4] It is obvious that a violation of the standard and of the 'esthetic canon' can only have the function of producing the meaning potential of a text and not the way in which that potential is actualized. The limitations of the deviationist model in relation to textual strategies can be gauged from the elementary problems

---

2 Cf. Stanley Fish, 'Literature in the Reader: Affective Stylistics,' *New Literary History* 2 (1970) 155

3 Jan Mukařovský, 'Standard Language and Poetic Language,' in *A Prague School Reader on Esthetics, Literary Structure, and Style*, ed. Paul L. Garvin (Washington DC: Georgetown University Press, 1964), 18

4 Ibid. 22

it raises. What *is* the norm of the standard language? What *is* the aesthetic canon? These two linchpins of the deviationist model must be constant – in order to guarantee an invariable effect. If deviation from them is a condition of 'poetic quality' – a province reserved for literary texts – then what is the status of conversational violations of the norm? The orthodox deviationist theory is evidently highly puristic – what is aesthetic in art is presumably non-aesthetic in real life. This distinction seems even more difficult to grasp than the thorny problem of how language norms and the aesthetic canon are to be ascertained. The concept of deviation offers a thoroughly one-dimensional definition of the literary text, resting its entire case on a single blanket assumption: that the text deviates from the norm or from the canon. Little attention is paid to the differences between component parts of the text, parts essential to the production of the aesthetic object; nor is there any analysis of those features of the aesthetic object that are considerably more concrete than the vague and highly suspect quality of 'poeticity.'

These glaring deficiencies in the deviationist theory have not altogether escaped the attention of its adherents. However, their attempts to perfect their theory simply bring to light more of its constitutive limitations. A series of corollaries sets out to define more closely what is meant by violation and deviation. Linguistically oriented poetics assembles a complete arsenal of deviations, not only from ordinary language, but also from accepted literary norms – the structuralist stylistics of Riffaterre being a prime example of this. The corollaries are all in the nature of classifications; they are simply lists that in principle could be extended indefinitely without ever ceasing to be lists. However useful such a catalogue might be, it tells us nothing whatsoever about functions. The fact that this objection would make little impression on the confirmed deviationist is due to his belief that the catalogue of deviations represents the fulfillment of what purports to be *the* structure of the literary text. But if 'there is such a thing as the *Ultimate Structure*, this must be indefinable: there is no metalanguage that could encompass it. If it is identified, then it is not the *ultimate*. The *ultimate* is that which – hidden and ungraspable and nonstructured – produces new phenomena.'[5] A mere register defining such a structure will therefore inevitably miss out its meaning.

However, despite this reification of structure basic to the deviationist theory, some aspects may be counted as its achievements in that they shed a good deal of light on the structure of the literary text. Deviations can range from violation of the norm or canon as far as total invalidation of the familiar. This very fact enhances the semantic potential of the text, which

---

5 Umberto Eco, *Einführung in die Semiotik*, transl. by Jürgen Trabant (Munich: W. Fink, coll. UTB 1972), 411 (quote trans. into English by W.I.)

thus produces a special kind of tension; the violation is transformed into an irritation, which begins to draw attention to itself. The tension demands relief, and this necessitates a reference that cannot be identical to those references that have originally produced the tension. This brings about the first phase of the relationship between text and reader: the 'poetic quality' is not linked to the norms of an abstract standard, nor to an equally abstract aesthetic canon, but to the disposition of the individual reader. Its function is to mobilize the reader's attention and so to accomplish the task which Austin – in relation to the illocutionary speech act – designated as 'securing uptake.'[6] Interpreted in this sense, deviation can no longer refer exclusively to a postulated linguistic norm; it is equally bound up with the expectations of the reader, the thwarting of which will lead considerably further than the mere production of a semantic potential. Generally speaking, the 'expectation norms'[7] of the text can be divided into two categories. First, the repertoire of social norms and literary references supplies the background against which the text is to be reconstituted by the reader. Second, the expectations may relate to the social and cultural conventions of a particular public for which a text is specifically intended. The latter type may be seen in didactic and propagandist literature from the Middle Ages to the present day; contemporary thought systems are incorporated into the text in order to provoke a confirmatory attitude towards the background they supply. Violations of such overt norms will, of course, produce a tension, but they will not themselves structure the attitude of the reader – if they did, the propaganda would fail. The enhancement of the semantic potential through violation of the norm clearly cannot be an end in itself but must be directed towards a possible recipient of the message, and it is precisely this pragmatic element of the text that eludes the grasp of the deviationists. For them, deviation is only significant, and can be so classified, in terms of a system of semantics, not in terms of pragmatics. One of the paradoxes of the deviationist theory is that its structuralist concept should prove incapable of structuring the communication process that arises between text and reader as a result of deviation.

It is evident that the deviationist theory offers an all too inadequate basis for a description of those strategies that structure the communication between text and reader. The necessity for a reorientation has been succinctly expressed by A.E. Darbyshire in his *Grammar of Style*: style, he says, is not 'a deviation from the norm' but 'a deviation into sense.'[8] He draws a vital distinction between meaning and information, showing that the strategies

6 J.L. Austin, *How to do Things with Words*, ed. J.O. Urmson (Cambridge, Mass.: Harvard University Press, 1962), 120

7 Cf. Broder Carstensen, 'Stil und Norm,' *Zeitschrift für Dialektologie und Linguistik* 37 (1970) 260ff

8 Cf. A.E. Darbyshire, *A Grammar of Style* (London: Deutsch, 1971) 98, 107, 111ff

cannot be confined merely to the technique of representation. 'I wish to make a distinction between the words *meaning* and *information* as technical terms used in the discussion of the grammar of style. To speak generally, one might say that information is provided by the encoders of messages in order to give the messages meaning, and that meaning, therefore, is a totality of the experiences of responding to a given amount of information.'[9]

Such observations also underlie Gombrich's ideas on the perception of pictorial art, as set forth in his book *Art and Illusion*. He introduces the concepts of 'schema' and 'correction,'[10] which are based on gestalt psychology though he develops them in his own way. Gombrich begins by using these two concepts to describe the act of representation in the pictorial arts; at no time, however, does he separate representation from the conditions of reception; on the contrary, he tries to comprehend representation in terms of reception. The schema functions as a filter enabling us to group data together: 'The idea of some basic scaffolding or armature that determines the 'essence' of things, reflects our needs for a schema with which to grasp the infinite variety of this world of change ... This tendency of our minds to classify and register our experience in terms of the known must present a real problem to the artist in his encounter with the particular.'[11] The schema reveals not only the economy principle, which gestalt psychology has shown to regulate all our everyday perceptions,[12] but also a drastic and necessary reduction in the contingency of the world, which is represented by the increasing complexity of the schema and is thereby made accessible to comprehension. The structure of the schema is evidently dialectical, in so far as it balances the economy principle (i.e. the exclusion of perceptual data) against its own increasing complexity through which it counters losses sustained by the reduction of the world's contingency. Only in this way can schemata prove themselves, and the more efficiently they can represent the real world, the more stabilized they become, until eventually they turn into reliable stereotypes.

This brings us to the second major point in Gombrich's argument. Each schema makes the world accessible in accordance with the conventions the artist has inherited. But when something new is perceived which is not covered by these schemata, it can only be represented by means of a correction to them. And through the correction the special experience of the new perception may be captured and conveyed. Here we have not only a renuncia-

---

9 Ibid. 141
10 Cf. E.H. Gombrich, *Art and Illusion: A Study in the Psychology of Pictorial Representation* (London: Phaidon Press, 1962) 24, 99
11 Ibid. 132ff, 144
12 Cf. Rudolf Arnheim, *Art and Visual Perception: A Psychology of the Creative Eye* (Berkeley and Los Angeles: University of California Press, 1966) 46ff

tion of the idea of naïve, imitative realism, but also the implication that the comprehension and representation of a special reality can only take place by way of negating the familiar elements of a schema. Herein lies the functional fecundity of the Gombrich model, for the schema embodies a reference which is then transcended by the correction. Whilst the schema enables the world to be represented, the correction evokes the observer's reactions to that represented world.

At this point, however, Gombrich appears to set limits to the operative character of his model. He suggests that the corrections of the schemata are guided by 'matching,'[13] by which he means the effort of the painter to match what he has observed to the patterns he has inherited. Thus the act of representation is seen as a continual process of modifying traditional schemata, the correction of which permits an ever more 'suitable' representation of the world – a process whose aim has been classified by Wollheim, in his justifiable attack on this concept, as ' a fully fledged Naturalism.'[14] Corrections in Gombrich's sense of the term presuppose a normative principle that regulates perception and representation of the world. Consequently schemata in painting have steadily lost their function ever since the Impressionist movement, so that Modern Art has rebelled against the schema, and the model has become virtually defunct.[15] What is important for our purposes, however, is the fact that the correction violates a norm of expectation contained within the picture itself. In this way the act of representation creates its own conditions of reception. It stimulates observation and sets to work the imagination of the observer, who is guided by the correction to the extent that he will try to discover the motive behind the change in the schema.

It is in this sense that the concepts of schema and correction have a heuristic value for the strategies of literary texts. If we apply these concepts to the description of such texts, however, we must make one important modification, which will also remove Wollheim's objection. The literary correction of schemata cannot come about through a special perception, as it does in the pictorial arts, for there is no special objective reality against which the text can be measured. The relation of the text to the world can only be discerned by way of the schemata which the text bears within itself, namely the repertoire of social norms and literary conventions which condition the particular 'picture' offered by the work. Now if these schemata are to be changed, the 'correction' cannot be guided by perceptual data from the existing outside world, because in literary texts the correction is meant to

13 Cf. Gombrich, *Art and Illusion*, 121
14 Richard Wollheim, 'Art and Illusion,' in *Aesthetics in the Modern World*, ed. Harold Osborne (London: Thames and Hudson, 1968), 245
15 Gombrich, *Art and Illusion*, 149, 169, 301, 330ff

evoke something not found and not formulated in the outside world. The correction can therefore only take place through the restructuring of points of *significance* in the schemata. Herein lies the particular function of the literary schemata; in themselves they are elements of the text, and yet they are neither aspect nor part of the aesthetic object. The aesthetic object signals its presence through the deformations of the schemata; and the reader, in recognizing these deformations, is stimulated into giving the aesthetic object its shape. It is the very insubstantiality of the aesthetic object that spurs on the reader's imagination. This, however, does not mean that the imagination is left completely free to produce what it will. It is here that the strategies play their part, in laying down the lines along which the imagination is to run. But how these strategies fulfill their function is explained neither by the deviationist model nor by Gombrich's schema and correction.

THE BACKGROUND-FOREGROUND RELATIONSHIP

If we take a term from R. Posner, the schemata of the text stand as the first code, while the aesthetic object stands as the second code, which the reader himself must produce: 'it [the aesthetic object] does not exist prior to the text that concretises it, but only assembles itself *in* the text, and it is not known to all participants, but is only ascertained during the reading process. It is mainly from this activity – the deciphering of the "second code" – that is derived the aesthetic pleasure which the reader feels as he reads.'[16] Now if the function of the primary code is to give the reader directions for deciphering the secondary code, the primary cannot be a pure denotation, because the selected schemata are not an end in themselves. They are component parts of a structure which transcends both the individual schema and the original context from which the schema has been taken. This structure consists of the relationships between the now depragmatized schemata, and thus sets out the conditions under which the new arrangement is to be experienced. But these conditions in turn cannot be binding, for while the primary code (the schemata) remains invariable, the secondary (the aesthetic object) certainly does not. It will vary in accordance with the social and cultural code of each individual reader. The strategies, then, carry the invariable primary code to the reader, who will then decipher it in his own way, thus producing the variable secondary code.

The basic structure of these strategies arises out of the selective composition of the repertoire. Whatever social norms may be selected and encapsulated in the text, they will automatically establish a frame of reference in the form of the thought system or social system from which they were selected.

16 Roland Posner, 'Strukturalismus in der Gedichtinterpretation: Textdeskription und Rezeptionsanalyse am Beispiel von Baudelaires "Les Chats," '*Sprache im technischen Zeitalter* 29 (1969) 31 (English transl. and emphasis W.I.)

The very process of selection inevitably creates a background-foreground relationship, with the chosen element in the foreground and its original context in the background. And indeed, without such a relationship the chosen element would appear meaningless. Now the norms of social realities have a definite meaning within their particular pragmatic context, but when they are removed from that context, hitherto unsuspected meanings are bound to make their presence felt. The same applies to literary allusions; in a parody, for instance, the change of context results in a complete reversal of the original meaning. And so once the norm is lifted from its original context and transplanted to the literary text, new meanings come to the fore. But at the same time the norm drags its original context in its wake, so to speak, because only against the background of that context can it take on its new form. The selections that underlie all literary texts will always give rise to this foreground-background relationship: the chosen element evokes its original setting, but is to take on a new and as yet unknown function. By means of this foreground-background relationship the principle of selection exploits a basic condition for all forms of comprehension and experience, for the as yet unknown meaning would be incomprehensible were it not for the familiarity of the background it is set against.

There are certain similarities between this background-foreground concept and that of redundancy and innovation in information theory, as there are similarities between that of figure and ground in gestalt psychology. In all cases this relationship is clearly central to processes of perception and comprehension, but there are definite differences between the literary concept and the others, and these are no doubt due to the different functions which the structure has to perform. Information will be innovative to the degree that it stands out from the redundancy in which it is embedded. 'Redundancy provides a guarantee against errors of communication, as it allows the information to be reproduced on the basis of the knowledge which the recipient already has of the structure of the language used.'[17] Consequently redundancy 'is to be regarded as the expression of a constraint which restricts the sender's freedom of choice,'[18] thus making the information 'measurable in quantity.'[19] Now the background of the literary text does not have this character of redundancy, for it is not actually formulated by the text itself but depends for its quantity and quality on the competence of its readers. In the communication of information, however, the redundancy must be formulated so that the newness of the information can be conveyed.

---

17 Abraham A. Moles, *Informationstheorie und ästhetische Wahrnehmung*, transl. Hans Ronge et al. (Köln: Du Mont, 1971), 82 (this and the next two quotes transl. into English by W.I.)
18 Ibid.
19 Ibid. 213, 259

This redundancy will also remain stable, for its sole function is to provide an unmistakable setting for the information to be imparted. In the literary text not only is the background unformulated and variable, but its significance will also change in accordance with the new perspectives brought about by the foregrounded elements; the familiar facilitates our comprehension of the unfamiliar, but the unfamiliar in turn restructures our comprehension of the familiar. This again reflects back on and so transforms the selected elements that have set the whole process in motion. Thus the background-foreground relationship in literary texts is dialectical in character, whereas the redundancy of the information model remains inactive and unactivated.

Gestalt psychology uses the terms figure and ground to describe the 'fields' of perception. The enclosed 'field' is the figure, and that which encloses it is the ground.[20] During the process of perception we always select specific items from the mass of data available to our senses, a selection governed by our expectations. The figure will remain surrounded by the diffuse data of which we have, so to speak, taken no account. Within this figure-and-ground-relationship, which is fundamental to the process of perception, certain distinctions must be drawn.

The most important of these is the fact that the perceived figure and the perceived ground are not formed in the same way, and in a certain sense the perceived ground has no form at all. A field which had previously been perceived as a ground, and is then for the first time perceived as a figure, can have a surprising effect, and this effect is due to the new form which the observer had not been conscious of before, and which he now perceives ... In order to draw the fundamental distinction between figure and ground, it is useful to introduce the contour, which may be defined as the borderline common to the two fields ... When two fields border on each other and the one is perceived as the figure and the other as the ground, what is directly perceived may be characterized by the fact that the common contour of the fields has a forming effect, which makes itself felt only in the one, or in the one more than in the other. The field that is most influenced by this forming effect is the figure, and the other field is the ground.[21]

If the order is reversed, with the forming effect of the contour being brought to bear on what had previously been the ground, there is a corresponding change in perception, with a corresponding element of surprise. Although the dividing line between background and foreground is by no means so clear in the literary text, the reversal of the two can have a similar effect. We find it, for instance, in social novels, where the norms represented by the

20 Cf. Edgar Rubin, *Visuell wahrgenommene Figuren: Studien in psychologischer Analyse* (Copenhagen: Gyldendal, 1921) 5, 68
21 Ibid. 36ff (trans. by W.I.)

characters often serve to draw attention to the social context from which they are taken. Then the background becomes the 'figure,' and the reader's surprise indicates that he now begins to perceive the system he is caught up in, a perception not possible as long as his own conduct was guided by that system. Dickens, for example, made great use of this effect in order to enable his readers to experience the social system that governed the world in which they were living.[22]

Despite these similarities between the two sets of concepts, the literary background-foreground relationship differs in several ways from the figure-and-ground-relationship in gestalt psychology. First, figure and ground are structures relating to existing data, whereas in literature the background and foreground are not given, but are dependent on selections made prior to 'perception'. Secondly, figure and ground can be interchanged, with a resultant surprise effect, but this exchange is nearly always occasioned by outside influences, whereas in literature the reversal is manipulated by structures within the text. Finally, the figure-and-ground concept involves a straightforward switch from 'formed thing' to 'unformed material,'[23] whereas in literature this switch, though it takes place continually, is not an end in itself, but is simply the precondition for a process which might be described by Arnheim's colourful phrase: 'mutual bombardment.'[24] The background-foreground relation is a basic structure by means of which the strategies of the text produce a tension that sets off a series of different actions and interactions, and that is ultimately resolved by the emergence of the aesthetic object.

THE STRUCTURE OF THEME AND HORIZON

In describing the background-foreground relation underlying all textual strategies we have so far talked only of the link between the repertoire (norms and literary allusions) and the systems to which the repertoire refers, for herein lies the external frame of reference of the work; it is the selection of norms and allusions that enables the background to be built up, which in turn allows the reader to grasp the significance of the elements selected. However, the main task of the textual strategies is to organize the *internal* network of references, for it is these that pre-structure the shape of the aesthetic object to be produced by the reader. The elements selected have to be combined. Selection and combination are, in Roman Jakobson's words,

22 Cf. Kathleen Tillotson, *Novels of the Eighteen-Forties* (Oxford: Oxford University Press, coll. Oxford Paperbacks, 1961) 73–88
23 Rubin, 48
24 Cf. Rudolf Arnheim, *Toward a Psychology of Art: Collected Essays* (Berkeley and Los Angeles: University of California Press, 1967) 226ff

'the two basic modes of arrangement used in verbal behaviour,' from which he concludes that 'the poetic function projects the principle of equivalence from the axis of selection into the axis of combination.'[25] Selection brings about the background-foreground relation, which allows access to the world of the text. Combination organizes the chosen elements in such a way as to allow comprehension of the text. Selection establishes the outer link, combination the inner.

What is combined within the narrative is a whole system of perspectives, for the work is not just the author's view of the world, it is itself an assembly of different perspectives – and indeed only through the combination of these different perspectives can the non-given reality of the aesthetic object be built up. Generally speaking, there are four perspectives through which the pattern of the repertoire first emerges: that of the narrator, that of the characters, that of the plot, and that marked out for the reader. Naturally, narrative texts need not always deploy the full range of these different orientations. If the function of the different perspectives is to bring out the production of the aesthetic object (i.e. the meaning of the text), it follows that this object cannot be totally represented by any one of those perspectives. And while each perspective offers a particular view of the intended object, it also opens up a view on the other perspectives. The interaction between perspectives is continuous, because they are not separated distinctly from one another, nor do they run parallel; authorial comment, dialogue between characters, developments of plot, and the positions marked out for the reader, all these are interwoven in the text and offer a constantly shifting constellation of views. These, then, are the 'inner' perspectives of the narrative text, to be distinguished from the 'outer' perspective which links the narrative to outside reality.

The inner perspectives form the framework within which the selected elements are combined, but they too must be structured in such a way that the combination may be regulated. In describing this structure, perhaps we might borrow a pair of terms from Alfred Schütz, *Thema und Horizont*,[26] theme and horizon. Because textual perspectives are continually interweaving and interacting, it is not possible for the reader to embrace all perspectives at once, so that the view he is involved with at any moment is what constitutes for him the 'theme.' This, however, always stands before the 'horizon' of the other perspective segments in which it had previously been

25 Roman Jakobson, 'Closing Statement: Linguistics and Poetics,' in *Style in Language*, ed. Thomas A. Sebeok (Cambridge, Mass.: Harvard University Press, 2nd prt 1964), 358
26 Cf. Alfred Schütz, *Das Problem der Relevanz* (Frankfurt: Suhrkamp, 1971) 30f and 36ff, who uses this concept in a different context and thus refers to something different from that intended here.

situated. 'The horizon is that which includes and embraces everything that is visible from one point.'[27] Now the horizon is not a purely optional one; it is composed of all those segments which had supplied the themes of previous phases of reading. For instance, if the reader is at present concerned with the conduct of the hero – which is therefore the theme of the moment – his attitude will be conditioned by the horizon of past attitudes towards the hero, from the point of view of the narrator, of the other characters, the plot, the hero himself, etc. This is how the structure of theme and horizon organizes the attitudes of the reader and at the same time builds up the perspective system of the text. It is a structure that constitutes the basic rule for the combination of textual strategies and its effects are manifold.

1 It organizes a relationship between text and reader that is essential for comprehension. As an author's perspective of the world, the text clearly cannot claim to represent the reader's view. The gap cannot be bridged just by a 'willing suspension of disbelief,' because, as has already been pointed out, the reader's task is not simply to accept but to assemble for himself that which is to be accepted. The manner in which he assembles it is dictated by the continual switching of perspectives during the time-flow of his reading, and this in turn provides a theme and horizon structure which enables the reader gradually to take over the author's unfamiliar view of the world on the terms laid down by the author. The structure of theme and horizon constitutes the vital link between text and reader, because it actively involves the reader in the process of synthesizing an assembly of constantly shifting viewpoints, which not only modify one another but also influence past and future syntheses.

2 The continual interaction of perspectives throws new light on all positions linguistically manifested in the text, for each position is set in a fresh context, with the result that the reader's attention is drawn to aspects hitherto not apparent. Thus the structure of theme and horizon transforms every perspective segment of the text into a two-way glass, in the sense that each segment appears against the others and is therefore not only itself but also a reflection and an illuminator of those others. Each individual position is thus expanded and changed by its relation to the others, for we view it from all the perspectives that constitute the horizon. In this respect the literary text avails itself of a mechanism that regulates perception in general, for what is observed changes when it is observed, in accordance with the particular expectations of the observer. In the case of the reader, these expectations are conditioned by the preceding perspective segments of the text. The individual segments, then, take on their significance only through interaction with other segments, and if we bear in mind the fact that all the

27 Hans-Georg Gadamer, *Wahrheit und Methode: Grundzüge einer philosophischen Hermeneutik* (Tübingen: Mohr, 1960) 286

perspectives (narrator, hero, etc.) represent something determinate and that these determinate elements are transformed by their interplay, it is obvious that the ultimate meaning of the text – or the aesthetic object – transcends all the determinate elements. Furthermore, every position incorporated into the text becomes an object of observation, and as such is inevitably changeable; and if these positions represent selections from the social or literary world outside the text, it follows that the reader, as he produces the aesthetic object, may react to the 'world' incorporated into the text, in other words he may see the selected norms in a new light. This is the ultimate function of the aesthetic object: it establishes itself as a transcendental viewpoint for the positions represented in the text, positions from which it is actually compiled and which it now sets up for (critical) observation. It is clear that if a literary text represents a reaction to the world, the reaction must be to the world incorporated in the text; the forming of the aesthetic object therefore coincides with the reader's reactions to positions set up and transformed by the structure of theme and horizon.

3 If the aesthetic object can only be built up by transformations of positions in the text, it cannot be as Ingarden conceives it in his theory of art. According to this theory, the schematized views of the text constitute a medium allowing access to what Ingarden calls the intentional object of the work.[28] He implies that each schematized view represents a facet of the object, whereas in fact these views, which we have called perspective segments, represent references to the world incorporated into the text. As we have seen from our discussion of the repertoire, these can be very heterogeneous, and it is only their mutual modification (impossible if they were truly representative) that brings about the equivalences which lead to the production of the aesthetic object. Ingarden certainly acknowledged that the 'intentional object' had to be formulated by the reader, but the access afforded by his schematized views cannot be sufficient for this formulation. Although they are schemata for the guidance of the reader, Ingarden tells us virtually nothing about the way in which they can be combined. They seem only to create a need for determinacy, an 'unfulfilled quality' which is then fulfilled by the subsequent view.[29] This, however, indicates nothing more than a process of completion, which serves to confirm Ingarden's postulate of the polyphonic character of the work of art rather than to illuminate the properties of the aesthetic object. If the schematized views represent specific positions, the question remains how the aesthetic object, which always transcends the individual positions, can be constituted.

As we have seen, the structure of theme and horizon allows all positions to be observed, expanded, and changed. Our attitude towards each theme is

28 Cf. Roman Ingarden, *Das literarische Kunstwerk* (Tübingen: M. Niemeyer, 1960) 294ff
29 Ibid. 277

influenced by the horizon of past themes, and as each theme itself becomes part of the horizon during the time-flow of our reading so it too exerts an influence on subsequent themes. Each change denotes not a loss but an enrichment, as attitudes are at one and the same time refined and broadened. It is the resultant accumulation of equivalences that constitutes the aesthetic object. The system of equivalences is therefore not to be found in any one of the positions or perspectives of the text and is not formulated by any one of them; on the contrary, it is the formulation of that which has not yet been formulated, and as such it offers the reader a transcendental vantage point from which he can see through all the positions that have been formulated. To sum up, then, the structure of theme and horizon exploits the basic mode of comprehension common to information theory and perception, but differs from these in that, first, its frame of reference is imaginary and not real, and, second, it initiates a process of communication through transformation of positions, as opposed to pinpointing of information and grouping of data.

VARIATIONS OF THE THEME-AND-HORIZON STRUCTURE

The structure of theme and horizon underlies the combination of all the perspectives, and it enables the literary text to fulfil its communicatory function: namely, to ensure that the reaction of text to world will trigger off a matching response in the reader. An all-important aspect of this process of communication is the allocation of selected norms to individual textual perspectives. A certain value will automatically be set on the social norms and literary allusions, in accordance with their distribution amongst characters, plot, narrator, etc. Thus not only does the repertoire reflect a process of selection but so too does the allocation of its elements. This principle of selection-within-selection can perhaps best be illustrated through the perspective of the characters. In general there are two possibilities here: the selected norms will be represented either by the hero or by the minor characters. The consequences of each choice may be totally different: if the hero represents the norms, the minor characters will fall short of or diverge from them; and if it is the other way round then the hero is likely to initiate a critical view of the norms. In the first case the norms will be affirmed, and in the second they will be undermined. Thus the distribution of the repertoire amongst the different perspectives brings about criteria for the evaluation of the elements selected. Such criteria only become effective, of course, through the interaction of theme and horizon, which permits the reader to view the old norms in their new context and so to produce for himself a system of equivalences. This is how the structure of theme and horizon absorbs the reader into the historical situation of the text, to which he is then to react. But even more important in this respect is the following. While the elements of the repertoire are allotted to the different perspectives, these perspectives are themselves arranged in a specific relationship to one another. In narrative texts we tend to find four basic types of perspective arrangement, which we might call counterbalance, opposition, echelon, and serial. Counterbalance entails a very definite hierarchy of perspectives; not only are the qualities and defects of the perspectives clearly graded but the communicatory function of the text is also clearly indicated. Bunyan's *Pilgrim's Progress* is a good example of this type. The hero represents the principal perspective; through him a catalogue of norms is unfolded, and these must be conformed to if the goal of salvation is to be reached. The norms represented by the central perspective are therefore affirmed, and any violation of them is punished. The perspective of the minor characters is clearly subordinate to that of the hero; those who conform most closely to the norms represented remain longest in the pilgrim's company, Hopeful being the obvious example. The historical background to these norms was the religious despair of the Calvinists, countered here by the affirmative description of an exemplary search for salvation. Thus the literary text offers a solution which had been explicitly excluded by the doctrine of predestination. The continual affirmation of the norms represented by the hero draws attention to the deficiencies of the system from which those norms have been drawn, and in this sense the arrangement of the perspectives provides a stabilizing counterbalance. Whatever the minor characters lack is supplied by the hero, and whatever the hero lacks he learns to supply for himself. The two perspectives therefore dovetail into each other, with the hero's norms demonstrating their validity in proportion to the invalidity of those of the minor characters, who disappear at greater or lesser speed, again in proportion to the invalidity of their norms. They are there to illustrate the negative aspects of the hero, and as these diminish so the minor characters themselves become superfluous. Here, then, the interaction between theme and horizon brings about a systematic reduction of existing uncertainties, and indeed this is the frame of reference set up quite deliberately by the text. As a result, the transformation of individual positions is conspicuously restricted, for the scope of these positions is strategically limited and the text itself already formulates the transformation. Nevertheless, even here, the structure of theme and horizon is the basic rule of combination; only here it is confined – in unmistakable terms – to an effective visualization of that which Calvinist theology excluded, namely individual certainty of salvation.

The counterbalancing arrangement of perspectives is mainly to be found in devotional, didactic, and propagandist literature, for its function is not to produce an aesthetic object that will rival the thought system of the social world but to offer a compensation for certain deficiencies in specific thought systems.

The oppositive arrangement of perspectives has none of the determinacy of the counterbalancing structure. It simply sets norms against one another by showing up the deficiencies of each norm when viewed from the standpoint of the others. When the reader relates these opposing norms to one another he produces a kind of reciprocal negation, with themes and horizons in continual conflict. The negation consists in the fact that as each norm becomes thematic it implicitly shuts out the others, and these in their turn become thematic, thus undermining what went before. And so each norm takes its place in a context of negated and negating norms, a context quite different from the system out of which they were all originally selected. The context is a product of switching perspectives, and the producer is the reader himself, who removes the norms from their pragmatic setting and begins to see them for what they are, thus becoming aware of the functions they perform in the system from which they have been removed. This is tantamount to saying that he begins to understand the influence the norms have on him in real life.

This oppositive arrangement of perspectives may be put to a variety of uses. An interesting example is Smollett's *Humphry Clinker*, where it serves to present topographical as well as everyday realities. As an epistolary novel, *Humphry Clinker* offers a whole range of highly individual perspectives, frequently directed toward the same phenomena, and yet frequently presenting totally opposing views. Reality is made imaginable here through precise, opposing, and yet mutually derestricting formulations of it.[30] The reader is made aware of the extent to which reality can and indeed must be made to conform (or appear to conform) to such formulations. Every view recedes into the horizon of its possible changeability, so that the aesthetic object of this novel emerges as the actual nature of these images of reality, which are composed in accordance with the social and personal dispositions of the characters – and this in turn shows us that we too only grasp reality by way of the images that we compose.

The echelon and serial arrangements of perspectives are without the referential element that still characterized the oppositive structure. The latter was stabilized mainly by the contrast between hero and minor characters and by the perspective of the narrator in relation to this contrast. A novel without a hero, as written for instance by Thackeray, eliminates this hierarchical structure of perspectives. The main and minor characters all serve the same purpose, which is to evoke a multiplicity of referential systems in order to bring out the problematic nature of the norms selected. If all the characters tend to negate the chosen systems, it is difficult for the reader to

---

30 I have given a detailed discussion of this particular problem in my book, *The Implied Reader: Patterns of Communication in Prose Fiction from Bunyan to Beckett* (Baltimore: Johns Hopkins Press, 1974).

grasp any reliable guidelines. Instead we have an echelon of references and perspectives, none of which is predominant. Even the narrator, despite his apparent position of superiority over the characters, deprives us of the guidance we might expect by neutralizing and even contradicting his own evaluations. This denial of orientation can only be offset by attitudes the reader may adopt towards the events in the text, which will spring not so much from the structure of the perspectives but from the disposition of the reader himself. The stimulation of these attitudes, and the incorporation of them into the structure of theme and horizon, is what characterizes the echelon arrangement of perspectives in novelists ranging from Thackeray to Joyce.

However, in Joyce this process is intensified, and the arrangement of perspectives is clearly serial. There is no clearly discernible trace of any hierarchy, for the narrative presentation is segmented, with perspectives changing even from one sentence to another, so that one's first task is often simply to find out which perspective is represented by any one particular section. The same structure underlies the arrangement of perspectives in the *nouveau roman*. The reader is forced to try to identify the perspective and the referential context of each individual sentence or section, which means that he must constantly abandon the connections he had established or had hoped to establish. The alternation of theme and horizon is so accelerated that reference becomes virtually impossible, and in its place is a continual process of transformation that leads back into itself and not into a composite image of reality. The result of this process, triggered and sustained by the serial arrangement of perspectives, is that the reader, in striving to produce the aesthetic object, actually produces the very conditions under which reality is perceived and comprehended.

University of Konstanz

EUGENE VANCE

Pas de trois: Narrative, Hermeneutics, and Structure in Medieval Poetics

If I may dare speak as a medievalist in a colloquium on literary theory, I should like to bring a certain historical perspective to the subject, which is the very problematical relationship between what we call 'narrative' and 'interpretative' discourses. Given that European vernacular literature emerged in an intellectual climate where both the nature of narrative and the theory of interpretation were matters of active debate, I believe that a historical glimpse at this cultural problem might be pertinent to contemporary theory of 'interpretation.'

From the outset I shall take several things for granted. First, both modern structuralists and hermeneutists are capable of caricaturing each other's dogmas with relative ease, and it would be silly to review the polemic here. Secondly, one can (and perhaps even should) submit medieval narrative to structural analysis, and this analysis 'works.' Indeed, long before attacking Baudelaire's 'Les Chats,' structuralism had sharpened its claws on folk narrative which was itself partially a legacy of the Middle Ages. Moreover, certain structuralists have looked on the great French medievalist Joseph Bédier as an important precursor.[1]

Thirdly, I shall assume that it is possible to approach medieval narrative with any one of several variants of modern hermeneutics. Though modern medievalists have all too often either forgotten or ignored the constitutive postulates of their discipline, it is perhaps fair to say that orthodox medievalism has always been predominantly a hermeneutic science. Wilhelm Dilthey, however, one of the early spokesmen for modern hermeneutics, did state very clearly the epistemological solidarity of hermeneutics with philology as a method. In his remarkable essay 'The Rise of Hermeneutics,' recently translated by Fredric Jameson, Dilthey underscores the bond between hermeneutics as a science of understanding (*Verstehen*) and philology, stating that texts are but 'written monuments' and that the true philologist (as hermeneutist) must devote himself to understanding these vestiges of an original reality now scarcely intelligible:

---

1 Claude Brémond, 'Joseph Bédier, précurseur de l'analyse structurale des récits,' in his *Logique du récit* (Paris: Seuil, 1973) 48–58

That is why the art of understanding centers on the exegesis or *interpretation of those residues of human reality preserved in written form.*

The exegesis of such residues, along with the critical procedures inseparable from it, constituted the point of departure for *philology.* Philology is in its essence a *personal skill and virtuosity in the scrutiny of written memorials.* Other types of interpretation of monuments or historically transmitted actions can prosper only in association with philology and its findings.[2]

Thus, the great Spanish Romanist Ramon Menéndez-Pidal practised a very strict hermeneutics in his laborious efforts to reconstruct the human drama of the year 778, which was purportedly the moment of origin of the eleventh- or twelfth-century epic, the *Chanson de Roland.*[3] Modern hermeneutics has shown itself to be flexible as well as persistent. Without denying in the least a primacy of the linguistic in literary structures, it has been possible, as Hans Robert Jauss has done, to bring hermeneutic theory to bear on problems of medieval allegory, on genre-theory, and on the more basic question of *Rezeptionsgeschichte.*[4]

My motive for speaking about what we call the Middle Ages grows out of my discomfort over the fact that when modern critics, whether structural or hermeneutical, speak of 'narrative' they seem to take for granted, first, that they are referring to an object of science that exists as some kind of universal in human culture and, secondly, that the object of their science is perfectly distinct from the cognitive instruments brought to bear upon it by the perceiving subject. My purpose in this paper is to explore some of the consequences of the fact that the performance of narrative in the Middle Ages was *not* understood as being distinct from what we might call a 'structural' or 'hermeneutical' performance. Before doing so, however, it would be appropriate to venture a few speculative remarks about the problem as it occurs in the critical context of our time.

One of the great disappointments of modern structural linguistics and its daughter disciplines is that they have not, finally, allowed us to define with any formal rigour the distinct discourses that we intuitively understand to

2 Wilhelm Dilthey, 'The Rise of Hermeneutics,' transl. F. Jameson, *New Literary History* 3 (1971–72), 233

3 Ramon Menéndez Pidal, *La Chanson de Roland et la tradition épique des Francs*, transl. I. Cluzel (Paris: A. et J. Picard, 1960), 481ff

4 Hans Robert Jauss, 'Chanson de geste et roman courtois,' in *Chanson de geste und höfischer Roman* (Heidelberg: Carl Winter, 1963); 'La Transformation de la forme allégorique entre 1180 et 1240,' in *L'Humanisme médiéval dans les littératures romanes du XIIe au XIVe siècle,* ed. A. Fourrier (Paris: C. Klincksieck, 1964), 105–46; 'Littérature médiévale et théorie des genres,' *Poétique* 1 (1970) 79–101; *Literaturgeschichte als Provokation der Literaturwissenschaft* (Frankfurt-am-Main: Suhrkamp, 1970), esp. 'Geschichte der Kunst und Histoire,' 208–51

constitute our culture (the political, the poetic, the erotic, the philosophical, the publicitary, etc.),[5] nor to distinguish these discourses from discourse in general, nor, finally, to distinguish 'discourse' from 'language.'[6] Logically speaking, it would not be possible to define any discourse without first defining the *defining* discourse with respect to all other existing discourses – not to mention all possible discourses. It follows that structuralism has not equipped us to discern with any certainty what different semiological layers are implicated in a given utterance: for instance, to know when or at which level the erotic is political or the political is erotic, or when the poetic is political, or when the poetic is publicitary, and so forth.

This is a problem endemic to hermeneutics as well. For example, in his recent book, *La Métaphore vive*, Paul Ricoeur argues for a 'plurality of the modes of discourse' but for the 'independence of philosophical discourse.'[7] He believes that instances of metaphor in fiction instigate a 'double reference,' both to the truth of the internal structure of the poetic message and to the truth of external, non-linguistic 'reality,' which is *re*described or *reviv*ified by poesis: 'Thus, metaphor presents itself as a discursive strategy which, by preserving and developing the creative power of language, preserves and develops the *heuristic* power unleashed by *fiction*.'[8] Taking for granted a discontinuity between poetic discourse and that of philosophy, Ricoeur believes that there can be a fulfilment of this only partial 'distantiation' of poetic metaphor in the more reflexive and systematic discourse of the philosopher: 'poetic discourse, as text and work, prefigures the distantiation that speculative thought carries to its highest degree of reflexion.'[9] Given his view that the poetic is a mere precursor of a more masterly 'reflexive' discourse, it is not surprising that Ricoeur remains very distant in this book from the actual substance of poetry: not only are all of his references (as far as I recall) to authors within or closely related to the high romantic tradition, *la poésie pensante*, but most of the snippets of verse cited, or even his allusions to poets by name, are mediated to him by the texts or by the prejudices of other critics whose philosophical bent is compatible with his own: no wonder we are told that poetry may derive from philosophy but philosophy may not derive from the poetic.

My purpose is not to mortify *La métaphore vive*, but it seems to me

5 For an interesting attempt at such 'discourse analysis,' see *Le Discours politique*, in *Langages* 23 (Sept. 1971), esp. the article by L. Guespin, 'Problématique des travaux sur le discours politique,' 3–24

6 See Pierre Kuentz, 'Parole/discours,' in *Langage et histoire*, a collection of essays edited by Jean-Claude Chevalier and Pierre Kuentz as a special number of *Langue française* 15 (Sept. 1972) 18–28

7 Paul Ricoeur, *La Métaphore vive* (Paris: Seuil, coll. L'Ordre philosophique, 1975) 11, 323ff

8 Ibid. 10

9 Ibid. 398f

obvious that Ricoeur has confused the poetic with what he considers to be poetry, the former being only a tendency in linguistic behaviour,[10] the latter being the canon of literary departments which are the institutional offspring of romantic ideologies of culture. There is nothing specifically poetic (in the latter sense of the term) about metaphor; nor is it obvious that the only proper response to metaphor as a 'distancing' discursive act (if it is that at all) is necessarily reflexive or philosophical. How de we distinguish the *fiction* of poetry from that of propaganda? Or advertisement? Do Virgil and Milton write texts that are above all poetic? Are they at their worst if they propagandize? Should we be banished from the republic if the voice of *poesis* inspires us to buy an automobile, to vote for the Ike that we like, to seduce our neighbour, or worse, to put down the philosopher's book (as I shall shortly do)?

Broadly speaking, the problem that Ricoeur's book raises involves the criteria for identifying and the justification for our ranking one discourse with respect to another in the search for 'reality,' and it implicates not only the philosopher but the historian and the critic as well – indeed, anyone who deliberately aspires to analyse, in language, objects that are themselves constituted only by language. Hayden White, for instance, has attempted to show to what extent historiography, whose mode is basically narrative, tends to organize its data into configurations identical to those of the basic plots of literature, and his observations invite us to see how the rhetorical strategies and the plot structures of historiography determine the selection and disposition of evidence and, more crucially, the ideological value judgments brought to bear upon that evidence.[11] In the realm of criticism, both structuralism and hermeneutics suffer from a similar confusion about the relationship of their discourse to that of the object of analysis. More practically, if we speak of narrative fiction as a 'discourse,' we are saying in effect that any instance of narrative is a discursive act which must be decoded in the context of other such discursive acts which have provoked it or which it provokes; this autotelic dimension of narrative implies that any instance of narrative fiction is in itself already to some degree a hermeneutic enterprise (of a hermeneutic enterprise); similarly, if we claim that narrative fiction is a structure that derives from language, which is its vehicle, then to practise

---

10 Roman Jakobson defines the poetic as follows: 'The poetic function projects the principle of equivalence from the axis of selection into the axis of combination.' See his well-known article, 'Linguistics and Poetics,' in *Language and Style*, ed. T.A. Sebeok (Cambridge, Mass.: Harvard University Press, 1960), and often reprinted since. I have quoted from *Essays on the Language of Literature*, ed. S.B. Chatman and S.R. Levin (Boston: Houghton Mifflin, 1967), 303.

11 Hayden White, *Metahistory: The Historical Imagination in Nineteenth-Century Europe* (Baltimore: Johns Hopkins, 1973) 1–42

structural analysis is little more than to renarrate in metalanguage (whose vehicle is also language) structures that are already pre-eminently linguistic: structures, then, of structures ... stories of stories ... interpretations of interpretations, and so on.

I wish now to explore some of the consequences of the fact that in classical antiquity the notion of hermeneutics, as Jean Pépin has recently reminded us, enjoyed many different connotations, some of which already began to be filtered out by the Latin translation of the Greek *hermeneuein* by *interpretare*, others of which have since been all too willingly ignored in phenomenology.[12] Today, except in certain restricted uses, such as when we speak of a musical performance as an 'interpretation,' the term 'interpretation' has come to signify, mainly because of its prefix, the more limited notion of 'go-between.' Pépin writes

The result of this contamination is that the Greek word has come to signify 'interpretation,' and that hermeneutics today commonly has as its synonym 'exegesis.' However, the original meaning *hermeneuein* and of related words – or, in any case, their principal meaning – was not that at all, and was not far from being its exact contrary, if we grant that exegesis is a movement of penetration into the intention of a text or message. For *hermeneia* designates most commonly the act of expressing, whose character of extroversion is ... strongly marked.[13]

Pépin gives examples where *hermeneuein* implies different types of 'expressions': to 'translate,' to 'augur,' to 'allegorize,' to 'prophesy,' and to 'narrate,' as in the case of *rhapsodes*. Even the notion of 'story' (*mythos*) was identified with the hermeneutic.

Parallel to the apparent ambivalence in the early meanings of *hermeneuein* as the act of both receiving and emitting some truth or reality, one may mention Quintillian's twofold definition of grammar, which is the science of speaking and writing correctly (*recte loquendi*) and also the art of 'explicating the poets' (*enarratio poetarum*).[14] For Bede, grammar is first of all 'the science of interpreting the poets and historians' ('Grammatica est scientia interpretandi poetas atque historicos') and secondly, the science of 'speaking and writing correctly' ('recte scribendi loquendique').[15]

The idea that *hermeneuein* could consist in a kind of extroverted, narrative performance remained central, of course, to the pragmatic side of Christian

12 Jean Pépin, 'L'Herméneutique ancienne,' *Poétique* 23 (1975) 291–300
13 Ibid. 291 (transl. E.V.)
14 I am indebted here to James J. Murphy's excellent study, *Rhetoric in the Middle Ages: A History of Rhetorical Theory from St. Augustine to the Renaissance* (Berkeley: University of California Press, 1974) 25.
15 Quoted from Murphy, 83; see his discussion, 82–4.

spiritual life, so much of whose theology was either expressed initially as, or interpreted by means of, narrative. For St Augustine, the act of catechism was primarily a *narratio*. His *Confessions*, consisting first of a narrative of his life story and secondly of an exegesis (*enarratio*) of the Book of Genesis, may seem disunified to us, yet this is because we have forgotten that narrative and interpretation could be seen by St Augustine as one and the same act.[16] In his *De doctrina christiana*, the term *interpretatio* covers the three activities of translation, exegesis, and teaching. (It is interesting that the root sense of the word 'narrate' is to 'know,' and that in the Middle Ages the term came to mean, among other things, the formal act of delineating one's property or possessions. Certainly this territorializing function of narrative is asserted in the performance of oral epic, if we are to judge by the *Chanson de Roland*, where even personal identity tends to be conflated with the territorial.) Broadly speaking, if by hermeneutics we mean not just the grasping of truth, but the production, the performance, of truth, then in the judicial sphere we may also see medieval trials by duel and by ordeal as a class of hermeneutic gesture in which truth is not so much discovered as produced. Similarly, Hamlet's doubts about the authenticity of his father's ghost and his subsequent staging of a regicide before Claudius may be seen as two complementary aspects of a single hermeneutic quest.

In the later Middle Ages, the link between hermeneutics and the performance of narrative was conscious and explicit, as is indicated by the thirteenth-century rhetorician and grammarian, John of Garland. John mentions a broad category of narrative that is called 'hermeneutic' (*ermeneticon*).[17] It includes all narrative that is alien to legal causes. Hermeneutic narrative is of two types: 'One kind is rooted in plot, the other in character.'[18] The kind rooted in plot or in structure has three species or parts, namely, *fabula, historia*, and *argumentum*. 'A fable,' John says, 'contains events that are untrue, and do not pretend to be true; it follows that avoiding vice in fabulous narratives means lying with probability, as it says in the *Art of Poetry*.'[19] 'A history,' John continues, 'reports an event which has taken place long before the memory of our age.'[20] The third term, *argumentum*, is more elusive – I am not satisfied, for example, with the term 'realistic fiction,' which is Traugott Lawler's translation. The definition of *argumentum*, though it implies a sense of the probable, seems to suggest a plot which

16 See Eugene Vance, 'Augustine's *Confessions* and the Grammar of Selfhood,' *Genre* 6, no. 1 (March 1973) 1–28
17 *The Parisiana Poetria of John of Garland*, ed. and transl. Traugott Lawler (New Haven and London: Yale University Press, coll. Yale Studies in English 182), 101
18 Ibid.
19 Ibid.
20 Ibid.

is above all architectonically or formally coherent, that is, structured, as an argument must be logically structured in order to be (probably) correct or 'true': '*Argumentum*,' says John, 'is a fictitious event which nevertheless could have happened, as in the case of comedies. And no invocation should be made in a comedy, except for an insoluble complication in the plot, as Horace [*Art of Poetry*, 191–2] says: "Let no god intervene, unless a knot develops that deserves such a deliverer." That is, a god should not be called on unless an insoluble complication develops.'[21]

It seems to me that John of Garland's notion of narrative as an essentially 'hermeneutic' discourse, and more specifically as an *argumentum* that obeys an inner logic of its own, is a development of an overwhelmingly important cultural fact of the twelfth century, that is, the rediscovery or reassimilation of the logical works of Aristotle, especially the *Categories* and the *Peri hermeneias*. And though it is well known that this intellectual revolution affected almost every aspect of the mental universe of the twelfth century, I should like to venture a few simple remarks about the *Categories*, the *Peri hermeneias*, and the poetics of medieval narrative.

Until the return of Aristotle in the twelfth century, the dominant hermeneutics in the West had been Augustinian (the Aristotelianism of Boethius, Porphyry, and others notwithstanding), and as a discipline it had been centred most specifically upon interpreting the Bible, the term 'interpretation' including, as I said earlier, the activities of translation, exegesis, and teaching or preaching. Although Augustine himself knew and transmitted theories of grammar and logic that were at least partially compatible with the teachings of the Peripatetics, Augustine's hermeneutical priorities were fundamentally mystical and intuitive in orientation, and their operations depended for their success upon reciprocal movements of human love and divine illumination, that is, upon our ability to invoke and to hear God's voice not as a physical but as a spiritual presence: listening, as Augustine says, 'through the ears of the heart.'

As is well known, the science of hermeneutics became demystified and systematized in the twelfth century under the impact of Aristotelianism, becoming above all a rational discipline no longer centred directly upon deciphering and teaching the Scriptures, but rather upon the analysis of the syntactic structures of language and of proper argumentation as a precondition for speaking or understanding truly and not falsely. We are dealing here of course with rather limited features of a vast epistomological fissure in the intellectual life of the Middle Ages, some of whose other features have been described by many others, most recently by Brian Stock in his book *Myth and Science in the Twelfth Century* (1972). With regard to practices of

21 Ibid.

narrative, this fissure accentuated the opposition between two fundamentally different modes or types of hermeneutic narrative, one rooted in a mystical intelligence of the universe and expressed as open-ended myth and encyclopedism, the other, more abstractive and (though still capable of drawing heavily upon the material of myth) rationally structured. It was in this intellectual climate that vernacular writers such as Chrétien de Troyes and Marie de France brought rigorous formal structure to written narrative.

This is not the place to recall the program of the *Organon*, which is Aristotle's logical corpus. Suffice it to say that Aristotle undertakes an integrative analysis of language, showing how syllables, words, composite words, and propositions combine to produce acts of synthesis (*sýnthesin*) and division (*diaípesin*) that are either true or false,[22] truth being nothing other than the proper conjunction, in our utterances, of our knowledge of what is universal (*kathólon*) and what is individual (*pragmáton*).[23] The goal of the dialectician is to argue correctly, the form of a proper argument being primarily understood in this context as the syllogism. The syllogism is a discursive syntagme composed of several propositions within which there has been proper inference.

That the rediscovery of the *Organon* brought to medieval thought a very pure kind of formalism grounded in the analysis of syntax is obvious; moreover, the fact that there are important correspondences between dialectics as an art of affirming and negating and the semantic structuralism of Greimas must remain unexplored here.[24] What is noteworthy for our purposes is that medieval logic was strongly antisubjectivistic and made an effort not only to transcend the equivocal nature of conventional verbal signs but also to avoid contradictions and errors in reasoning that arise from an uncritical, intuitive, or mystical approach to texts, especially the scriptures, as objects of understanding. Logic seemed to promise, in short, the power to articulate truths that could be divorced from the consciousness of the individual uttering them, truths that could be held by any rational man to be universally evident. Thus, Abelard says in his glosses on the *Peri hermeneias* that there are three degrees of knowledge: sensation (*sensus*), imagination (*imaginatio*), and intellection (*intellectio*), the latter process being abstractive and leading to the correct knowledge of universals.[25] The

---

22 Aristotle, *Peri hermeneias* I, ed. Harold P. Cooke (Cambridge, Mass.: Harvard University Press, 1938), 115
23 *Peri hermeneias* VII, 125ff
24 See especially *Sémantique structurale* (Paris: Larousse, 1966) and *Du Sens: essais sémiotiques* (Paris: Seuil, 1970)
25 See Jean Jolivet, *Arts du langage et théologie chez Abélard* (Paris: Vrin, 1969), est. 356–74. I wish to record here my very extensive debt to this book: its influence on this text is pervasive.

controversy generated in the twelfth century by the method of the *Peri hermeneias* and the other logical treatises (as opposed to a more intuitive, exegetical hermeneutics) was massive, and, if we take John of Salisbury as an apostle of the new intellectualism, his complaints that the reactionary detractors of trivium persisted in preaching that there was no letter to be sought in the liberal arts but only 'spirit,' sound very much like a caricature of certain 'interpretative' critics of our own time whose sensibilities have been sorely abused by the anti-subjective aspect of modern structuralism.[26]

With regard to medieval poetics, which was a branch of rhetoric overlapping with certain exercises in the discipline of *grammatica* (the science of *grammata*, or *letters*, hence, *litteratura*),[27] if we may safely assume that there was constant cross-fertilization amongst the three liberal arts of the *trivium*, or the arts of language (*arts sermocinales*), we may also safely suppose that logic provided to twelfth-century poets new criteria for order and system in narrative as a hermeneutic performance, useful criteria not found, for example, in rhetorical treatises under the concept of *dispositio*. (Indeed, *dispositio* is part of formal rhetoric that seems to have benefited from rather little careful consideration in rhetoricians following Cicero, compared, at least, to the elaborations given to the other parts of rhetoric.) For instance, let us consider the potential implications of the fact that the *Categories* furnishes a rigorous definition of the term 'substance' (*ousia*), which includes, of course, the notion of 'person'; Aristotle says that what seems to be the most general characteristic of substance is that, although it remains numerically one and the same, it is capable of receiving contrary properties (hot, cold, white, black, good, bad) at different moments in time.[28] A substance (or person) is capable, then, of change: 'It is by a change in itself that a thing that was hot becomes cold (having passed from one state to another) or a thing that was white becomes black or a thing that was good becomes bad.'[29] With the theory of substances (which extended, I repeat, to what we mean by 'person' or 'character') came a new awareness of narrative as a system in which certain basic transformations within binary oppositions could be expressed by means of the proper predication of those accidents by which substances (or persons) manifest their being in time and space. Put more simply, with the theory of substances came not only a quest for a

---

26 John of Salisbury, *Metalogicon* I. ii, ed. C.C.I. Webb (Oxford: Oxford University Press, 1929), 10, transl. D. McGarry (Berkeley: University of California Press, 1955), 14

27 Marc-René Jung, 'Poetria: Zur Dichtungstheorie des ausgehenden Mittelalters in Frankreich,' *Vox Romanica* 30 (1971) 44–64; see also Paul Zumthor, 'Rhétorique et poétique,' in *Langue, texte, énigme* (Paris: Seuil, 1975) 93–124

28 Aristotle, *Categories*, ed. Harold P. Cooke (Cambridge, Mass.: Harvard University Press, 1938), 33

29 Ibid.

rigorously coherent narrative plot (*argumentum*, in John of Garland's terms) but also a notion of personal identity that was dynamic; poets could now admit to the possibility (if not to the necessity) of change in the human consciousness. One thinks right away, for instance, of the psychological dynamism demanded of (and attained by) Erec and Yvain in Chrétien's romances. Epic, by contrast, centres on characters in whom any inner change is fatal and, as in the *Roland*, tends to build its plot and its ethical values around the intractibility of the heroic will. But the sudden rise of logic in the twelfth century no doubt brought a new technical sense to other aspects of poetic theory as well. Especially since Curtius, we have been familiar with the rhetorical notion of *topos* as implying a 'commonplace' or as a conventional but effective means of 'inventing' or 'amplifying' the *materia* of narrative[30]; however, one may suspect that the return of Aristotle's *Topica* to the liberal arts (in 1128 as part of the New Logic) inaugurated a less rhetorical sense of the term 'topic' in that it taught not just the practical utility of exploiting *topoi* in the process of invention, but taught above all how to argue properly from commonplaces.[31] As John of Salisbury put it, the *Topica* taught *doctrinam localium argumentationum.*[32] A logical notion of topical invention does not in the least exclude typical or conventional predications but does imply predication where there is truth because there is structure (*constructorius*) and coherence in our utterances.[33] The rediscovery of the *Topica* (as well as of the other three Aristotelian treatises forming the New Logic) no doubt instilled in poets a deep attraction for formal virtuosity as a conscious goal in narrative art. With the science of propositions that grew out of Aristotelian logic there appears to have come also a much clearer notion, among poets, of the nature of the event as a structuring of meaning – in contrast again with the *Chanson de Roland*, where events do not tend to be presented as being ontologically distinct from one another. This art of 'making' the event in language – let us call it a 'poetics' of the event – demanded, moreover, increasing perfection in manipulating the tenses of language so that there could be accurate or coherent diachronism within the event as a formal construct. A logical sense required in the practice of predication also no doubt encouraged poets to exploit mechanisms of

30 E.R. Curtius, 'La topique,' in *La Littérature européenne et le Moyen Âge latin*, transl. J. Bréjoux (Paris: Presses universitaires, 1956), 99–130
31 For an interesting discussion of the relationship between poetics and *topoi*, I refer the reader to an unpublished lecture by Douglas Kelly, 'The Value of "Semantic Range" in Interpreting Medieval Writing,' available on tape, presented at the International Conference on Medieval Grammar, University of California, Davis, 19–20 Feb. 1976, James J. Murphy, Conference Chairman. If I have correctly understood Professor Kelly's talk, he does not, however, stress the logical import of the 'topic,' but remains, rather, on the side of the rhetoricians.
32 *Metalogicon* III.6, 176–78
33 *Metalogicon* III.10, 189–202

hypotaxis or *subordination* in description and, no less, to distinguish between causes and effects (in medieval terms, between 'passion' and 'action').

Of course, it is hard to prove that this or that writer of narrative was necessarily influenced by logic as a direct source of models for generating narrative form, but I suspect that Chrétien's famous notions of *sens* as a consequence of *conjointure* is less rhetorical than grammatical or logical.[34] A minimal proposition is a *conjunctio* of a *nomen* (by which we name a substance) with a *verbum* (by which we predicate something about that substance: 'Socrates runs'). Moreover, for those who would hope to explain the sudden manifestation of structure in twelfth-century narrative more easily by citing the influence of Virgil and Ovid, both of whom display an obvious structural consciousness, one may answer, first, that these classical authors were themselves probably influenced by Stoic and/or Aristotelian logic and, secondly, that such borrowing could take place in the twelfth century only after the assimilation of logic had made such borrowings both possible and desirable, if not downright prestigious. Certainly one very salient difference between the narrative art of a Chrétien or a Marie de France and that of the *romans d'antiquité* is the intervention of a consciousness of structure in narrative. Moreover, many of the effects of what critics have loosely called the realism and the psychological insight of medieval narrative derive neither from a truly scientific pragmatism nor from an upsurge in psychotheory, but rather from the perfection of narrative as a logical system.

If there is indeed any warrant for suggesting that medieval logic and what we may call medieval vernacular narrativity (understood as a consciously motivated formalism in the art of telling) are historically conatural, I find it interesting to note that among modern hermeneutical critics I have read (Gadamer, Ricoeur, Jauss, Iser, Hirsch, and others) there is no attention given to the role of the *Categories* and the *Peri hermeneias* (or indeed, the *Organon* as a whole), as a determining force in European literary culture. One cause of this neglect is no doubt the reluctance of literary medievalists themselves to explore the intellectual repercussions of logic (and later of speculative grammar) within the area of poetics. For a number of reasons,

---

34 The transformations of meaning that have occurred in the basic vocabulary of medieval poetic theory are, admittedly, difficult to show. Douglas Kelly, in *Sens and Conjointure in the Chevalier de la Charette* (The Hague: Mouton, 1966) and in 'The Source and Meaning of Conjointure in Chrétien's *Erec* 14,' *Viator* 1 (1970) 179–200, has undertaken an exhaustive study of the terms *sens* and *conjointure* in rhetorical and poetic theory of classical and medieval writers. I believe that these terms acquired a more specialized sense in the later twelfth century owing to the renewal of interest in Aristotelian logic; however, this specialized sense does not contradict earlier notions of *conjunctio*, but does invite narrative poets to become more precise in their understanding of narrative whose truth lies in the mastery of narrative understood as a coherent system.

medievalists have become methodologically locked into an *episteme* of philology which tends to depreciate the specificity of the syntagmatic organization of the text-object at hand in order to regress to some anterior event, reality, or source of which the extant text is but a trace; *this* is the 'reality' of the text which we must come to 'understand.'

If the prevalence of a logical over a mystical hermeneutics in the twelfth century may be said to have contributed to an initial confidence among poets in structural perfection as a worthy and perhaps adequate artistic goal, and if the optimism of poets led them to assume that they could fictionalize both truth and its interpretation without making the status of their own text seriously problematical, later scholastic thinkers called into question man's power to formulate (must less to communicate) intelligible ideas and concepts freed from all their sensory and individual associations. Poets, on their side, exploited the polysemy of language and sought out strategies to make the relationship between the well-wrought text and the reader more complicated; it is as if the writer wanted to fictionalize his own difficult relationship to the written word (which was understood to be a mere sign of a sign) by staging it as a problem of reading. Such epistemological games correspond, I believe, to a scepticism of late medieval thought which took the form of an intense belief in the individual basis of all experience. Gordon Leff has recently written of Ockham:

Ockham's epistemology is founded upon the primacy of individual cognition. As coming first in the order of knowing, it is the complement to his view of the individual nature of all being ... If we except the limited efforts of Abelard, Ockham was the first thinker to incorporate universal knowledge into an individual ontology, systematically reducing ... concepts, terms and propositions to their individual import. He thereby reversed the direction which Christian thought had for the most part followed from the time of Augustine. Instead of asking how the individual derives from a universal nature or essence he sought to explain how in a world of individuals we come to have knowledge which is not individual. What had been an ontological question became a psychological and logical question.[35]

More schematically (and simplistically), in late scholasticism the role of the self in the four-sided relationship between the knower, the thing he knows, the concept of the thing that he holds in his mind, and the conventional sign by which he signifies the thing (or the concept) became more and more a matter of reflexion. For convenience, we may draw the terms of this prob-

35 Gordon Leff, *William of Ockham: The Metamorphosis of Scholastic Discourse* (Manchester: Manchester University Press, 1975) 2

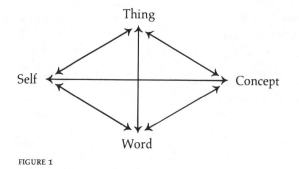

Thing

Self

Concept

Word

FIGURE 1

lematic as in Figure 1. The growing interest among late medieval philosophers such as Scotus and Ockham in the discrepancy between words, concepts, and things as they relate to individual experience gave an ample rational basis (if one was necessary) for semiological strategies among poets that would subject the reader's relationship to the written text to a rigorously controlled ambiguity. In Duns Scotus, for example, one may find an adequate semiological basis for what modern critics call dramatic irony, by which they commonly mean situations in stories where the understanding of the discrete intelligence of a character differs from the understanding which has been given either to those around him or to the audience of readers or spectators. Dramatic irony tends to instigate a double referentiality to utterances, hence is necessarily a source of a metalinguistic consciousness in which speech acts (in the sense of Austin, Searle, and others) become defined through their contextual effects. Duns Scotus held, as did almost all medieval theoreticians of language, that words are significant only by convention. Because they are conventional, they refer at once to individual objects that we know immediately or directly through experience and to the plurality of concepts that we (and others) may hold of these things. Asserting, then, the individual basis of all experience, yet the conventional nature of verbal signs, Scotus inferred that it was possible (if not inevitable) that whenever we employ conventional signs we should signify more than we ourselves have understood: 'distinctius potest significari quam concipi.'[36] In their wish to correlate the ontological with the cognitive in signification, Scotus and his pupil Ockham attributed great importance to the so-called theory of supposition, which attempted to make distinctions between man as a concept-maker and as a signifying creature. Peter of Spain, who is credited with having demonstrated the importance of supposition theory to problems of cognition, defined supposition as follows:

36 Laurent Renaud, 'Le Problème de la signification chez Jean Duns Scot,' thesis, École Pratique des Hautes Études, 5e Section, 1968, 79–80

Supposition (*suppositio*) is the acceptance of a substantive term as denoting some-thing. Supposition and signification differ, however, because signification is ac-complished through the imposition of a word to signify a thing, while supposition is the acceptance of a term, already significant, as denoting something; as when one says: 'Man runs,' the term 'Man' is taken to denote Sortes [Socrates], Plato and the rest of men. Thus signification is prior to supposition. They also differ in that signification belongs to the word, whereas supposition belongs to the term already composed of the word and its signification. Therefore, to denote (*supponere*) and to signify (*significare*) are not the same, but rather are different.[37]

Although such theories originated in a problematics of proper argumenta-tion, as they were transformed, by Ockham, into a problematics of psychol-ogy and cognition, they implicated not just the concept-making apparatus in the speaking subject but also man's *will* to signify or to understand. Thus, Ockham held that the intellect is not in itself sufficient as an agent in the discovery of truth but depends also upon the proper functioning of the will. As Gordon Leff puts it,

For once it [the intellect] knows it will continue to know in the same way unless circumstances change; and if these are not the result of some natural impediment, or the loss of something which was previously present, they must be due to another agent which decides either to know or not to know or to know differently or more intensely or to accept or reject what is known: namely the will. In consequence all changes in the mode of knowing which are not merely natural are due to the will either wanting or refusing to know.[38]

The will, then, is the agent which, acting upon the preceding cognition of the intellect as partial cause, brings about the actions of proposition-making and syllogizing, i.e. the production of knowledge that is inferential.[39]

Abstract though they may seem, such ideas were at the centre of the most acute intellectual debates of the late middle ages, and though I believe it would be silly to assume that any serious, literate poet of the time, that is, one who had studied the *trivium*, was not at least indirectly aware of these issues, it would be equally silly to deny that poets had their own ways of apprehending and their own practical strategies for dramatizing these ideas. For instance, Dante and Chaucer were obviously more disposed than were the philosophers to explore the relationship between the will and significa-tion as an ethical or moral question, and to create dramatic structures involving the acts of speaking individuals, rather than to explore faulty

37 Peter of Spain [Joannes XXI], *The Summulae logicales*, ed. and transl. J.P. Mullally (Notre Dame: University of Notre Dame Publications in Mediaeval Studies VIII, 1945), 3–4
38 Leff, 539
39 Ibid. 539–40

arguments or sophisms. Unlike logicians, poets were also inclined to see the problem of individual experience as a dimension of historicity, one which also implicated the vernacular language that is given to the speaking individual at birth, according to the conditions of race, milieu, and moment; as Chaucer put it, 'in forme of speche is chaunge.'[40] From the thirteenth century onward, poets began to internalize into their fiction (res ficta) their awareness that the encoding and decoding of messages (written or not) were radically different acts, whether the cause of that difference was perceived as humorous or tragic. By creating an 'I' whose referent is not the personal identity of the poet, but only the poetic message in which it is proffered, poets fictionalized not only the process of literary creation but also the process of literary response, to the degree that we as readers assume this same 'I' as masks of ourselves when we read.

I am suggesting that with the return of the Categories, the Peri hermeneias, and the other logical works of Aristotle to the medieval curriculum, the hermeneutic act, whether one of performance or interpretation, came to implicate two fundamentally different, and perhaps opposed, gestures before the poetic text. First, there was the essentially Augustinian impulse either to express or to grasp intuitively something conceived as existing prior to, but also immanent in, the text – a meaning, a truth, an identity, an intention; secondly, there was the impulse either to produce (or to deduce) a narrativity existing above all as an autonomous, self-sufficient, transsubjective system. 'Meaning' in the latter case resides in the relationship between its propositions. Spare and untechnical though it is, John of Garland's use of the term argumentum to describe narrative indicates a conception of the story surely not incompatible with that of Greimas, when he says

a story is a discursive unit which ought to be consider as an algorithm, that is, as a succession of state-actions oriented towards an end. As a succession, the story possesses a temporal dimension: the actions which are distributed in it assume with regard to each other relationships of anteriority and posteriority.

In order to have a meaning, a story must be a significant whole: it manifests itself, therefore, as a simple semantic structure.[41]

Challenged by the ambivalence of the notion of hermeneutics, poets of the later middle ages tended to exploit the dual nature of the story, whose purely formal potential derives from inherently linguistic structures but whose 'presentation' must take place as an act of living speech, that is, in a medium of individual expression which is always equivocal because it is also conventional. Poets experimented with strategies of composition by which the goal

40 Geoffrey Chaucer, Troilus and Criseyde II.22
41 A.J. Greimas, Du Sens: essais sémiotiques (Paris: Seuil, 1970) 187 [transl. E.V.]

of structured narrative, whose meaning lay in a presence of the story to itself – in wholeness – would be disrupted by the process of uttering, by *énonciation* in the sense that Benveniste gives to that term.[42] Such artistic cross-purposes were not heady ventures of 'deconstruction,' as we might be tempted to see them, but were more likely consequences in part of the chastening reminder of theologians to poets that their art, as a vehicle of truth, was *infima inter omnes doctrinas*, and that their figures and fictions could only obscure, rather than disclose, truth. By positing in their art both a consciousness of formalistic virtuosity and a disruptiveness of form that occurs as a kind of slippage or drifting in signification devolving from the irreducible difference between *signans* and *signatum*, poets expressed what may be seen as a more general dilemma in the condition of fallen man, in whom the instinct of innocent desire has been doubled by a desire to desire.

By way of conclusion I shall briefly indicate six major poetic strategies which tend to unleash the disruptive arbitrariness of language upon 'meaningful' fiction, strategies which I believe to be functional in a large, and perhaps representative, group of later medieval narrative texts. Although the value of any theory lies in its applicability, the goals of this colloquium obviously cannot include application of such theories at present, if only for the lack of time and space. Therefore, I submit this list of what we may perhaps call strategies of decomposition only as a tentative and incomplete effort to encourage readers of narrative, especially readers of medieval narrative who are not content with the results of orthodox genre-theory, to find new criteria for describing and classifying their materials:

1 *Intertextualization of the instance of narrative discourse*: this occurs whenever a poet dramatizes within his seemingly closed fiction the status of his text both as a performance and as a reception and transformation of a multiplicity of other texts. By doing so he practises the art of *grammatica* (or *litteratura*) as a twofold operation involving, simultaneously, both a production of the new and an interpretation of the old. The text is seen more as a productivity than as a product.

2 *Hybridization of narrative discourse*: this occurs when a single story is told (whether once or more) in more than one discourse, thereby relativizing 'truth' and disrupting the monopoly of a single code as a condition of integral meaning. When hybridization occurs, the author does not point to or postulate the existence of any hidden, all-comprehending, redeeming arch-code. It is similar to Bakhtin's notion of the 'dialogic' as taken up by Kristeva.[43] To the degree that the informing discourses are socially marked,

42 Emile Benveniste, *Problèmes de linguistique générale* (Paris: Gallimard, 1966) 224–76
43 Julia Kristeva, 'Le mot, le dialogue et le roman,' in *Séméiôtiké: Recherches pour une sémanalyse* (Paris: Seuil, coll. Tel quel, 1969) 143–73

the hybridized text may be said to be totemic in function. Narrative, here, may be seen as a medium of exchange.

3 *The encasement of narrative*: stories are told within stories, perhaps within stories. Equivocation occurs; it involves the non-equivalence of the fictive teller's meaning and the meaning produced by the tale told by interlocutors within the fiction, and, finally, meaning as a production of our own needs and desires.

4 *The interlacing of discrete narratives*: this consists in an overelaboration of form occurring as a multiplicity of intersecting plot lines, without there being expressed, within the universe of narrative events, adequate causal relationships, except perhaps the gratuitousness of chance. This device has been studied under the term 'interlacing' by many medievalists, including Eugene Vinaver and John Leyerle, and is prevalent in several late medieval and renaissance genres (romance, epic, theatre).

5 *The fragmentation of narrative syntax*: this usually occurs as the dispersion of a plot line into disjunctive utterances, between which there are blank spaces compelling the reader to construct meanings, yet to do so without succeeding in validating their truth. This typically occurs in lyric sequences centred on an 'I' with no definite centre (historical, ideological, personal) and whose referent is, finally, only the code of the discourse in which it is manifested.

6 *The allegorization of narrative*: this occurs when the actants, actors, and functions constituting a recognizable narrative sequence are resemanticised through a process of substitution. This process of substitution is usually effected by devices such as metaphor, metonymy, or synecdoche. In such instances, both the original terms and their substitutes must be discernible, though the motive for substitution may remain ambiguous.

I am aware, finally, that the poetic strategies that I have tried to name here are not specifically medieval and may be found to occur in the literatures of other periods and cultures. So much the better if we find that medieval literature is not 'just' medieval; and so much the better if, in our concern about our inability to place medieval narrative properly within what we take to be medieval history, we are led to ponder once again the problem of history itself as narrative, as does Hayden White, or Jean-Pierre Faye when he says so tautologically 'because history is made only by being told, a critique of history may be practised only in telling how history, by being narrated, is produced.'[44]

Université de Montréal

44 Jean-Pierre Faye, *Théorie du récit: Introduction aux langages totalitaires, critique de la raison, l'économie narrative* (Paris: Hermann, 1972) 9 [transl. E.V.]

PART THREE

METACRITICISM

HANS ROBERT JAUSS

Theses on the Transition from the Aesthetics of Literary Works to a Theory of Aesthetic Experience

The following propositions evolved originally in the context of the German debate concerning new theories of the so-called aesthetics of reception,[1] the literary theory aiming at the inclusion of the reader, listener, or observer as a mediating moment in the history of authors and works. This debate has again brought to light the opposition between an 'idealist' and a 'materialist' point of view. My theses represent an attempt to give this discussion a new goal. Until now, the idealist and the materialist schools – as well as the formalist and hermeneutic methods – were primarily concerned with an understanding of texts which corresponds to the classical concept of the autonomous work. All schools of literary theory confront new difficulties once they abandon the substantialist idea of a self-contained work, which is not appropriate to either medieval or modern literature. Difficulties also result when the problem of interpretation and verification is extended to instances of intertextuality, which until now has scarcely been explained historically or systematically.

CLARIFYING THE TENDENCIES

The difference between a structuralist or formalist and an historical or hermeneutic camp has proven to be productive in the field of literature and has encouraged a reciprocal development of new theories. Since the antinomy between the synchronic and the diachronic, between system and change, has been recognized as a not insurmountable barrier by research in linguistics and history, since, from a methodological point of view, we have started to benefit considerably from the complementarity of structure and event, description and narration,[2] those engaged in areas of literary theory, aesthetics, and hermeneutics need no longer dogmatically adhere to former positions. Upon closer examination we indeed discover a new line of demarcation which has already evolved in Germany during the past few years. It cuts across former camps and promises to make literary theory and practice

---

1 For the status of this debate see *Rezeptionsästhetik – Theorie und Praxis*, ed. R. Warning (München: W. Fink, 1975)

2 Cf. Eugenio Coseriu, *Synchronie, Diachronie und Geschichte – Das Problem des Sprachwandels* (München: W. Fink, 1974); R. Koselleck and W.D. Stempel, eds, *Geschichte – Ereignis und Erzählung* (München: W. Fink, coll. *Poetik und Hermeneutik* V, 1973)

more productive. Although traditional bourgeois as well as orthodox Marxist aesthetics still cling to the classical priority of the work over the reader, a new aesthetic theory has on both sides replaced the authority of the work by the reader's experience of it. Consequently, its function in society and its history of reception have taken the place of the work's timeless meaning.

RELATED TRENDS IN AESTHETICS

To the classical concept of the autonomous work of art corresponds the reader's solitary contemplation as the paradigmatic behaviour of the receiver. This premise is shared by aesthetic theories of such various origins and intentions as those of Adorno, Gadamer, and Lukács. Benjamin's aura concept also remains dependent upon the classical notion of the autonomous work and individual aesthetic appreciation. The aesthetic properties of the work are defined by criteria such as perfection, form as a complete entity, reconciliation of the parts into an organic whole, correspondence between form and content, and unity between the general and the particular. The paradigmatic quality of a work of art is legitimized by means of what may be called the 'exemplary' in a positive sense (the Platonic triad of the true, good, and beautiful), but also in a strictly negative connotation (Adorno's new version of l'art pour l'art). In this case the ideal reader would be the classical philologist who reduces the meaning of the text through an objective revelation, given once and for all, and who, as an interpreter, must disappear in his object.

RELATED TRENDS IN THE THEORIES OF AESTHETIC EXPERIENCE

The step from a substantialist conception of a work towards a definition of art arising from its historical and social function is synonymous with granting to the receiver (reader or audience) those rights so long denied. The notion of the work as an entity which supports or represents the truth is replaced by the progressive concretization of meaning. This meaning is constituted by the continuous convergence of text and reception, of the given structure of the work and the appropriating interpretation. The productive and receptive aspects of the aesthetic experience are dialectically related. The work does not exist without its effect; its effect presupposes reception, and in turn the audience's judgment conditions the author's production. Thus literary history is represented as a process in which the reader as an active but collective subject confronts the individual producing author. As the mediating, long-forgotten element in literary history, the reader can no longer be ignored.

THE VARIOUS STRATA OF A 'LITERARY HISTORY OF THE READER'

It is as impossible to give an independent history of the reader as it is to create one dealing only with *viri illustres*, or with pure institutions (as, for instance, the so-called art history without names). However, the concept of a literary history of the reader, to which current scholarship is contributing much, certainly represents a necessary corrective to the kind of history which has prevailed up until now: that of genres, styles, authors, and works. As I see it, modern scholarship still does not sufficiently differentiate between various levels of reception. Pascal as a reader of Montaigne, Rousseau as a reader of Saint Augustine, Lévi-Strauss as a reader of Rousseau are examples of the highest level of individual dialogue between authors, a dialogue which may be epoch-making in literary history owing to the assimilation and re-evaluation of the predecessor whose influence has been recognized as crucial. Such changes are taken into account by society only once the innovative understanding of the individual reader has been publicly acknowledged, accepted by the academic canon of exemplary authors, or sanctioned by cultural institutions. In this middle level of institutionalized reading, the power of literature to transgress norms is again co-opted and transformed into traditionalized and authorized meaning. However, the need for reading, like any other aesthetic pleasure, cannot be totally channeled or manipulated. What the next generation of students finds interesting will not coincide with the aesthetic judgments of their teachers' and parents' generation. Their needs for admiration or sympathetic identification, for protest and for new experience, fall into the lower, or shall we say prereflective, level which represents a subversive process of canon formation. In this way institutionalized thought may become equally subject to change, as much by the lower level of subversive canon formation as by the highest level of dialogue of 'great authors.'

THE READER AS A PROTOTYPE OF BOURGEOIS LITERARY HISTORY

Differentiating three levels of canon formation through reading – the reflective at the high level of authors, the social at the level of cultural institutions, and the prereflective at the underground level of immediate aesthetic experience – may help us to see more clearly the historical boundaries of reader-oriented aesthetics. The 'summit-dialogue' among authors creates the impression of a continuity from Homer to Beckett, whereas reading as a socially formative institution represents an historical period of a few centuries of the bourgeois era. Whoever is interested in the aesthetic experience of the overwhelming majority of humanity which is not yet, or no longer, reading, must search through the realms of listening, watching, and playing, the manifestations of which have scarcely entered the history of art. The theory of the active reader who raises himself to the level of the literary public has its original scene in an era in which, according to Jean-Paul Sartre, the freedom of writing appealed to the freedom of the bourgeois reader. Rousseau, who continually addresses himself as the representative of the entire *genre humain*, has characterized the absolute high point of the reader's emancipation at the beginning of the first book of his *Confessions* with the following provocative description. He summons the vast multitude of readers ('l'innombrable foule de mes semblables') to judge him as well as themselves when he presents his book to God on Judgment Day. This book, however, claims to reveal all the inner secrets known hitherto only by the *souverain juge*, who is now no longer indispensable. The excessive nocturnal readings of father and son in the first book of the *Confessions* also describe the other side of the coin: the fascination of the imagined world of novels, the temptation of unlived adventures, the inaccessible emotions and artificial paradises. It demonstrates that subterranean pleasure which from Don Quixote to Emma Bovary has again and again been sublimated or suppressed in vain. In the case of the bourgeois reader, this aesthetic experience should be analysed as a narcotic or a fantasy escape from his everyday world, as well as a factor contributing to his sentimental education (as in Rousseau's 'Je n'avais aucune idée des choses, que tous les sentiments m'étaient déjà connus').

THE READER'S HORIZON OF EXPECTATIONS: AN OVERDUE CLARIFICATION
In recent years, not only has the concept of the horizon of expectations attracted much attention but its methodological implications have also produced misunderstandings which I would partly attribute to myself. In my studies on medieval animal poetry (*Untersuchungen zur mittelalterlichen Tierdichtung*, 1959), I discovered that the character of the *Roman de Renart* as a counterpoint to heroic poetry and a parody of courtly love only became recognizable if one reconstructed the horizon of the works and genres which, in the prologue to the oldest sections, Pierre de Saint-Cloud had assumed to be generally accepted. Thus I began to test the analysis of horizons as a hermeneutic instrument in intrinsic literary interpretation. The inaugural lectures at Constance in 1967 went a step further with the claim that the literary experience of the reader must be sought out where it 'enters the horizon of expectations of his everyday life, predetermines his understanding of the world, and thus also influences his social behaviour.'[3] My first definition of the horizon of expectations did not do full justice to this claim, which considers the social functions of literature not only from the representative point of view but also from that of the formation and mediation of social norms by literary tradition: 'The analysis of the reader's literary experience is kept from the dangers of psychologism when the reception and effect of a work is described in terms of the frame of reference pertaining to

3 *Literaturgeschichte als Provokation* (Frankfurt: Suhrkamp, 1970) 199

verifiable expectations. At the moment of a work's appearance, this frame of reference results from a prior understanding of the genre, from the forms and themes of previously known works, and from the opposition of poetic and practical language.'⁴ The distinction which has become necessary between the literary horizon of expectations implied by the new work and the social horizon of expectations indicated by an historically given *Lebenswelt* is suggested here in the contrast between poetic and practical language; however, it is not yet explicitly worked out.

An analysis of the reader's, or, if you will, a reading community's, experience in the past or present must encompass both aspects of the text-reader relationship. It must include the effect as that which is stipulated by the text, as well as the reception as that which depends upon the receiver; both these elements constitute the concretization of meaning in the fusion or mediation of two horizons. The reader begins to understand the unknown work to the extent that he establishes the inner literary horizon of expectations while sensing the pre-orientations ('signals' in Harald Weinrich's sense and *Rezeptionsvorgaben* in Manfred Naumann's sense). Behaviour towards the text, however, is both receptive and active at the same time. The reader can make the text 'speak to him,' that is, he can concretize the potential meaning of a text in the direction of contemporary significance only to the extent that he introduces his own pre-understanding of the lived world into the framework of textual expectations and those of the implied reader. His pre-understanding includes his concrete expectations arising from the horizon of his interests, desires, needs, and experiences. The social horizon of expectations is thereby conditioned by the reader's biography, social group or class, education, generation, etc. It goes without saying that literary experiences have their role, through the creation of models such as the hero, in the formation of the social horizon of expectations. The fusion of the two horizons, one of which is implied by the text, the other supplied by the reader, may be carried out through the spontaneous enjoyment of fulfilled expectations, in the relief from the restraint and monotony of everyday life, in the acceptance of an invitation to identify with a model, or more generally, in the enrichment of a new or widened experience. But this fusion may also take place more reflectively as a distanced contemplation, the recognition of a challenge to our comprehension, the discovery of a stylistic or aesthetic device, the response to a flight of thought, and, in all this, an appropriation or a refusal of a new aesthetic experience. With this explanation I also hope to have demonstrated that the concept of the 'fusion of horizons' introduced by H.G. Gadamer is not as 'conservative' as it is imputed to be. Instead, his concept permits us to discover and define different achievements of the

4 Ibid. 173–4

literary experience which work to transgress or to fulfil, but also to invent new norms of behaviour.

THE HERMENEUTIC PRIORITY OF THE IMPLIED READER

The distinction between the intrinsic literary horizon of expectations and the extrinsic horizon of expectations related to a given lived world simplifies the typology of reader roles which is now expanding; there are ideal, normal, fictitious, real, and implied readers, to say nothing of the ominous super-reader. Our distinction presupposes the 'implied' reader (in Wolfgang Iser's meaning) on one side and the 'explicit' reader on the other. According to Iser, the implied reader means 'the necessary requirements of the act of reading as indicated in the text,' or more specifically 'the reader's role noted in the novel,' which is to be understood as the condition for the possibility of effects and which pre-orients, but does not pre-determine, the actualization of meaning.[5] Just as the intrinsic literary horizon of expectations is counter-pointed by a given *Lebenswelt*, so the implied reader stands in opposition to the explicit or historically differentiated one. The latter is a historically, socially, and biographically distinct reader who, as an ever-changing subject, accomplishes the fusion of horizons. To contrast the role of the actual with the implied reader – or in other words the code of a historically determined reader with the code of his role as indicated in the text – is an indispensable prerequisite to a hermeneutically enlightened analysis of the receiver's experience. The implied reader's role may be discerned from the text's objective structures. For this reason it is easier to grasp the implied rather than the explicit reader's role, with its often concealed social dependencies and subjective conditions. Therefore, the role of the implied reader deserves methodological preference. Once we have reconstructed this role in a text, we may with much more assurance ascertain the structures of pre-understanding and thereby uncover the ideological projections of different strata of readers.

This hermeneutic priority of the implied reader may be denied in favour of the materialist principle that production must always be the primary and all-encompassing factor. However, we would then very quickly fall into the well-known dilemma that a strata-specific pre-understanding or 'ideology' could be attributed to a given group of readers which, however, could not be directly deduced from their material or productive conditions. Certainly material relations influence a reader's aesthetic attitudes, but they are by nature mute; they do not spontaneously express themselves in 'analogies' or 'homologies,' but must be obtained from reflection on the subject's be-

---

5 Wolfgang Iser, *Der implizite Leser: Kommunikationsformen des Romans von Bunyan bis Becket* (München: W. Fink, 1972) 8, 92

haviour towards the text. I have not been able to discover how a so-called materialist hermeneutics would proceed otherwise than through the analysis of horizons with the aid of the tools of dialectic. If this kind of scholarship were to revert to the empirical investigation of readers, it would expose itself to all the reservations that Adorno has raised against strict empiricism in sociological research. Remaining in the realm of market studies or limiting behavioural roles to a census-like enumeration (sex, age, income, education, number in family, etc.) are reifications of a method which inevitably fail as a result of the biased use of its population sample and which falsify the data to conform to a previous ideology.[6] If the role of the implied reader does not serve to grasp the divergent forms of reception of historical and social groups, it is not surprising to be faced in the end not with aesthetic attitudes and judgments but with simple hypostases of role behaviour or prejudices which depend upon stratum or status, both incapable of articulating an aesthetically mediated experience. The implied reader cannot totally sacrifice the universal claim made by Rousseau if the text is to appeal to the aesthetic freedom of historical readers. Whoever reduces the role of the implied reader to the behaviour of an explicit reader, whoever writes exclusively in the language of a specific stratum, can only produce cookbooks, catechisms, party speeches, travel brochures, and similar documents. He will not excel in these genres either, as may be seen from eighteenth-century cookbooks which aimed at universal good taste and not at limited structures of pre-understanding.

AN ATTEMPT TO DIFFERENTIATE BETWEEN MODES OF RECEPTION UNRELATED TO THE WORK OF ART AS A WHOLE

The above explanation of the distinctions between the implied and the explicit reader is based on a premise the historical delineation of which is often overlooked and needs discussing. Reading behaviour towards the text by far exceeds what has been said about a historically defined reader who assumes the receiver's role as outlined in a novel and who reconciles it with the horizon of his own experience. As in the case of other genres, such as the lyric, aphorisms, or homilies, which are supported through their very quality as written text by a specific reading process, the mode of reception is not indicated by means of an explicit role. And not every reception of a novel is brought to a complete actualization of the discrete multiplicity and structural unity of a self-sustained work. Upon closer historical examination the reader's experience of the text as a literary work appears more episodic than one might think; however, the single instance of appreciation is a postulate of humanist aesthetics and the typical relation of readers to books in the

6 'Soziologie und empirische Forschung' (1957), in *Logik der Sozialwissenschaften*, ed. E. Topitsch (Köln/Berlin: Kiepenheuer u. Witsch, 1966), 511–25

144 / Hans Robert Jauss

bourgeois period of literature and art. As the history of aesthetic experience shows, such a postulate cannot be generalized to include the eras of pre- or post-autonomous art, nor does it encompass the various levels of reading reception. If we have read a single detective novel and are content with that, it would still be impossible to say that we know what the pleasure of the reader of detective novels is. The specific experience of the detective novel begins only with the need to read more of them, to observe the hero in other situations, and to become acquainted with a variety of other detectives and other procedures of entering into and solving riddles. In the case of a lyric poem or a play the aesthetic enjoyment may begin and be fulfilled with the first work. The hypothetical reader who reads only one detective novel as a 'work' misses the specific attitude from which the enjoyment of the 'crime story' derives. The pleasure does not arise from the self-sufficient immersion in a work qua work but rather from a generic expectation which is at play between works. This expectation, together with each new variation of the basic pattern, enhances the reader's enjoyment of the detective novel. In this fashion it exists for its reader only as a *plurale tantum*, that is, as a way of reading which must negate the character of the text as a unique work in order to renew the charms of a well-known game with familiar rules but unknown surprises. This structure of reception which I call *plurale tantum* is obviously also present in other serial productions of consumer-oriented writing and *Trivialliteratur*. It requires a more thorough examination in accordance with a semiotic model that Charles Grivel has so impressively established for the *roman à consommation* and its ideological archetype during the Second Empire.[7] Here a genuine field is still open for the application of semiotic methods which are most appropriate for the sign systems of such texts. However, these methods meet with difficulties, that is, they are forced to revert to more and more complex secondary sign systems, when they are used to describe the particularity of a text, the singularity of art as a 'sign sui generis.' The fascination of the *plurale tantum* structure of reception may be grasped in an exemplary manner at that moment when it asserted itself for the first time. This occurred in the 1830s when the daily press expanded, thereby permitting a new production and reception of the *roman-feuilleton*. The overwhelming success of these serials among large sections of the population may be compared with today's irresistible television series. In view of this phenomenon we might ask whether trivial literature and art, which distinguished themselves so clearly from the 'entertaining arts' of earlier periods, did not in fact arise in the nineteenth century as a result of the techniques of reproduction (called *art industriel!*) but rather as a correlative to the needs which could not be filled by the suspense-oriented serial novel.

7 *La Production de l'intérêt romanesque* (The Hague/Paris: Mouton, 1973)

Such forms of aesthetic experience which are not related to the classical idea of a self-contained work are already common in eras of pre-autonomous art, to the extent that the reader's relation to the book as a work seems to be but one episode in literary history. If we accept this hypothesis, some difficulties that medievalists continually encounter may be resolved. The prevailing scholarship, which considers itself strictly positivistic, had to suffer, for instance, the ruinous criticism of Eugène Vinaver on the question of the 'unity of the *Song of Roland*,' a topic treated in thousands of essays during the past hundred years. Vinaver pointed out that the quarrel about unity was without foundation in the current debate, but was rather the unrecognized consequence of an applied aesthetics that every French positivist carries with him from his classical training in Corneille and Racine.[8] Indeed, the old Romance epic is part of an oral tradition which cannot be traced back to the closed form of the 'original' work, nor can it be reduced to 'impure' or 'corrupt' variants which require special editorial attention. The *chanson de geste* was performed in instalments with a serial structure of reception. It was poetry meant for recitation and permitting, by means of the *style formulaire*, a certain amount of improvisation so that each performance resulted in a different, and never definitive, form of the text. Increasing continuations and variations had the effect of making the work's boundaries seem still more flexible and of secondary importance. Thus, the epic fable itself could not be regarded as definitive. In the cycle of the *Roman de Renart* I encountered a noteworthy phenomenon; the cycle's core fable about the court day of the lion is retold by a series of narrators who continually alter the trial of the rogue-figure of the fox by changing both the initial motive and the final outcome. What positivist scholarship considered to be a series of 'corrupt variants' of a lost original version was received by the medieval audience as a sequence of instalments introducing an element of suspense within a static framework. This principle, running counter to humanist understanding of original versions and their reception by a reading audience as well as to the ideal of the purity of a work and the faithfulness of imitation, is not only to be found at the level of popular literature or lower style. The great Latin works which were written in the elevated style of philosophical and theological epic and composed in the aftermath of the allegorical tradition of Claudian and Boethius by the twelfth-century Chartres school may also be explained by the principle of what I would call the continuation within an imitation. These series, wherein every new variant of one allegorical fable represents a new answer, could be read according to the perspective of constantly formulated questions. I found this phenomenon in the series of *De universitate mundi* by Bernhard Silvestris,

8 *A la Recherche d'une poétique médiévale* (Paris: Nizet, 1970)

the *Planctus Naturae* and the *Anticlaudianus* by Alanus ab Insulis, the *Roman de la Rose* in the thirteenth century, and finally Brunetto Latini's *Tesoretto*.⁹ Examples in other genres which were neither conceived nor received in terms of definitive form will be mentioned here only in passing. The religious drama, because it was related to the story of the Passion, transcended with every performance the *telos* of a created work. Lyrics passed on through song sheets (*canzone*) or improvised in accordance with rules of public competition (*partimen*) were also subject to similiar fluidity. And finally, the so-called *poésie formelle* of the Middle Ages did not exist in definitive form; this is proven by the instability of textual tradition as well as by the serial reception of the poems. Its particular charm, as Robert Guiette shows us, consisted in perceiving the variations from text to text. What today's critics call 'intertextuality'' finds its best manifestation in the medieval enjoyment of poetry.

All in all, these examples confirm a situation already pointed out by C.S. Lewis: 'We are inclined to wonder how men could be at once so original that they handled no predecessor without pouring new life into him, and so unoriginal that they seldom did anything completely new.'¹⁰ A particular work in the medieval literary tradition should be considered neither as a unique and final creation closed in itself nor as an individual product of its author. The categories of classical aesthetics of production were first proclaimed by the Renaissance after poetry's autonomous quality had attained a new status. The notion of the uniqueness of the original hidden in the distant past, the pure form of which was first to be sought and reconstructed from the distortions of its usage through time, then saved from future profanation by an *editio ne varietur*, made the work into a hypostasized product. If it can be confirmed that the classical equation of the work with the original has its origin with humanism, we could add a further hypothesis on the formation of the concept of autonomous art during the bourgeois period. Has not the rising bourgeois class, in competition with humanism and with the representative art of the aristocratic courts, attempted to create for itself its own works of art, or in other words, 'contemporary originals?' How then otherwise could this new bourgeois art compete with the originals of antiquity, the number of which could no longer be increased?

Post-romantic modernity may again in many respects be understood in terms of a suspension of the classical aesthetics of the self-contained, fetichized work matched by the solitary interpreter. This statement requires

9 See my 'Brunetto Latini als allegorischer Dichter,' in *Formenwandel – Festschrift zum 65. Geburtstag von Paul Böckmann*, eds W. Müller-Seidel and W. Preisendanz (Hamburg: Hoffmann. Campe, 1964), 70

10 *The Discarded Image: An Introduction to Medieval and Renaissance Literature* (Cambridge: Cambridge University Press, 1964) 209

only a few references. All the camps of literary theory have by now absorbed Benjamin's famous essay *Das Kunstwerk im Zeitalter seiner technischen Reproduzierbarkeit* (*The Work of Art in the age of its Technical Reproducibility*, 1936, full text in 1963). In this article Benjamin associates, not without nostalgia, the concept of the aura of uniqueness with the status of the autonomous work of art, a notion at which he has arrived, *via negationis*, through the loss of his own aura by mass-reception. Not as well known is the fact that André Malraux's *Les Voix du silence* (1951) represents an unavowed case of 'Benjamin-reception.' Once the original work is separated from its cultural or historical context it becomes a 'not-original,' an aesthetic object no longer related to the work's concept. It can then be enjoyed by aesthetic consciousness, an attitude often unjustly slandered. The negation of the work's aura of uniqueness and the growing activation of the receiver is most notable in modern painting since Duchamps' 'ready-mades' in which 'the act of provocation itself replaces the status of what has been the work.'[11] The term 'text' also belongs in this context, which once would have been unthinkable in this function but today has been promoted to describe a genre unto itself, thereby presupposing an actualization by a reader as its very mode of existence. Being one of the spiritual fathers of our time, Paul Valéry should hold a central position in an historical re-examination of the problem with which we are concerned. His provocative statement 'mes vers ont le sens qu'on leur prête' denies both the teleology of the completed work and the ideal of its contemplative, but passive, reception.

If it is true that the concept of the 'auratic' work of art remains, in its historical significance, limited to the idealist period of art which is that of bourgeois society, then it must now be asked how, post factum, the entire history of art has been conceived and represented in terms of the priority of works over their experience, of authors over their readers.

University of Konstanz

---

11 Peter Bürger, *Theorie der Avantgarde* (Frankfurt: Suhrkamp, 1974) 77

J. HILLIS MILLER

Ariadne's Thread: Repetition and the Narrative Line

Ich bin dein Labyrinth. Nietzsche, 'Klage der Ariadne,' *Dionysos-Dithyramben*[1]

Now, in the pictures of this imaginary maze, you are to note that both the Cretan and Lucchese designs agree in being composed of a single path or track, coiled, and recoiled, on itself. Take a piece of flexible chain and lay it down, considering the chain itself as the path: and, without an interruption, it will trace any of the three figures. (The two Cretan ones are indeed the same in design, except in being, one square, and the other round.) And recollect, upon this, that the word 'Labyrinth' properly means 'rope-walk,' or 'coil-of-rope-walk,' its first syllable being probably also the same as our English name 'Laura,' 'the path,' and its method perfectly given by Chaucer in the single line 'And, for the house is crenkled to and fro.' And on this note, farther, first, that *had* the walls been real, instead of ghostly, there would have been no difficulty whatever in getting either out or in, for you could go no other way. But if the walls were spectral, and yet the transgression of them made your final entrance or return impossible, Ariadne's clue was needful indeed.

Note, secondly, that the question seems not at all to have been about getting in; but getting *out* again. The clue, at all events, could be helpful only after you have carried it in; and if the spider, or other monster in midweb, ate you, the help in your clue, for return, would be insignificant. So that this thread of Ariadne's implied that even victory over the monster would be vain, unless you could disentangle yourself from his web also.   John Ruskin, *Fors Clavigera*, xxiii[2]

String is my foible. My pockets get full of little hanks of it, picked up and twisted together, ready for uses that never come. I am seriously annoyed if any one cuts the string of a parcel instead of patiently and faithfully undoing it fold by fold. How people can bring themselves to use india-rubber rings, which are a sort of deification of string, as lightly as they do, I cannot imagine. To me an india-rubber ring is a precious treasure. I have one which is not new – one that I picked up off the floor,

1 Friedrich Nietzsche, *Werke in Drei Bänden*, ed. Karl Schlechta, ii (Munich: Carl Hanser, 1966), 1259: 'I am your labyrinth.'
2 *Works*, ed. E.T. Cook and Alexander Wedderburn, 27 (London: George Allen, 1907), 407–8. See Plates 1 and 2 for the illustrations to which Ruskin refers in the first sentence of this citation.

nearly six years ago. I have really tried to use it, but my heart failed me, and I could not commit the extravagance.   Elizabeth Gaskell, *Cranford*[3]

Devilry, devil's work: – traces of such you might fancy were to be found in a certain manuscript volume taken from an old monastic library in France at the Revolution. It presented a strange example of a cold and very reasonable spirit disturbed suddenly, thrown off its balance, as by a violent beam, a blaze, of new light, revealing, as it glanced here and there, a hundred truths unguessed at before, yet a curse, as it turned out, to its receiver, in dividing hopelessly against itself the well-ordered kingdom of his thought. Twelfth volume of a dry enough treatise on mathematics, applied, still with no relaxation of strict method, to astronomy and music, it should have concluded that work, and therewith the second period of the life of its author, by drawing tight together the threads of a long and intricate argument. In effect, however, it began, or, in perturbed manner, and as with throes of childbirth, seemed the preparation for, an argument of an entirely new and disparate species, such as would demand a new period of life also, if it might be, for its due expansion.

But with what confusion, what baffling inequalities! How afflicting to the mind's eye! It was a veritable 'solar storm' – this illumination, which had burst at the last moment upon the strenuous, self-possessed, much-honoured monastic student, as he sat down peacefully to write the last formal chapters of his work ere he betook himself to its well-earned practical reward as superior, with lordship and mitre and ring, of the abbey whose music and calendar his mathematical knowledge had qualified him to reform. The very shape of Volume Twelve, pieced together of quite irregularly formed pages, was a solecism. It could never be bound. In truth, the man himself, and what passed with him in one particular space of time, had invaded a matter, which is nothing if not entirely abstract and impersonal. Indirectly the volume was the record of an episode, an interlude, an interpolated page of life. And whereas in the earlier volumes you found by way of illustration no more than the simplest indispensable diagrams, the scribe's hand had strayed here into mazy borders, long spaces of hieroglyph, and as it were veritable pictures of the theoretic elements of his subject. Soft winter auroras seemed to play behind whole pages of crabbed textual writing, line and figure bending, breathing, flaming, into lovely 'arrangements' that were like music made visible; till writing and writer changed suddenly, 'to one thing constant never,' after the known manner of madmen in such work. Finally, the whole matter broke off with an unfinished word, as a later hand testified, adding the date of the author's death, *'deliquio animi.'*   Walter Pater, 'Apollo in Picardy'[4]

What line should the critic follow in explicating, unfolding, or unknotting these passages? How should he thread his way into the labyrinthine prob-

---

3 *Works*, The Knutsford Edition, 2 (London: Smith, Elder and Co., 1906), 49–50
4 *Miscellaneous Studies* (London: Macmillan and Co., 1895) 141–3

lems of narrative form and in particular into the problem of repetition in fiction? The line of the line itself? The motif, image, concept, or formal model of the line, however, far from being a 'clue' to the labyrinth, turns out, as the passage from Ruskin suggests, to be itself the labyrinth. To follow the motif on the line will not be to simplify the knotted problems of narrative form but to retrace the whole tangle from the starting place, from a certain point of entry.

This overlapping of the part, even a 'marginal' part, with the whole is characteristic of all such theoretical investigations. The same thing would happen in a different way if the problems of narrative form were entered by way of the question of character in the novel, or of interpersonal relations, or of the narrator, or of temporal structure, or of the role of figurative language and mythological references, or of irony as the basic trope of fiction, or of realism, or of multiple plots, and so on. The motif of the line may have the advantage of being a less used point of entry, a back door, and of being at once a local motif, microscopic, and an over-all formal model, macroscopic. The image of the line, it might be noted, has by an unavoidable recrossing already contaminated this topological placing of the image of the line. Since the line is more figure than concept (but is there any concept without figure?) the line can lead easily to all the other conceptual problems I have mentioned: character, intersubjectivity, narrator, time, mimesis, and so on. Perhaps it less begs the questions from the start, or begs the questions at any rate in a different way.

Ariadne's thread, then. Dionysus's 'I am your labyrinth,' said to Ariadne, marks the moment of the happy ending of her story. This moment has entered almost as deeply as the other two crucial moments of Ariadne's life into the classical, Renaissance, and post-Renaissance imagination, all the way down to Richard Strauss's *Ariadne auf Naxos*. The latter is the latest in a long genealogical line in opera going back through Jiři Benda in the eighteenth century to Claudio Monteverdi in the seventeenth.[5] The other two moments of the story are the one in which the enamoured girl offers Theseus the thread with which to save himself and offers in the thread herself, and the one which shows Ariadne betrayed, watching from the shore at Naxos the perjured sails diminishing toward the horizon:

---

5 Monteverdi's famous 'Lament of Ariadne' is all that remains of his opera on Ariadne. Jiři Benda (1722–1795) was a Czech musician and composer, more important than Rousseau in the development of the melodrama, or recitation with musical accompaniment. His *Ariadne auf Naxos* (1774) influenced Mozart, who planned to write a 'duodrama' modelled on those of Benda. For a history of melodrama, duodrama, and monodrama, in its connection with Tennyson's 'Maud: A Monodrama,' see A. Dwight Culler, 'Monodrama and the Dramatic Monologue,' *Publications of the Modern Language Association* 90 (May 1975) 366–85.

PLATE 1 Cretan coins referred to by Ruskin in *Fors Clavigera*

And to the stronde barefot faste she wente,
And cryed, 'Theseus! myn herte swete!
Where be ye, that I may nat with yow mete,
And myghte thus with bestes ben yslayn?'
The holwe rokkes answerede hire agayn.
No man she saw, and yit shyned the mone,
And hye upon a rokke she wente sone,
And saw his barge saylynge in the se.
                Chaucer, *The Legend of Good Women,* 11.F 2189–2196[6]

Though in one version Ariadne in her forlorn despair hangs herself with her thread, the story is most often given a happy ending. Dionysus rescues Ariadne and marries her. As Walter Pater says:

Of the whole story of Dionysus, it was the episode of his marriage with Ariadne about which ancient art concerned itself oftenest, and with most effect ... And as a story of romantic love, fullest perhaps of all the motives of classic legend of the pride of life, it survived with undiminished interest to a later world, two of the greatest masters of Italian painting having poured their whole power into it; Titian with greater space of ingathered shore and mountain, and solemn foliage, and fiery animal life; Tintoret with profounder luxury of delight in the nearness to each other, and imminent embrace, of glorious bodily presences; and both alike with consummate beauty of physical form.[7]

The story of Ariadne has, as is the way with myths, its slightly asymetrical echoes along both the narrative lines which converge in her marriage to Dionysus. Daedalus it was who told Ariadne how to save Theseus with the

6 *Works,* ed. F.N. Robinson, 2nd ed (Boston: Houghton Mufflin, 1961), 513
7 'A Study of Dionysus,' *Greek Studies* (London: Macmillan and Co., 1895) 16.

thread. Imprisoned by Minos in his own labyrinth, he escapes by flight, survives the fall of Icarus, and reaches Sicily safely. Daedalus is then discovered when he solves the puzzle posed publicly by Minos with the offer of a reward to the solver: How to run a thread through all the chambers and intricate windings of a complex seashell? Daedalus pierces the centre of the shell, ties a thread to an ant, puts the ant in the pierced hole, and wins the prize when the ant emerges at the mouth of the shell. Thread and labyrinth, thread intricately crinkled to and fro as the retracing of the labyrinth which defeats the labyrinth but makes another intricate web at the same time; pattern is here superimposed on pattern, like the two homologous stories themselves.

This notion of a compulsion to repeat, intrinsic in the pattern of the story, is present in the legend of the 'dance of Theseus.' Theseus, surely the anti-Dionysus of the myth, man of reason and Apollonian clarity, nevertheless cannot free himself from his bondage to the Dionysian irrationality of the maze or from the unreason of Ariadne herself, however much he tries to forget her. When Theseus has escaped from the Daedalian labyrinth and, later on, has abandoned Ariadne, he goes to the island of Delos, makes sacrifice to Apollo and to Aphrodite, and institutes in their honour a dance performed by his consort of youths and maidens saved from the Minotaur. The dance in its intricate turnings is a ritual copy of the labyrinth. It becomes a religious institution at Delos and is performed periodically henceforth in honour of Aphrodite. The Delians call it *Geranos*, the crane dance, by analogy, apparently, with the movements of that bird.[8]

Along the other line, the line of Dionysus, in one direction there is the story of Erigone, in the other that of Pentheus and the Baccantes, subject of

---

8 See Pausanias, *Description of Greece*, ix, xi, 4, Plutarch, *Theseus*, 21, and, for a valuable analysis of the motif, Hubert Damisch, 'La Danse de Thésée,' *Tel Quel* 26 (1966) 60–8. See especially 61:

> L'élément dionysiaque qui transparaît ici pourra sembler timide, mesuré qu'il était par la cithare de l'aède (accompagné, il est vrai, de deux porteurs de tambourins): il importe à notre propos de souligner que pareille farandole, au moins si l'on en croit Plutarque, ne reproduisait pas tellement le cheminement du héros qu'elle ne redoublait de labyrinthe lui-même par le détour d'une danse qui mettait en mouvement tous les membres des corps entraînés par elle dans une course sans autre terms assignable que l'étourdissement ou l'ivresse légère qui ne pouvaient manquer de s'emparer des danseurs livrés à ses méandres, leur individualité étant appelée à se consommer dans des figures collectives dont l'entrelacement et la succession, entraînant la rupture répétée de la chaîne, étaient faits pour évoquer la structure de ce lieu obscur et sauvage, saturé d'un réseau de chemins sans mémoire bientôt refermés, pour ne le laisser plus échapper, sur celui qui en avait passé le seuil.

PLATE 2 Labyrinth on the southern wall of the porch of the Cathedral of Lucca. Illustration from *Fors Clavigera*

the extraordinary late play by Euripides, still controversial in purport. The story of Pentheus, doubter of Dionysus, murdered by his Bacchus-maddened mother, is well known, that of Erigone more obscure. Daughter of Icarius, one of the two Erigones, she is seduced by Dionysus, who repays her father with wine. Icarius's people murder him when they believe they have been poisoned by the wine. Led to her father's unburied corpse by the barking dog Marra, Erigone hangs herself on a nearby tree. Dionysus, in revenge, drives all the daughters of Athens mad so that they hang themselves. Erigone is made into the constellation of the Virgin.

Again the slightly askew matching of the three stories is striking. Dionysus is in each case the ambiguous seducer-rescuer in a family romance involving defeat or death for the father-figures, with a complex role for the female-figures as murderous mothers, self-slaying victims, and transfigured mates for the god. Dionysus liberates the latter from their repression by fathers or by self-righteous perjuring lovers. The relation among the various stories is uncanny. It cannot be wholly rationalized. The need for a permutation of the somewhat mysterious elements of the story is intrinsic to the story itself. It is as if no telling of it could express clearly its meaning. It has to be traced and retraced, thread over thread in the labyrinth, without ever becoming wholly perspicuous. Each telling both displays the labyrinthine pattern of relations again and at the same time leaves its 'true' meaning veiled. Generations of scholars have quarrelled over the meaning of Euripides' *Bacchae*. Even Daedalus, fabulous artificer, could not with all his cunning escape from the labyrinth he had made to hide Pasiphaë's monster son, product of her unnatural lust. Daedalus escaped his labyrinth only by flying out of it, by cutting the Gordian knot, so to speak, rather than by untying it, though at the cost of his too bold son, rash youth, defier of the sun. The stories turn on enigmatic oppositions: making/solving, hiding/revealing, male/female, or is it female/male, united in ambiguous or androgynous figures, like Dionysus himself, or like Ariadne, who is perhaps too aggressive to be purely 'feminine,' in the male chauvinist sense of the word, or like Arachne, devouring phallic mother, weaver of a web, *erion* in Greek, which also, as Jacques Derrida observes in *Glas*, means wool, fleece, the ring of pubic hair.

The conflation of Arachne and Ariadne is implicit in Ruskin's image of the victim of the labyrinth eaten by the 'monster in midweb.' The superimposition of the myths of Ariadne and Arachne, two similar but not wholly congruent stories, both involving the images of thread or of weaving, is already present in Shakespeare's splendid portmanteau word 'Ariachne's' in Act v of *Troilus and Cressida*. As 'This is, and is not, Cressid,' so Ariachne is and is not Ariadne and at the same time is and is not Arachne, is both and neither at once. To the similarity and dissimilarity of stories in the same mythical or narrative line must be added the lateral repetition, with a difference of distinct myths, here brought to our attention by the 'accidental' similarity of the names. This clashing, partial homonymy perfectly mimes the relation between the two stories.[9]

The convergence of two narrative lines, in the marriage of Dionysus and Ariadne, that of Dionysus, that of Ariadne, is traditionally symbolized by the starry crown Dionysus gives her. This crown is immortalized after her death as the corona in the region of the constellation Taurus. It is also symbolized by the ring that Dionysus slips on Ariadne's finger. Ring of the marriage tie, knotting the two stories, ring of stars, each ring divinizing the fragmented and linear sequence of episodes in a round of recurrence, the

9 I.A. Richards, as far as I know, was the first to accept 'Ariachne's' and to interpret its 'bifold' meaning. See his '*Troilus and Cressida* and Plato,' *Speculative Instruments* (London: Routledge and Kegan Paul, 1955) 210

round of eternal return: 'o wie sollte ich nicht nach der Ewigkeit brünstig sein und nach dem hochzeitlichen Ring der Ringe, – dem Ring der Wiederkunft?' ('Oh, how should I not lust after eternity and after the nuptial ring of rings, the ring of recurrence?')[10] This double ring, marriage ring and crown of stars, is in fact a spiral, coil-shaped, labyrinth-shaped, or ear-shaped. Even an exact repetition is never the same, if only because it is the second and not the first. The second constitutes the first, after the fact, as an origin, as a model or archetype. The second, the repetition, is the origin of the originality of the first. Ariadne, originally herself a goddess of love, is doubled, in Tintoretto's magnificent painting, by Venus. Venus gives Ariadne the crown, and, in another doubling, the marriage ring of Ariadne and Dionysus matches the small labyrinth-shaped ears of the two lovers. The ears appear in Nietzsche's revision, for the version in the *Dionysos-Dithyramben*, of Dionysus's response to the lament of Ariadne, sung grotesquely by the magician-shaman in *Zarathustra*, vi, 5:

Sei klug Ariadne! ...
Du hast kleine Ohren: du hast meine Ohren:
Steck ein kluges Wort hinein! –
Muss man sich nicht erst hassen, wenn man sich lieben soll? ...
Ich bin dein Labyrinth ...

(Be clever, Ariadne! ...
You have small ears, you have my ears:
Put a clever word into them!
Must people not first hate each other if they are to love each other? ...
[Or: Must one not first hate himself if he is to love himself? Or: Must people not first hate each other if each is to love himself? Or: Must one not first hate himself if people are to love each other? The phrase in German is undecidable. It has four possible readings.]
I am your labyrinth ...)[11]

I am your labyrinth! Ariadne's lament is pervaded by the imagery of Dionysus's penetration of her inmost being: '*willst* du *hinein*, / ins Herz, einsteigen, / in meine heimlichsten / Gedanken einsteigen?' ('*Wouldst* thou

---

10 F. Nietzsche, *Also Sprach Zarathustra*, iii, 'Die sieben Siegel,' 2, *Werke*, ed. Schlechta, ii, 474: 'On, how should I not lust after eternity and after the nuptial ring of rings, the ring of recurrence?' trans. Walter Kaufmann, *The Portable Nietzsche* (New York: Viking Press, 1954), 340
11 Schlechta ed., ii, 1259, my translation

deeply/ The heart climb in / Into my most secret thoughts / Climb in?')[12] When Dionysus speaks, he offers himself in turn as a maze for her to penetrate and retrace with her thread. This reciprocity, in which each is the container or labyrinth for the other, is echoed by the matching of their small spiral-shaped ears, as in Tintoretto's painting. It is echoed also in the mirroring oscillations of meaning in the enigmatic wisdom Dionysus puts in Ariadne's ear. This is the wisdom of a doubling interpersonal relation between the sexes. It is a relation of simultaneous love and hate which is at the same time the Narcissistic mirroring of an androgynous self by itself, in self-hate and self-love: 'Muss man sich nicht erst hassen, wenn man sich lieben soll.' The line of Ariadne's thread is at once the means of retracing a labyrinth which is already there, and at the same time is itself the labyrinth, a 'rope-walk' according to Ruskin's false etymology, spun from the belly of a spider in mid-web, Ariadne anamorphosed into Arachne. The line, Ariadne's thread, is both the labyrinth and a means of safely retracing the labyrinth. The thread and the maze are each the origin of which the other is a copy, or the copy which makes the other, already there, an origin: *Ich bin dein Labyrinth.*

The tangles of love and hate and the question of who penetrates whom, in a love which, in its intensity of self-abnegation, is a fatal labyrinthine betrayal, is expressed at a crucial moment of *The Golden Bowl* in a reference to Ariadne's thread. It will be remembered that the Biblical source of the title of James's novel contains the image of a broken or untied line: 'Also when they shall be afraid of that which is high, and fear shall be in the way, and the almond tree shall flourish, and the grasshopper shall be a burden, and desire shall fail: because man goeth to his long home, and the mourners go about the streets: Or ever the silver cord be loosed, or the golden bowl be broken, or the pitcher be broken at the fountain, or the wheel broken at the cistern' (*Ecclesiastes* 12:5–6). Desire and the failing of desire in death, broken containers of the bounty of life, interrupted lines for holding or drawing those vessels – the Biblical passage 'contains' already the elements of the Ariadne story. James's reference to Ariadne comes just after Mrs Assingham, one of James's most brilliant *ficelles*, has broken the bowl and has left Maggie to confront her adulterous husband and to offer him the 'help' of a delay. She sets the outrageous price he must pay for her complicity in her own betrayal. He must allow her penetration into the winding corridors of his inmost self. He must be her labyrinth: 'It had operated within her now to the last intensity, her glimpse of the precious truth that by her helping him, helping him to help himself, as it were, she should help him to help *her*.

12 Ibid. 1257, my translation

Hadn't she fairly got into his labyrinth with him? – wasn't she indeed in the very act of placing herself there for him at its centre and core, whence, on that definite orientation and by an instinct all her own, she might securely guide him out of it?'[13] Maggie, like Ariadne/Arachne, is both the source of the thread which will make it possible for her husband to escape his labyrinth and at the same time a central energy spinning a web to entangle him inextricably. His labyrinth is both his own and one she has made inescapable for him by penetrating it and retracing it.

The image of the line cannot, it is easy to see, be detached from the problem of repetition. Repetition might be defined as anything which happens to the line to trouble or even to confound its straightforward linearity: returnings, knottings, recrossings, crinklings to and fro, suspensions, interruptions, fictionalizings. As Ruskin says in *Fors Clavigera*, the Daedalian labyrinth, made from a single thread or path curved and recurved, may now serve as a model for everything 'linear and complex.' The phrase is an oxymoron; it names the line which is not simply linear, not merely a straightforward movement from beginning to middle to end. In what follows, I shall briefly explore the way the 'simple' linear terminology and linear form of realistic fiction subverts itself by becoming 'complex' – knotted, repetitive, doubled, broken, phantasmal.

To put down first, pell-mell, like the twisted bits of string in the pockets of the narrator of *Cranford*, some of the images of the line as they are associated with narrative form or with the ordinary terminology of story-telling: narrative line, life line, by-line, main line, drop me a line, break up their lines to weep, linotype, what's my line?, genealogical line, genetic strain, affiliation, defile, thread of the story, *ficelle*, lineaments, crossroads, impasse, denouement, cornered, loose thread, marginal, trope, chiasmus, hyperbole, crisis, double bind, tie that binds, circulation, recoup, reproduction, engraving, beyond the pale, trespass, crossing the bar, missing link, marriage tie, couple, coupling, copulation, plot, double plot, sub-plot, spin a yarn, get an angle on, the end of the line.

It may be possible gradually to untwist these hanks, to lay them end to end in a neat series, to make an orderly chain of them, knot added to knot in macramé, or to crochet them into a fabric making a visible figure, a figure in the carpet. At the beginning the thing to be most emphasized is the richness and complexity of the family of terms involving the image of the line – figures of speech, idioms, slang, conceptual words, or narrative motifs like Hercules at the crossroads. Dozens of examples spring to mind in proliferat-

13 Henry James, *The Golden Bowl*, New York Edition of *The Novels and Tales*, 24 (New York: Charles Scribner's Sons, 1909), 187

ing abundance, like a tangled skein of bits of yarn. This especially is the case if the line is extended slightly to include the adjacent figures of cutting, weaving, and setting limits, drawing boundary lines. How can one find the law of this tangled multitude or set limits to the limitless? The notions of legislation (imposed from without or found within) and of boundary are themselves already images of the line. (*Lex* is from the root *lege*, to collect. It is the same root as that for 'logic' and 'coil.') The thing to be defined enters into and contaminates the definer, according to an inescapable aporia.

One can see from the beginning that the image of the line, in whatever region of narrative terms it is used, tends to be logocentric, monological. The model of the line is a powerful part of the traditional language of Occidental metaphysics. It cannot easily be detached from its implications or from the functions it has within that system. Narrative event follows narrative event in a purely metonymic line, but the series tends to organize itself or to be organized into a causal chain. The chase has a beast in view. The end of the story is the retrospective revelation of the law of the whole. That law is an underlying 'truth' which ties all together in an inevitable sequence revealing a hitherto hidden figure in the carpet. The image of the line tends always to imply the norm of a single continuous unified structure determined by one external organizing principle. This principle holds the whole line together, gives it its law, controls its progressive extension, curving or straight, with some *arché, telos*, or ground. Origin, goal, or base: all three come together in the gathering movement of the *logos*: transcendent word, speech, reason, proportion, substance, or ground, from *legein*, to gather, as in English collect, legislate, legend, or coil.

What is the status of these etymologies? Identification of the true meaning of the word? Some original presence rooted in the ground of immediate experience, physical or metaphysical? By no means. They serve rather to indicate the lack of enclosure of a given word. Each word inheres in a labyrinth of branching interverbal relationships going back not to a referential source but to something already, at the beginning, a figurative transfer, according to the Rousseauistic or Condillacian law that all words were originally metaphors. Moreover, one often encounters for a given word, not a single root, but forks in the etymological line leading to bifurcated or trifurcated roots or to that philologist's confession of archeological ignorance: 'Origin unknown.' There is, in addition, no reason (that I can see) why there should not be bends or absolute breaks in the etymological line. The realm of words is a free country. Or is it? There seems no reason why a given sound or sign should not be deployed to uses entirely without affiliation to its figurative roots. Or can it? What coercion does the word itself, as a material base, exert over the range of meanings one can give it? Can one bend, but not break, the etymological line? In any case, the effect of etymological retracing is not to ground the word solidly but to render it unstable, equivocal, wavering, abysmal. All etymology is false etymology, both in the sense that there is always some bend or discontinuity in the etymological line, and in the sense that etymology always fails to find an *etymon*, a true literal meaning at the origin. If the line suggests always the gatherings of the word, at the same time, in all the places of its use, the line contains the possibility of turning back on itself. In this turning it subverts its own linearity and becomes repetition. Without the line there is no repetition, but repetition is what disturbs, suspends, or destroys the linearity of the line, and plays with its straightforward logic.

Moreover, one can also see, at the beginning, that the narrative terminology of the line tends to organize itself into links, chains, strands, figures, configurations, each covering one of the topographical regions I have identified as basic to the problematic of realistic fiction: time, character, the narrator, and so on. To identify the terminology of the line, even in an apparently random way, bit of string by bit of string, will be to cover the whole ground, according to the paradox of Ariadne's thread. That thread maps the whole labyrinth, rather than providing a single track to its centre and back out. The thread is the labyrinth, and at the same time it is the repetition of the labyrinth.

The bits of string I have gathered may be organized in nine areas of linear terminology.

First there are the physical aspects of writing or of printed books: letters, signs, hieroglyphs, glyphs, and anaglyphs, as well as letters in the sense indicated in the phrase 'drop me a line.' The linearity of the written or printed book is a powerful reinforcement of logocentrism, though there is no writing without the possibility of repetition or of the breaking of the line.

A second region of linear terminology involves all the words for narrative line: dénouement, curve of the action, turn of events, broken or dropped thread, line of argument, story line, figure in the carpet, narration as the retracing of a story which has already happened. Note that these lines are all figurative. They do not describe the actual physical linearity of the lines of type or of writing, nor do they even describe the sequence of chapters in a novel. They name rather the imagined sequence of the events narrated.

A third topic is the use of linear terms to describe character, as in the phrases, line of life, life-line, or what's my line? Physiognomy is the reading of character from facial lineaments. The word character itself is a figure meaning the outward signs in the lines on a person's face of his inward nature. A character is a sign, as in the phrase, 'Chinese written character.'

A fourth is all the terminology of interpersonal relations: filiation, affiliation, marriage tie, liaison, genetic or ancestral line, and so on. One cannot talk about relations among persons without using the image of the line.

The next region is that of economic terminology. The language of interpersonal relations borrows heavily from economic words, as in 'expense of spirit in a waste of shame,' or when one says, 'Pay him back,' or 'Repay him with interest,' or speaks of someone as 'out of circulation.' Many, if not all, economic terms involve linear imagery: circulation, binding promise or contract, recoup, coupon, margin, cutback, line your pockets, on the line (which means ready for immediate expenditure), currency, current, and pass current.

Another area of narrative terminology involves topography: roads, crossroads, crossings, paths, frontiers, gates, windows, doors, turnings, journeys, narrative motifs like Oedipus at the forks.

Another topic for investigation is the illustrations for novels. Most nineteenth-century novels were of course illustrated by engravings, that is, by pictures printed from plates incised with lines. Ruskin in *Ariadne Florentina* (1873–75) has investigated this use of the line to make a repeatable design.

Another region is figurative language in the text of a novel. The terminology for figures of speech is strongly linear, as when one speaks of tropes, of *topoi*, of chiasmus, of ellipsis, of hyperbole, and so on.

A final *topos* in the criticism of fiction is the question of realistic representation. Mimesis in a 'realistic' novel is a detour from the real world which mirrors that world and in one way or another, in the cultural or psychic economy of production and consumption, leads the reader back to it.

Each of these topological areas requires separate discussion. The image, figure, or concept of the line threads its way through all the traditional terms for story-writing or story-telling as the dominant figure in the carpet. The peculiarity of all these regions in their relation is that there are no terms but figurative ones to speak of any of them. The term 'narrative line,' for example, is a catachresis, the violent, forced, or abusive use of a term from another realm to name something which has no 'proper' name. The relationship of meaning among all these areas of terminology is not from sign to thing but a displacement from one sign to another sign which in its turn draws its meaning from another figurative sign, in a constant *mise en abyme*. The name for this displacement is allegory. Story-telling, the putting into language of man's 'experience' of his life, is in its writing or reading a hiatus in that experience. Narrative is the allegorizing along a temporal line of this perpetual displacement from immediacy. Allegory in this sense, however, is precisely the expression of the impossibility of expressing unequivocally, and so dominating, what is meant by experience or by writing. My exploration of the labyrinth of narrative terms is in its turn to be defined as an impossible search for the centre of the maze, the minotaur or spider which has created and so commands it all.

The reasons for this impossibility may be variously formulated. Perhaps it might be better to say, since what is in question here is the failure of reason, that the inability of the mind to reach the centre of the labyrinth of narrative terms and so command it may be variously experienced. One way is in the blind alley encountered when any term or family of terms is followed as far as it will go, either linguistically, 'in itself,' or as a means of talking about objective aspects of specific novels. No one thread (character, realism, inter-personal relation, or whatever) can be followed to a central point where it provides a means of overseeing, controlling, and understanding the whole. Instead it reaches, sooner or later, a crossroad, a blunt fork, where either path leads manifestly to a blank wall. This double blind is at once the failure to reach the centre of the labyrinth and in fact the reaching of a false centre, everywhere and nowhere, attainable by any thread or path. These empty corridors are vacant of any minotaur. The minotaur, as Ruskin saw, is a spider, Arachne – arachnid who devours her mate, weaver of a web which is herself, and which both hides and reveals an absence, the abyss. Her text is a *mise en abyme*.

The impasse in the exploration of a given novel or of a given aspect of the terminology of the criticism of narrative occurs differently in each case. In every case, however, it is experienced as something irrational, alogical. The critic suffers a breakdown of distinctions, for example that between figura-tive and literal language, or between the text and that extra-textual reality which the text mirrors, or between the notions that the novel copies some-thing or that on the other hand it makes something happen. The critic may be unable to decide, of two repeating elements, which is the original of which, which the 'illustration' of the other, or whether in fact they repeat or are heterogeneous, unassimilable to a single pattern, double-centred or acentric. The critic may be unable to tell whether a given textual knot is 'purely verbal' or has to do with 'life.' The reader may experience the impossibility of deciding, in a given passage, who is speaking, the author, the narrator, or the character, where or when, and to whom. Such a passage in its undecidability bears the indelible traces of being a written document, not something that could ever be spoken by a single voice and so returned to a single *logos*. There is always in such passages something left over or something missing, some-thing too much or too little. This forbids translating the written text back to a single mind, imagined or real. In one way or another the monological becomes dialogical, the unitary thread a Möbius strip, with two sides and yet only one side. An alternative metaphor would be that of a complex knot of many crossings. Such a knot may be in one region untied, made un-perplexed, but only at the expense of making an inextricable tangle of knotted crossings at some other point on the loop. The number of crossings remains stubbornly the same.

The critic, in a further frustration, may experience the impossibility of detaching a part of the problem of narrative form from the whole knot of problems and so understanding that. He cannot separate one piece and explore it in isolation. The part/whole, inside/outside division breaks down. The part turns out to be indistinguishable from the whole, the outside already inside. Character in the novel, for example, may not be defined without talking about interpersonal relations, about time, about figures of speech, about mimesis, and so on.

The critic, on the other hand, may experience the impossibility of getting outside the maze altogether and seeing it from without, giving it its law or finding its law, rather than the impossibility of reaching a commanding centre. Any terminology of analysis or explication is already inextricably folded into the text the critic is attempting to see from without. This is related to the impossibility of distinguishing critical and analytical terminology, the terms the critic needs to interpret novels, from terminology used inside the novels themselves. Any novel already interprets itself. It uses within itself the same kind of language, encounters the same impasses, as are used and encountered by the critic. The critic may fancy himself safely and rationally outside the contradictory language of the text, but he is already entangled in its web. The same blind forks, double blinds, or double binds, are encoun-tered in the attempt to develop a general 'theoretical' terminology for the interpretation of prose fiction and in the attempt to eschew theory, to go to the text itself and, without theoretical presuppositions, to explicate its meaning.

Criticism of a given novel or body of novels should therefore be the following of one or another track until it reaches, in the text, one or another of these double blinds, rather than the attempt to find a presupposed unity. Such a unity always turns out to be spurious, imposed rather than intrinsic. This can be experienced, however, only through the patient work of follow-ing some thread as far, deep into the labyrinth of the text, as it will go. Such an effort of interpretation is not the 'deconstruction' of a given novel but rather a discovery of the way it deconstructs itself in the process of construct-ing its web of story-telling. The blind alleys in the analysis of narrative may not by any means be avoided. They may only be veiled by some credulity making a substance where there is in fact an abyss, for example, in taking consciousness as a solid ground. The thinly veiled chasm may be avoided only by stopping short, by taking something for granted in the terminology one is using rather than interrogating it, or by not pushing the analysis of the text in question far enough that the impossibility of a single definitive reading emerges.

The impasse of the analysis of narrative is a genuine double blind. It results first from the fact that there is in no region of narrative or of its analysis a literal ground – in history, consciousness, society, the physical world, or whatever – for which the other regions are figures. The terminology of narrative is therefore universally catachresis. Such tropes break down the distinction between figure and ground, so reassuringly open to the experience of a theoretical seeing. The other fork of this double blind is the fact that the terminology of narrative may by no effort be compartmentalized, divided into hanks of different colored thread. The same terms must be used in all regions. All the *topoi* overlap. Neither the critic nor the novelist can, for example, talk about sexual relations without using economic terminology (getting, spending, and so on), or without talking about mimetic representation (reproduction, etc.), or about topography (crossings), and in fact about all the other topics of narrative at the same time. The language of narrative is always displaced, borrowed. Therefore any single thread leads everywhere, like a labyrinth made of a single line or corridor crinkled to and fro.

Take, as an example of this, the letter x. It is a letter, a sign, but a sign for signs generally and for a multitude of relations involving ultimately interchanges among all nine of my places. x is a crossroads, the figure of speech called chiasmus, a kiss, a fish, Christ, the cross of the crucifixion, an unknown in mathematics, the proofreader's sign for a broken letter, a place marked on a map (x marks the spot), an illustration (See fig. x), the signature of an illiterate or unlettered person, the sign of an error or erasure (crossed out), the indication of degrees of purity, as in the x's on a sack of flour or sugar, the place of encounters, reversals, and exchanges, the region of both/and and either/neither ('She is my ex-wife'), the topos as gap, gape, or yawning chasm, the undecidable, the foyer of genealogical crossings, of crossing oneself, of the x chromosome, of crisis, of the double-cross, of star-crossed lovers, of cross-examination, of cross-stitching, of cross-purposes, of the witch's cross, of the criss-cross (originally Christ-cross), and of the cross child. x is finally the sign of death, as in the skull and crossbones, or the crossed eyes, or crossed-out eyes of the cartoon figure who is baffled, unconscious, or dead: x x. In all these uses, the ex means out of, beside itself, displaced. The real and visible rises, exhales, from the unreal – or is it the unreal appearing as the always intervening veil or substitute for the absent real? – as, in stanza 18 of Wallace Stevens's 'The Man with the Blue Guitar,'

daylight comes,
Like light in a mirroring of cliffs,
Rising upward from a sea of ex.[14]

The daylight, the visible and namable, is always doubly derived, secondary. It rises from the sea and then is further displaced by its mirroring from the cliffs in a wandering like that of all those terms I have been examining. This movement, however, makes the source itself unreal, a sea of ex, as Stevens speaks, in 'An Ordinary Evening in New Haven' (xiii), of the approach of night, from which the light comes and to which it returns, as 'the big x of the returning primitive.'[15] The real and the unreal, the metaphorical and the literal, the figure and the ground, constantly change places, in oscillating chiasmus, for 'ex'ample in Stevens's contradictory explanation of 'sea of ex' in his letters. To Renato Poggioli he wrote' 'A sea of ex means a purely negative sea. The realm of has-been without interest or provocativeness.' To Hy Simons: 'Sea of Ex. The imagination takes us out of (Ex) reality into a pure irreality. One has this sense of irreality often in the presence of morning light on cliffs which then rise from a sea that has ceased to be real and is therefore a sea of Ex.'[16] Which is unreal, which real, the sea or the light? It can not be decided. Whatever one sees is unreal and creates as its ground a phantasmal real, which becomes unreal in its turn, when one turns to it.

I shall come full circle, in conclusion, to one of the texts with which I began, Cranford. Cranford is a novel about a village in danger of becoming entirely populated by old maids and fastidious bachelors. It is in danger of dying out through a failure of ancestral lines to continue, a failure of sexual doubling or genealogical crossing, as if there had been some loss of the masculine power of capitalization in an effeminate or effeminizing doubling, as in Freud's recognition that the multiplying of the images of the phallus means its loss: 'As Miss Pole observed, "As most of the ladies of good family in Cranford were elderly spinsters, or widows without children, if we did not relax a little, and become less exclusive, by-and-by we should have no society at all." '[17] The passage in question in Cranford has to do with generation and with the passing on of names from generation to generation in family

14 The Collected Poems of Wallace Stevens (New York: Alfred A. Knopf, 1954) 175
15 Ibid. 474
16 The Letters of Wallace Stevens, selected and edited by Holly Stevens (New York: Alfred A. Knopf, 1966), 783, 360
17 Elizabeth Gaskell, Works, The Knutsford Edition, II, 77

crossings. It has to do with the letter f, in fact with a double f. F is genealogically derived from G, gamma in Greek, which is another kind of crossing, the fork in the road, a truncated X, in this like Y. The f is a doubling of that turn, a *digamma* or 'double gamma,' as it was called in Greek. The cursive or minuscule gamma is of course y-shaped, while the capital gamma is like a right-angled turn: Γ. In the passage in *Cranford* the f or double g is further doubled in an effete purity of family names and family blood lines which almost, but not quite, makes further genealogical crossings impossible. It is as though the double f or quadruple G were the true doubleblind or end of the line, as it is the end of my line of argument here.

The passage, in its admirably quiet but devastating irony, speaks for itself, though it should be noted that it is doubled, dialogical. In fact it is alogical, not only in its irony but also in its use of that Möbius-strip form of language, indirect discourse. The passage has quotation marks around it and is presented as spoken by Mrs Forrester at the convocation of the ladies of Cranford brought together to decide whether or not to call upon the parvenu Mrs Fitz-Adam, née Mary Hoggins, a farmer's daughter. Mrs Forrester's words are not presented directly, however. They are expressed in the third person past tense of indirect discourse as if what she says were, absurdly, printed in a newspaper as reported from a parliamentary debate. The words on the page, the tenses and the pronouns, are neither the narrator's nor Mrs Forrester's. The language belongs properly to no one. It is a double diegesis, that kind of narration Plato so deplored in *The Republic*. In fact the passage is a double double diegesis, if the reader thinks, as he should, of the narrator of *Cranford* as an invented character not identical to Elizabeth Gaskell. The words on the page could not be spoken, in the real world of person-to-person dialogue, by man or woman. They are a pure invention of writing, like the double f in the names ffaringdon or ffoulkes. The passage is not so much dialogical, with two originating voices, like an ellipse with two focii, as alogical, parabolical, hyperbolical, thrown permanently off-base. It has no conceivable ground in any *logos*, not even in a double one:

She had always understood that Fitz meant something aristocratic; there was Fitz-Roy – she thought that some of the King's children had been called Fitz-Roy; and there was Fitz-Clarence now – they were the children of dear good King William the Fourth. Fitz-Adam! – it was a pretty name; and she thought it very probably meant 'Child of Adam.' No one, who had not some good blood in their veins, would dare to be called Fitz; there was a deal in a name – she had had a cousin who spelt his name with two little ffs – ffoulkes – and he always looked down upon capital letters, and said they belonged to lately-invented families. She had been afraid he would die a bachelor, he was so very choice. When he met with a Mrs ffaringdon, at a watering-place, he took to her immediately and a very pretty genteel woman she was – a widow, with a very good fortune; and 'my cousin,' Mr ffoulkes, married her; and it was all owing to her two little ffs.'[18]

Yale University.

18 Ibid.

PAUL HERNADI

So What? How So? and the Form that Matters

In an ideal world of consistent systems, Formalism and Hermeneutics might exemplify disparate critical orientations to be defined as follows. The first approaches literary works as instruments of mimesis, words representing worlds. The other sees them as instruments of communication, messages from authors to readers. In reality, of course, all instances of spoken or written discourse represent and communicate at the same time. As a result, it simply won't do for the Formalist critic to say 'I only want to tell you what the work is,' nor for the Hermeneutic critic to say, 'I only want to tell you how the work functions.' If a work works, its very being is tied up with its function, and vice versa. This is why the most painstakingly objective answer to the question *what* often provokes a rather blasé response: 'So what?' and the most probingly introspective answer to the question *how* often prompts a no less embarrassing, sceptical 'How so?' To answer those loaded counter-questions, the Formalist is expected to prove that this form matters and the Hermeneutist that his response has indeed been informed by the work. Any successful attempt to validate analysis or interpretation thus takes the originally one-sided critic into his imagined opponent's presumably hostile territory – a circumstance clearly suggesting that the two approaches not so much oppose as presuppose each other. Together they can help us explore both the what and the how of literature. In conflict, they make us vulnerable to the nasty questions so what? and how so? and even to the implied charge of producing criticism which tends to be so-so.

Of course it is one thing to proclaim the need for critical brotherhood and quite another to demonstrate the tacit co-operation of brotherly principles in some of the best theoretical frameworks available to the contemporary critic. I shall try to do the latter with the aid of a map (Figure 1) co-ordinating four main areas of critical concern along a horizontal and a vertical line: from West to East the rhetorical axis of communication which connects (but also goes beyond) writer and reader, from South to North the mimetic axis of representation which connects (but also goes beyond) language and information. Obviously all such diagrams simplify, yet they have the advantage of

This article was published in part in 'Literary Theory: A Compass for Critics,' *Critical Inquiry* 3, No 2 (Winter 1976), 369–86

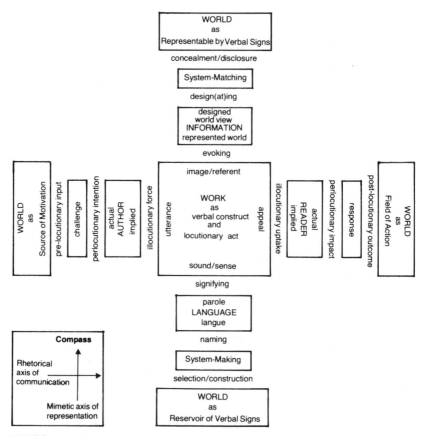

FIGURE 1

offering easier targets than a narrative presentation would for focused at-
tacks. For better or worse, you are invited to take your aim at my sitting
pigeon, a modification and amplification of similar models suggested by Karl
Bühler, M.H. Abrams, Roman Jakobson, and other students of verbal
discourse.

What does the chart show? In its centre is the WORK: an uttered or (more
frequently) utterable verbal construct signifying concepts, evoking images,
verbalizing intentions, and making appeals. On the periphery and beyond is
the WORLD as the reservoir of potential signs, as the totality of all that can be
represented by signs, as the source of motivation, and as the field of action.
Despite the first impression such a chart might create, no WORK is suspended
in a timeless net of relationships between language, information, author,
and reader; those four apparently sturdy entities are, after all, subject to

historical change. The youthful author of *The Comedy of Errors*, for example, can hardly be regarded as identical with the mature author of *The Tempest*. Likewise, the sophomore reading *Macbeth* for the first time is no longer (one hopes) the same reader when he returns to the text in preparation for a term paper. While works outlast the situation in which they were produced, authors and readers live in the WORLD serving for both as a source of motivation and as a field of action. Along the axis of communication every text may thus be seen as responding to 'worldly' challenges (some of them literary) and in turn challenging the reader to respond in his day and age, under his particular circumstances. But even language and what it represents are far from stagnant. In a matter of years, the slang term 'cool' could end up conveying just about the same value judgment as 'hot' used to convey, and the originally fantastic worlds evoked by the early science fiction of a Jules Verne have come to be seen as a kind of prophetic realism.

De Saussure's distinction between *parole* and *langue* has greatly helped linguists to clarify the difference between a fixed, concrete instance of employed language and a permanently changing system of verbal signs and combinatory rules. It seems to me that the more recent literary distinction between the implied author of a work and its actual author (or between the implied and actual reader) relies on a strikingly similar principle. For example, the respective authors implied by *The Comedy of Errors* and by *The Tempest* are in a sense fixed, concrete manifestations of the actual author whose permanently shifting potential of manifesting himself in literary works or otherwise was only partially realized between 1564 and 1616; his full potential has thus for ever remained virtual. The congenial readers implied by the respective plays are in turn two of many 'roles' which an actual reader may attempt to slip into for the length of time it takes him to read one work or another. Even a book like *Mein Kampf* will be adequately understood only by men and women able and willing temporarily to become Adolf Hitler's implied readers; the price may be high, but having shed the mental mask and costume required for the proper 'performance' of the text, a discerning person will emerge from the ordeal with a keener sense of the despicable part assigned to that book's actual readers. Works of imaginative literature naturally tend to imply readers whose intellectual, emotive, and moral response is far less predetermined than is the response of the reader implied by the typical work of assertive discourse.

The analogy between the virtual system of *langue* and the actual writer and reader becomes clear as we consider that Shakespeare's unrealized or even unconceived projects of further works could have revealed further aspects of his personality by implying other, more or less different authors. Likewise, any text left unread by a given person has simply not challenged him to test whether the particular constellation of personality traits required to play the part of that work's implied reader might have been produced from the virtual resources of his imaginations. The mental 'growth' of a human being in consequence of having written or read a particular work is in turn analogous to the possible effect of slightly unconventional speech events on the very conventions of a language system.

But our map also suggests a third parallel to *langue* in the 'northerly' area of information. Here, too, the particular world evoked by a given text emerges as one of a theoretically unlimited number of verbalizations of a *Weltanschauung*. To be sure, the mimetic results of discourse are much harder to systematize than its verbal means. For example, we may never be able to contrast the characteristic world view of tragedy to that of comedy, or that of Existentialism to that of pantheism, with the same degree of precision as we can contrast hypotaxis to parataxis or the comparative form of adjectives to their superlative form. Yet the assumption of a *langue-parole* type interdependence between realizable potential and concrete event may well prove a fruitful hypothesis for the study of disclosable world views and represented worlds. As for the relative merit of divergent or even contradictory views of the world, the best human minds have not as yet agreed upon what the world consists of and what holds it together. Until they do, we may as well suppose that one man's ontology is another man's mythology. I would even say that all purported ontologies, including the most iconoclastic mythographer's categorical denial of the possibility of any ontology, are more or less comprehensive, more or less persuasive mythologies.

This view of a delicate reciprocal relationship between 'South' and 'North,' between language and what language is about, finds support in the so-called Seventh Epistle of Plato. (The author of this text may or may not have been Plato.) An intriguing passage of the Epistle suggests something like a ladder of four epistemological instruments on which the mind must repeatedly ascend and descend in its effort to grasp what Plato refers to as 'the fifth,' and which he circumscribes as 'the object itself, the knowable and truly real being.' The four rungs of the ladder are the name, the definition, the image, and the knowledge of 'the fifth,' – each a necessary but imperfect and thus potentially counterproductive factor in the epistemological enterprise. Take Plato's example, the circle. Its very name is arbitrary; Plato notes that we might as well have used 'straight line' for the name of the circle. Its definition ('the figure whose extremities are equally distant from its centre') seems to Plato likewise arbitrary since it consists, as he says, of 'arbitrary nouns and verbs.' The image (what we can 'draw or rub out') is in turn described as 'full of characteristics that contradict the "fifth," for it everywhere touches a straight line, while the circle itself ... has in it not the slightest element belonging to a contrary nature.' Even the fourth instrument, knowledge, is open to the charge of being 'just as much concerned with making clear the particular property of each object as the being of it.'

If I may 'update' Plato's terminology and project the four rungs of the ladder – name, definition, image, and knowledge – on my vertical 'axis of representation,' we have 1/ utterable words (verbal signifiers), 2/ lexically definable meanings (concepts signified), 3/ perceivable characteristics (images evoked), and 4/ mental referents (objects represented). Thus we can name, signify, evoke, and even know (that is, mentally re-present) Plato's mysterious 'fifth.' But we cannot penetrate its 'real being,' that is, we cannot prove the actual existence of that which we can nonetheless name, signify, evoke, and represent. We can of course assume its existence, and if we do we say that language has represented an object of knowledge in the sense of designating it. In contrast, words like 'mermaid,' 'unicorn,' 'Antigone,' or 'Othello' do not represent in that strict sense of (presumably) pointing to something 'on the other side' of language. Yet they design or help to design aspects of an imaginable world within which it is possible to name, signify, evoke, and mentally represent mermaids, unicorns, or the personalities of fictive characters.

The visual or otherwise perceptual images evoked to a mind by words like 'mermaid' or 'Santa Claus' (but also 'yellow' and 'skunk') tend to be more salient than our strictly conceptual response to what such a word lexically signifies. Conversely, so-called abstract words such as 'state' or 'economy' may make us skip Plato's third rung – the image – as we keep ascending and descending between their names, concepts (or 'definitions'), and referents. Theoretically speaking, however, all words name, signify, evoke, and design or designate to some – be it zero – degree. And larger linguistic units such as entire sentences or complete literary works can be even more profitably analysed with the aid of this fourfold framework. Indeed, Roman Ingarden's theory of the stratified structure of literary works distinguishes the four strata of sound, sense, schematized aspects, and represented objects along very similar lines.

Such a fourfold account of the structure of verbal representation amplifies J.L. Austin's threefold concept of the locutionary act: instead of distinguishing phonetic, phatic, and rhetic acts, it submits that we name, signify, evoke, and design (or designate) whenever we say something. Austin's main concern in *How To Do Things With Words* (1962) was of course not with locutionary acts (what we do as we say something). Rather, he drew an additional line of demarcation between illocutionary acts (what we do in saying something) and perlocutionary acts (what we do *by* saying something). For example: threatening and promising are illocutionary acts, frightening and raising hopes are perlocutionary acts. Now I propose to project that seminal distinction on my horizontal axis of communication. Let me illustrate some of the theoretical consequences with the aid of a well-known Shakespearian sentence involving speech acts on more than one level of possible analysis.

In saying 'Pray you, undo this button,' Lear performs the illocutionary act of making a request (v, iii, 309). If at least one of the other characters on stage can be assumed to realize that Lear is making a request, the illocutionary force of the utterance has worked, that is (in Austin's terminology), 'uptake' has been secured. But the understanding of Lear's words as a request does not necessarily mean that someone will decide to comply, as seems to happen in the play. Yet only if someone so decides can we say that Lear's perlocutionary intention of making someone 'undo this button' by uttering a request has led to its intended perlocutionary impact. Why he wanted his button undone and whether the person deciding to oblige Lear will actually be able to do so are questions linked to but not really integrated with the speech act under consideration. To answer those questions we must investigate what I would call the pre-locutionary input and the post-locutionary outcome of the illocution and perlocution involved.

On a deeper level of analysis, of course, the playwright rather than the character engages in the acts of locution, illocution, and perlocution. The locutionary act of saying (or writing) 'Pray you, undo this button' is in fact Shakespeare's; he only assigned the utterance with its illocutionary force of a request to Lear. But *in* doing so, Shakespeare too engaged in an illocutionary act – not, of course, in the act of making a request but rather in the act of suggesting the former ruler's utter helplessness. If a reader or spectator realizes that the words assigned to Lear carry the additional illocutionary force of that authorial suggestion, uptake has been secured once again. Now if we focus on this latter kind of illocutionary force and uptake, we in fact consider what the play's implied reader is meant to perceive the implied author as doing *in* making Lear say, 'Pray you, undo this button.' Only if we ask ourselves what Shakespeare did or was attempting to do *by* assigning the request to Lear can we refer to the actual author's perlocutionary intentions and the perlocutionary impact of Lear's request on the actual reader. At an almost ludicrously minimal level of sophistication we may say, for example, that Shakespeare – the actual author at the time of writing *King Lear* – wanted to scare readers and spectators of his play into avoiding the kind of actions and circumstances that can reduce even a Lear to utmost helplessness. If we assume this to be Shakespeare's most elementary perlocutionary intention we can further say that it is fulfilled to the extent that some people will decide to avoid such actions and circumstances whether or not they indeed succeed in doing so. That decision is the utterance's or the whole play's perlocutionary impact. Success or failure to carry out the decision would have to be considered the *post*-locutionary outcome, twice removed from any speech act within the play. The same relative independence characterizes the world's pre-locutionary input, whatever has challenged the actual author to form a particular perlocutionary intention.

Needless to say, my entire speech act analysis relies on the implicit premise that the characters on stage understand Lear's words and that we understand Shakespeare's. In the absence of such semantic 'uptake' with regard to the locutionary acts of naming, signifying, evoking, and designing or designating, no uptake of the illocutionary force could occur. Nor would the utterance have any perlocutionary impact and post-locutionary outcome commensurate with the actual author's perlocutionary intentions and pre-locutionary motivation. To speak metaphorically, that stalwart horizontal axis of communication would break right in the middle without the friendly support it receives from the vertical axis of representation. But the vertical axis, ambitiously pointing to Plato's 'fifth,' would also collapse if authors and readers (or, more generally, speakers and listeners) did not continually form, use, and modify what are ultimately their own systems of representation.

To sum up: Figure 1 is intended to show why representation is unthinkable without communication and vice versa. Just as language systems need users if they are to disclose and/or conceal views of the world, signs capable of containing information are required if one man's motivation is to be turned into another's action. With this constant interplay in mind, I have tried to interrelate, amplify, and perhaps also clarify some important distinctions first made or revived by Formalist as well as Hermeneutic critics. Is it really useful to insert so many terms and concepts between the WORK and various aspects of the WORLD. I think it is, for the following reason. Literature's verbal energy – generated between its rhetorical poles of motivation and action and between its mimetic poles of the means and results of representation – this energy can easily short-circuit any critical endeavour unless our conceptual wires are both connected and separated by a sufficient number of well-placed fuses.

University of Iowa

CONCLUSION AND EPILOGUE

URI MARGOLIN

Conclusion: Literary Structuralism and Hermeneutics in Significant Convergence, 1976

The subject of our panel involves, by definition, the relations between two kinds of theories or approaches, and my discussion will hence of necessity be metatheoretical. I shall restrict myself to the two approaches as manifested in the study of literature only, leaving out their philosophical roots and implications. I shall dwell primarily on the parallels and convergences between them at the present moment, following a brief description of the differences between their historical points of departure, since my central thesis is that structuralism has been moving steadily towards a rapprochement with hermeneutics.

Let me start with a few general observations. Both structuralism and hermeneutics are not just specific theories, but rather two basic modes of theorizing or kinds of theories. Each of them is represented by a whole family of specific theories which show a marked degree of similarity but no complete overlap. Furthermore, like all other cultural phenomena, theories too are historical dynamic entities which are constantly being modified, so that one cannot speak of any fixed essence of a given approach, only of its state at a given moment. The representation of each school which I shall shortly give is hence a vastly simplified ideal type, constructed solely for the purpose of indicating some major lines of development. Finally, no approach or mode of theorizing can be characterized by one parameter only. Any adequate definition of it has to take into account all of the following factors: its formal object or theoretical range (e.g. the work of literature as a manifestation of an individual creative consciousness or as a sum total of devices); its central problems and questions; its basic concepts and principles; the basic models in terms of which it represents its theoretical object; its methods and procedures of inquiry; its normative component, which includes a set of priorities for research, canons of evidence, and standards of theory-construction and validation; finally, the underlying set of metaphysical presuppositions of this approach. Two approaches may converge or even coincide in the case of some of these parameters, and diverge widely with regard to the rest. Any discussion of concord or discord between two approaches must hence specify the aspect which is being compared.

After these preliminaries, let me proceed to a simplified typological description of the literary versions of the two approaches at their original points of departure.

Structuralism (formalism) as I see it started out from one basic question: how are texts made as constructed objects or systems of signs? Attention was focused on the forms of expression (style and composition), on textual properties and patterns, their nature and interrelations. The aim was to give a general descriptive poetics of the major forms of literary texts. There was some interest in the methods of representation employed by different types of texts, but seldom in what was represented. The procedure was to move upwards from sound to sense and from micro to macro units. The textual properties described by the scholar were considered to be inherent in the text, existing objectively and open to scrutiny. The meaning of a text was supposed to be inherent in it, residing in the interrelations among its elements. At this point, description, categorization, typology, and correlation of textual features were the methodological goals, and explanation in terms of extratextual or extraliterary factors was rejected. Linguistics supplied the theoretical paradigm here, and its procedures and models were willingly followed.

Literary hermeneutics started out from a very different question: how does one make sense of texts beyond the literal-lexical level, and what are the conditions, rules, mechanisms, and kinds of sense-making? Many of its representatives argued that a text yields its sense only in a dialogue with the reader, that in fact its meaning is created in this dialogue. The reader's horizon and presuppositions play accordingly a decisive role in determining the meaning of the text. This meaning is also greatly influenced by the textual and cultural tradition in which the text is placed. Both aspects, reader and tradition, change historically, and so do textual meanings. Textual production in its turn is determined by the text-text and text-reader interrelations, and texts exist and operate only in situations or contexts of cultural communication.

The phenomenological school was primarily interested in the imaginary universe represented or constructed in literary texts, that is, in the intentional objects created by these texts. Questions were asked about the laws of its mythopoesis, the nature of the events, characters, space, and time projected in it, its over-all ideological (symbolic, philosophical, etc.) significance, and the metaphysical qualities and values (the sublime, grotesque, etc.) inherent in this universe. As one can see, the interest here was primarily in the forms of content, and the medium and its organization were regarded as a mere conduit of this content. The approach was global, integrative, 'from above,' starting from the totality of the text as a meaningful whole, from its most complex levels. The disciplines which served as theoretical paradigms here were phenomenological psychology and philosophy, the study of myth, and various forms of cultural anthropology. Many phenomenologists also regarded the imaginary universe of literary texts as the product or record of a unique centre of creative consciousness, its special mode of experiencing and constituting a world of some sort. The task of the literary scholar here is to enter this other consciousness and its unique vision and to reconstitute it through the text. One can penetrate into this consciousness only through an intuitive effort of deciphering, which by its very nature is holistic and circular, leading from part to whole and vice-versa. In this specific approach, e.g. that of Poulet, the meaning of the text is supposed to be inherent and immutable, and the sensitive reader strives to recapture it as fully as possible. The text itself is obviously seen as a closed totality.

How do matters stand between these approaches at the present moment? In my opinion the most fundamental, complex, and significant questions (Leitfragen, Problemstellungen) for the study of literature have long ago been posed by phenomenology and hermeneutics. Because of its own inner logic, and independently of hermeneutics, the structuralist approach has steadily moved towards an ever-increasing preoccupation with the kinds of questions and levels of analysis first formulated by phenomenology and hermeneutics. In addition, it has developed independently many of the parameters for the discussion of the literary system and of the assumptions about its nature first formulated by hermeneutics. Several of the models for the representation of the literary system and its subsystems currently used in structuralist studies are also of hermeneutic origin. The goals of literary theorizing now being advocated by scholars such as Todorov or Culler also bear striking resemblance to the traditional hermeneutic ones.

If we restrict our attention to the various waves of structuralist activity in Eastern Europe, we can say that the attention of each of them has moved constantly upwards from the lower to the higher levels of the text, and in ever-expanding concentric circles from the isolated text to its relation with other literary texts and with the cultural context as a whole. The upward movement signifies a shift in interest from micro to macro units, from the signifier to what it signifies, while the concentric circles move from the syntactic textual dimension through the semantic one to text pragmatics. From purely formal elements, the structuralists turned to mixed formal-representational units, such as dialogue, utterance and the act of narration which involve linguistic, ideological, and psychological points of view. From the forms of expression, they moved towards forms of content: the world-model created in the text, its laws and ideological polarities. From the study of patterns within the individual text, attention has shifted to intertextual relations, where each text is regarded as a multivoiced dialogue with other texts, as exemplified in stylization, parody, allusion, and metatext. The global over-all semantic features of texts are nowadays represented in the various generative text grammars, which aim at a derivation of stylistic features from a deep structure of macro semantic features. This deep structure serves as an underlying set of rules for the world projected in the text (Van Dijk, Petöfi). It may also be regarded as an over-all mechanism of sense-making from the point of view of the text producer, which is to be reconstructed by the reader. After the establishment of world models for different kinds of texts and their respective ideologies, the next step involves a juxtaposition of these models with those provided by other cultural series, from the common-sense world model to the systems of values and the polarities represented by the religion, ideology, and philosophy of the time. In this way the literary object is inserted into the wider cultural horizon.

The notions of code and tradition as systems of conventions to be reconstructed from actual literary works existed in structuralism from its very beginnings in the 1920s. A great change, which brought this approach in line with hermeneutic thinking, occurred when the locus of this code was shifted to the reader's awareness. This awareness is different in each generation and represents the literary culture of an age. Any text makes sense only relative to such a horizon of literary awareness (repertory of text models, regulative norms concerning how a text should be treated, and sets of interpretation rules), and its meaning and significance are largely determined by the nature of this code. The text is hence no longer regarded as possessing objective, inherent patterns of meanings. Meaning itself is now envisioned as a function or a relation between the text and the reader's code with which it is confronted. The text is merely a set of potentialities for many operations of patterning and sense-making by the reader on all levels. Metre and stylistic valency too are potentialities only. As the readers' codes change, so do the patterns one discerns in the text. The meaning of the text has thus been historicized and relativized. Tradition too does not exist as an objective factor; it resides in the ever-changing literary awareness of the readers. Since literary texts exist as cultural facts only in their realizations through readers' codes, it is of the utmost importance to study the various components of this awareness (Culler's 'literary competence') and the various forms in which it manifests itself in the activities of cultural text-processing (adaptation, translation, commentary, etc.). Literature itself is now regarded as a functional dynamic category, associated with and defined by a special mode of reception, by cultural status, and by rules of interpretation, all belonging to the reader, and not by any fixed set of textual features. The reader's literary code is obviously only a part of his total cultural code, and interacts with other subsystems of it. The reader's code thus forms a mediating link between the literary system and the other cultural systems. It interacts with these other systems and thus plays a crucial role in any attempt to explain how changes in the literary series are motivated by changes in other cultural series, and vice-versa. The explanation of literary dynamics is now a focal point of structuralist interest, and while literature is not reduced to any of the other systems its dynamic interaction with them is readily recognized. The isolating study of literature in early formalism now gives way to an integrative cultural perspective. In other words the literary text and the literary system are no longer regarded as closed systems but rather as open systems with two-way feedback (both positive and negative) between them and their cultural environment. The literary work is now seen as an *act* of communication and not as a self-contained object.

It is interesting to note that the perspectives, assumptions, and models nowadays shared by literary hermeneutics and structuralism are precisely those in which both approaches coincide with recent schemes proposed by communication theory and speech-act theory. In fact, one may even argue that both approaches have steadily been working towards such an integrated model, each from its own angle. Communication theory can therefore be regarded as a more powerful theory than either approach in isolation, and large portions of both can be mapped into this 'super theory.' As far as hermeneutics is concerned, communication theory can also be regarded as a non-metaphysical explication of many of its basic tenets. Similar observations could be made about the relations of both approaches, in their convergent parts, with semiotics, whether it is understood as the study of all aspects of sign systems or as the study of cultural codes and their interrelations. Since the two 'super theories' initially grew out of general philosophical considerations, their remarkable convergence with the two literary approaches tends to lend further corroboration to the schemes of literary communication developed by these literary approaches. A careful study of the various schemes of cultural communication proposed in semiotics, for example, may suggest to the literary scholar further areas of research. The hypotheses formulated in this 'super science' can be tested on literary material and modified if necessary, and the many different theoretical vocabularies proposed by various structuralist and hermeneutic scholars could probably be unified to a large degree through their translation into the language of communication theory. The multiple convergence noted above is in fact not accidental, since communication theory tried to do in the most general terms just what recent literary structuralism and hermeneutics sought to do for their special domains, namely, list all the factors relevant to the literary object and propose a coherent model of their interactions, giving primacy to the dynamic interference of readers' and writers' code over the text in isolation. One may also note in this context the significant convergence between communication theory and the recent schools of neorhetoric in the United States and Belgium, for example. This, too, is not surprising, since Rhetoric, from its Greek and Roman origins onwards, has always regarded the literary work as an act of communication in which textual strategies are deliberately employed by the author in order to elicit responses and reactions of specific kinds in the receiver. In other words, works of literature are to be regarded as goal-oriented messages whose impact depends on the reader's antecedent norms, conventions, and rules of construction.

In spite of the convergence between structuralism and hermeneutics as regards problems, basic assumptions, models, and goals, the two still diverge widely as far as their theoretical vocabulary, procedures of enquiry, and norms of theory construction and validation are concerned. In this respect structuralism is much closer to the super sciences of semiotics and communication theory, probably because it shares with them the theoretical paradigm of logic, linguistics, and logical empiricism, while literary hermeneutics was oriented towards *Geistesphilosophie* and philosophical anthropology. Structuralism has insisted on the minimal role of metaphysical presuppositions, on the development of an explicit and operational theoretical vocabulary, and on the correlation of every theoretical statement about the world created in the text with intersubjectively accessible textual features. When structuralists discuss such an imaginary universe and its laws, they employ the terminology of binary oppositions, hierarchy of features, and modal logic (Lotman, Todorov). Even though they too nowadays see genres primarily as specific sets of rules for sense-making, they insist on the textual clues which activate these rules (Culler). Instead of a synthetic intuitive approach to the text which is supposed to penetrate directly into its unique *vision du monde*, they require a step-by-step analytic progression from the lowest to the highest textual levels in which no level is skipped and all levels are interrelated and taken into account as contributing to the total meaning of the text. The structuralists thus insist on the meaning of form and seek to answer the crucial question how the imaginary universe of the text is constructed through its logico-semantic elements. The different forms of textual interrelations are formulated in terms of law-like statements which can be tested on additional sets of texts, so that their validity can be checked and their specific content modified when necessary.

While no method contains within itself the guarantee of success, it seems to me that the structuralist vocabulary and procedure have a clear advantage over the traditional hermeneutic ones because of their explicit and orderly nature, which enables us to generalize their precepts, learn them, and teach them to others. If this assumption is correct, then two urgent goals of structuralist study would be the explication and reformulation in operational terms of many of the insights and categories of traditional hermeneutics, and the extension of the structuralist 'machinery' to several traditional domains of literary hermeneutics, such as character analysis in narrative. This task should be rendered possible by the fact that research procedures and the logical form (as distinct from the specific content) of their resultant statements are independent of any specific domain of theorizing. I am in fact proposing to regard structuralism as a methodological paradigm for hermeneutics, in the same way that linguistics was for structural poetics in its turn. The Konstanz school of literary theory has been doing this with great success for some time now, marrying hermeneutic perspectives with structuralist procedures and terms.

Both approaches have already gained considerably from this process of clarification and explication. The structuralist method was shown to be capable of contributing to traditional humanistic theories, at least by making them more precise and intelligible, while these reformulated theories, or at least portions of them, could now for the first time be incorporated into the structuralist field for testing and eventual acceptance or rejection.

The study of formal narrative patterns in isolation is exposed to the danger of ending up in sterile calculi of plot functions which lead nowhere. The study of the imaginary universe of a fictional text without regard to its forms of expression often leads to the construction of another imaginary universe, to a series of metaphysical intuitions which cannot be tested in any way. New and highly instructive insights into the working of narrative texts can be gained only if these two extremes are avoided. The fruitful middle ground lies, in my opinion, in the study of the various correlations between forms of expression and forms of content and of the linking of the various possible thematic interpretations of texts with their textual features. Work in this area requires the close co-operation of the structuralist and the hermeneutic approaches. Let me then conclude with a few remarks on several possible directions such work may assume in the future.

One important area of problems here concerns the ways in which the building blocks of the world projected in the text, such as descriptions, situations, arguments, reflections (Iser's *Ansichten*, Jameson's 'frames'), are built up by means of logico-semantic elements. What, for example, is the method of portrayal used: generalization followed by exemplification or a sequence of details only; how general or specific, typological or individual, is the *Ansicht* created. Are time and space continuous or discontinuous; does the perspective shift or not, and in what ways; are the linkages between contiguous elements metonymic or metaphoric; what role does digression play in each *Ansicht*, and how far does it encompass/anticipate elements from earlier/later *Ansichten*; what kind of elements occur in each *Ansicht*, and in what proportion? This cluster of questions integrates a phenomenology of the constituted world coming from above with a stylistic analysis coming from below.

The conceptual tools provided by the linguistics of the utterance and linguistic pragmatics enable us to show how the receiver reconstructs the full communicative context, including the characteristics, attitudes, and values of the speaker, from the words he uses. The study of interaction among utterances in literary dialogue, for example, leads to the modelling of the interpersonal interaction in the fictional universe.

A further step involves the study of the various degrees and kinds of textual cohesion (text-logic) through an examination of the transitions between the *Ansichten*. Do they follow each other according to the rules of inference, or those of physical or psychological causality, or are they rather determined by linguistic and architectonic factors? Do they reveal a shift from one level/key of reality to another, and if so are the shifts motivated or not? Is there any attempt to naturalize the supernatural or not? Are the transitions between the *Ansichten* dictated by the logic of the fictional universe, or by that of the linguistic sign, or by both alternately? If we conceive of every fictional universe projected in the literary text as a possible/alternative world, we have to describe the laws governing it and the nature of its deviations, if any, from our common-sense space-time-causality-personal identity model. Modal logic will no doubt play a crucial role here, as well as film theory (Eisenstein, Ivanov).

Ingarden and Iser have pointed out the gaps (Leerstellen) between the *Ansichten* in the fictional text. We now have to study their extent, nature, and location in different kinds of texts. Do these *Ansichten* themselves yield some constraints on the ways in which the gaps can be filled and textual ambiguities resolved? Do they give us some positive instructions or clues how the text should be integrated, or do they at least exclude some fillings as incompatible with it? It would not do simply to replace the old doctrine of 'the one inherent meaning of the text which the reader has to uncover' with an opposite doctrine according to which 'anything goes' and texts mean 'all things to all people.' We do regard some interpretations of any given text as more plausible than others. What is it in the text then that leads us to this ranking of its different actualizations? What are the textual guidelines that impose internal constraints on the process of interpretation-as-filling-of-gaps? Why is it that some texts are more amenable to a variety of interpretations than others?

As Culler has recently shown, different types of texts are associated in the readers' literary code with different sets of global rules and procedures of sense-making. In addition, there are several such rules which apply to all literary texts and to them only. We ought to render explicit these culturally acquired and internalized sets of rules, which are accessible through introspection and the analysis of texts *about* literature and their underlying assumptions. We should also ask about the textual clues or indications which tell us what particular set of rules to activate when reading a given text. In other words, we are looking for correlations between types of texts (a morphological category) and sets of interpretative rules (a functional category). The number and the nature of these sets are different in different cultures and historical periods, and changes in them are somehow correlated with changes in the nature of the literary output itself. The study of these correlations is another important subject for future study. A significant beginning in this direction, as far as the notion of fictionality itself is concerned, has recently been made by several German scholars (Schmidt, Anderegg, Stierle).

University of Alberta

Epilogue

'If it be true that good wine needs no bush, 'tis true that a good play needs no epilogue: yet to good wine they do use good bushes; and good plays prove the better by the help of good epilogues.' Shakespeare's 'self-conscious' attempt, in the epilogue of *As You Like It*, to justify the very processes in which he is engaged mirrors not only the concerns of the present writer in giving the sense of an ending to this volume but also the implicit concerns that lie behind the papers on literary theory herein presented. The empirical objects to which they appear to be directed are literary works themselves. But, as Northrop Frye has reminded us, what one learns in literary studies is not literary works themselves but literary criticism, in other words the critical discourse that actualizes verbally the reader's or critic's thoughts about literary works. Literary theory then is a meta-meta-discourse whose object (if we can separate literary criticism from literary theory, a dubious contention to say the least) is critical discourse. The growth and interest in literary theory over the past few years is in many ways a response to uncertainties about the assumptions of the various critical discourses that have traditionally engaged literature. But especially it marks the degree of 'self-consciousness' that has crept into all critical discourses. Roland Barthes has expressed this concern aptly: 'Passer de la lecture à la critique, c'est changer de désir, c'est désirer non plus l'œuvre, mais son propre langage.' To move from reading to the act of practising criticism, is to cease to 'listen' and to begin to 'speak.'

It is here the question of 'verification' or 'verifiability' becomes problematic. For if it is accepted that the literary critic in seeking to create his own criticial discourse turns away from his object, 'the literary work,' to engage in his own struggle with language, and if we therefore contend that this critical discourse cannot be 'true' to the literary artefact but embodies its own truth in the sense that we say that a line is true, it follows that the meta-meta-discourse which we call literary theory (whether formalist, structuralist, or any other) must also embody its own truth and cannot be verified by reference to its object, critical discourses. Barthes' comments then relate not merely to problems of verification of a critical discourse entertained with respect to a literary work but to any meta-meta-discourse of literary theory entertained with respect to literary criticism. The problems to which this volume addresses itself reflect indirectly what is essentially a crisis of language or of all discourse. Few of the participants of this volume, if any, would accept that their own discourses on formalist or hermeneutic theory were not to some degree cognitive and verifiable with respect to their object. If one can no longer accept the inviolability of what might be called the correspondence theory of language, it is difficult to exclude it entirely and totally embrace what we might call the coherence theory of language.

Meyer Abrams in *The Mirror and The Lamp* offers us a pragmatic solution to the problem of verification. 'A good theory,' he claims, 'has its own kind of validity. The criterion is not the scientific verifiability of its single propositions, but the scope, precision and coherence of the insights that it yields into the properties of single works of art and the adequacy with which it accounts for diverse kinds of art.' It may appear on first sight that Abrams wants to have it both ways, asserting both that validity is established by the theory itself and that validity is measured by reference to the literary artefact. But the view advanced here is more sophisticated. It asserts, in our opinion, the notion that the validity of a literary theory or its lack of validity is established with respect to literary works in so far as the particular theoretical discourse enters into a dialectical relationship with the critical discourse that the critic or reader himself entertains with literary works; this validity is personal, individual, varying with each critic and reader.

Such a notion seems equally applicable, though still pragmatic, at the meta-meta-meta level, that is, to the various discourses presented in this volume whose object is ostensibly formalist and hermeneutic theories of narrative. Some papers challenge certain aspects or certain premises of established theories by confronting them with their own critical discourse on texts or with their own theoretical discourse on theory; others attempt to establish a particular theoretical or critical discourse that works within the assumptions of that literary theory and either operates on the various aspects of theory or operates on literary texts: yet others use a combination of these approaches. In each case an attempt is made at verification, established upwards, sometimes to the level of theories about theorizing, but always to the assertions generated in various discourses of the participants themselves or downwards to the level of critical discourses or the texts themselves. Finally, there are the discourses attempted in the introduction and conclusion, themselves establishing a dialectical relationship with those presented by the participants of this volume. To these must be added the comments of the preface and epilogue seeking not to achieve an ultimate and final level but opening the volume to the reader and attempting to engage him in a dialectical response. If the present volume raises more problems than it solves, that is because there is no ultimate solution to be found. To question a discourse involves creating a discourse at another level. In this act of language one pledges allegiance, but one betrays.

University of Toronto

REFERENCES AND INDEX OF AUTHORS

REFERENCES

ABRAMS, MEYER. *The Mirror and the Lamp: Romantic Theory and the Critical Tradition*. New York: Oxford University Press, 1953

ALLEN, JOHN J. *Don Quixote: Hero or Fool? A Study in Narrative Technique.* Gainesville: University of Florida Press, 1969

ARISTOTLE. *The Organon: The Categories. On Interpretation.* ed. Harold P. Cooke. London: Heinemann, Cambridge, Mass.: Harvard University Press, The Loeb Classical Library, 1938

ARNHEIM, RUDOLF. *Art and Visual Perception: A Psychology of the Creative Eye.* Berkeley and Los Angeles: University of California Press, 1965

– *Toward a Psychology of Art: Collected Essays.* Berkeley and Los Angeles: University of California Press, 1967

AUCH, LORD [G. BATAILLE]. *Histoire de l'oeil.* First edition Paris, 1928. Second edition Burgos, 1941 [*sic*]. Third edition Seville, 1940 [*sic*]. Fourth edition G. Bataille. *Histoire de l'oeil.* Paris: Pauvert, 1967. Fifth edition in G. Bataille. *Oeuvres complètes, I: Premiers Écrits 1922–1940.* Paris: Gallimard, 1970

AUSTIN, J.L. *How to Do Things with Words.* ed. J.O. Urmson. Cambridge, Mass.: Harvard University Press, 1962

BALZAC, HONORÉ DE. *La Comédie Humaine.* ed. Marcel Bouteron. 11 vols, Paris: Gallimard, Bibliothèque de la Pléiade, 1951

BARDÈCHE, MAURICE. *Balzac romancier.* Paris: Plon, 1940

BARTHES, ROLAND. 'Introduction à l'analyse structurale des récits,' *Communications* 8 (1966), 1–27

– *Critique et vérité.* Paris: Seuil, 1966

– 'La métaphore de l'oeil,' *Essais critiques.* Paris: Seuil, coll. *Tel quel,* 1964, 238–45

BATAILLE, G. *Histoire de l'oeil.* Fourth edition. Paris: Pauvert, 1967

BENJAMIN, WALTER. *Das Kunstwerk im Zeitalter seiner technischen Reproduzierbarkeit. Drei Aufsätze zur Kunstsoziologie.* Frankfurt: ed. suhrkamp (27), 1963

BENVENISTE, EMILE. *Problèmes de linguistique générale.* Paris: Gallimard, 1966

BERGIN, T.G. and M.H. FISCH, translators. *The New Science of Giambattista Vico.* Rev. transl. of 3rd edition. Ithaca: Cornell University Press, 1968

BOURNEUF, ROLAND and RÉAL OUELLET. *L'Univers du roman.* Paris: Presses universitaires de France, 1972

BREMOND, CLAUDE. *Logique du récit.* Paris: Seuil, 1973

BÜRGER, PETER. *Theorie der Avantgarde.* Frankfurt: Suhrkamp, 1974

CARSTENSEN, BRODER. 'Stil und Norm,' *Zeitschrift für Dialektologie und Linguistik* 37 (1970), 257–79

CHATMAN, SEYMOUR. 'New Ways of Analysing Narrative Structures, with an Example from Joyce's Dubliners,' *Language and Style* 2 (1969), 3–36

CHATMAN, S.B. and S.R. LEVIN, eds. *Essays on the Language of Literature*. Boston: Houghton Mifflin, 1967

CHAUCER, GEOFFREY. *Works.* ed. F.N. Robinson. 2nd edition. Boston: Houghton Mifflin, 1961

CLARK, RONALD W. *Einstein: The Life and Times*. New York: Avon, 1972

CONSTANT DE REBECQUE, HENRI BENJAMIN. *Adolphe*. Paris: Classiques Garnier, 1959

COSERIU, EUGENIO. *Synchronie, Diachronie und Geschichte – Das Problem des Sprachwandels*. München: W. Fink, 1974

CULLER, A. DWIGHT. 'Monodrama and the Dramatic Monologue,' *PMLA* 90, 3 (May 1975), 366–85

CURTIUS, E.R. 'La topique,' *La Littérature européenne et le Moyen Âge latin*, transl. J. Bréjoux. Paris: Presses universitaires, 1958, 99–130

DAMISCH, HUBERT. 'La Danse de Thésée,' *Tel Quel* 26 (1966), 60–8

DARBYSHIRE, A.E. *A Grammar of Style*. London: Deutsch, 1971

DERRIDA, JACQUES. *De la Grammatologie*. Paris: Minuit, 1967

DILTHEY, WILHELM. 'The Rise of Hermeneutics,' *New Literary History* 3 (1971–2), transl. F. Jameson, 229–44

ECO, UMBERTO. *Einführung in die Semiotik*. transl. Jürgen Trabant. Munich: W. Fink, coll. *UTB* 105, 1972

FAYE, JEAN-PIERRE. *Théorie du récit: Introduction aux langages totalitaires, critique de la raison, l'économie narrative*. Paris: Hermann, 1972

FISH, STANLEY E. 'Literature in the Reader: Affective Stylistics,' *New Literary History* 2 (1970), 123–62

FITCH, BRIAN T. *Dimensions et structures chez Bernanos*. Paris: Minard, 1969

– *Dimensions, structures et textualité dans la trilogie romanesque de Beckett*. Paris: Minard, 1977

– '"Jonas" ou la production d'une étoile,' *La Revue des Lettres Modernes* Nos 351–65 [Série] *Albert Camus* 6 (1973), 51–65

– '*La Peste* comme texte qui se désigne: analyse des procédés d'auto-représentation,' *La Revue des Lettres Modernes* Nos 479–83 [Série] *Albert Camus* 8 (1976), 53–71

– 'Temps, espace et immobilité chez Julien Green,' *Configuration critique du Julien Green*. Paris: Minard, 1966. *La Revue des Lettres Modernes* Nos 130–3, 93–136

FREGE, GOTTLOB. 'On the Scientific Justification of a Conceptual Notation,' *Conceptual Notation and Related Articles*. transl. and ed. T.W. Bynum. Oxford: Clarendon Press, 1972

FRYE, NORTHROP. *Anatomy of Criticism. Four Essays by Northrop Frye*. New York: Atheneum, Atheneum Paperbacks, 1966

GADAMER, HANS GEORG. *Wahrheit und Methode: Grundzüge einer philosophischen Hermeneutik*. Tübingen: Mohr, 1960

GASKELL, ELIZABETH. *Works*. London: Smith, Elder and Co., The Knutsford Edition, 1895

GENETTE, GÉRARD. *Figures III*. Paris: Seuil, 1972

GOMBRICH, E.H. *Art and Illusion: A Study in the Psychology of Pictorial Representation*. London: Phaidon Press, 1962

GREIMAS, A.J. *Du sens: essais sémiotiques*. Paris: Seuil, 1970
- *Maupassant: la sémiotique du texte*. Paris: Seuil, 1976
- *Sémantique structurale: recherche de méthode*. Paris: Larousse, 1966

GRIVEL, CHARLES. *La Production de l'intérêt romanesque*. The Hague/Paris Mouton, 1973

GUESPIN, L. 'Problématique des travaux sur le discours politique,' *Langages* 23 (Sept. 1971), 3–24

HAMON, PHILIPPE. 'Clausules,' *Poétique* 24 (1975), 495–526

HATZFELD, H. *'Don Quijote' als Wortkunstwerk: die einzelnen Stilmittel und ihr Sinn*. Leipzig/Berlin: B.G. Teubner, 1927

HEGEL, GEORG WILHELM FRIEDRICH. 'Vorrede,' *Phänomenologie des Geistes*. ed. Johannes Hoffmeister. 5 Aufl. Leipzig: F. Meiner, 1949

HEIDEGGER, MARTIN. *Erläuterungen zu Hölderlins Dichtung*. 3. Aufl. Frankfurt-am-Main: V. Klostermann, 1963

HEISENBERG, WERNER. *Physics and Philosophy: The Revolution in Modern Science*. New York: Harper, 1958

HENDRICKS, W.O. 'The Work and Play Structures of Narrative,' *Semiotica* 13 (1975), 281–328

HERNADI, PAUL. 'Literary Theory: A Compass for Critics,' *Critical Inquiry* 3, No. 2 (Winter 1976), 369–86

HIRSCH, E.D. 'Three Dimensions of Hermeneutics,' *New Literary History* 3, 2 (Winter 1972), 245–61
- *Validity in Interpretation*. New Haven: Yale University Press, 1967

HÖLDERLIN, FRIEDRICH. 'Anmerkungen zum Oedipus,' *Sämtliche Werke*. Große Stuttgarter Ausgabe V. Stuttgart: J.G. Cotta, 1954

HUNT, HERBERT J. *Balzac's Comédie Humaine*. London: The Athlone Press, 1964

HUSSERL, EDMUND. *Logische Untersuchungen*. 2. Aufl., 2 vols. Halle, 1913, 1921
- *Ideen zu einer reinen Phänomenologie und phänomenologischen Philosophie*. Halle: M. Niemeyer, 1913

INGARDEN, ROMAN. *Das literarische Kunstwerk*. Tübingen: M. Niemeyer, 1960

ISER, WOLFGANG. *Der implizite Leser: Kommunikationsformen des Romans von Bunyan bis Beckett*. München: W. Fink, 1972
- 'Indeterminacy and the Reader's Response in Prose Fiction,' *Aspects of Narrative: Selected Papers from the English Institute*. ed. J. Hillis Miller. New York/London: Columbia University Press, 1971, 1–45

- *The Implied Reader: Patterns of Communication in Prose Fiction from Bunyan to Beckett.* Baltimore: Johns Hopkins University Press, 1974
- 'The Patterns of Negativity in Beckett's Prose,' *The Georgia Review* 29, 3 (Fall 1975), 706–19
- 'The Reality of Fiction: A Functionalist Approach to Literature,' *New Literary History* 7 (1975–6), 7–38

JAKOBSON, ROMAN. 'Closing Statement: Linguistics and Poetics,' *Style in Language.* Ed. Thomas A. Sebeok. Cambridge, Mass.: Harvard University Press, 2nd prt., 1964
- 'Linguistics and Poetics,' *Language and Style.* ed. Thomas A. Sebeok. Cambridge, Mass.: Harvard University Press, 1960

JAMES, HENRY. *The Golden Bowl.* New York Edition of *The Novels and Tales of Henry James.* New York: Charles Scribner's Sons, 1909

JAUSS, HANS-ROBERT. 'Brunetto Latini als allegorischer Dichter,' *Formenwandel – Festschrift zum 65. Geburtstag von Paul Böckman.* ed. W. Müller-Seidel and W. Preisendanz. Hamburg: Hoffmann und Campe, 1964, 47–92
- 'Chanson de geste et roman courtois,' *Chanson de geste und höfischer Roman.* Heidelberg: Carl Winter, 1963, 61–83
- 'La Transformation de la forme allégorique entre 1180 et 1240, *L'Humanisme médiéval dans les littératures romanes du XIIᵉ au XIVᵉ siècle.* ed. A. Fourrier. Paris: C. Klincksieck, 1964, 105–46
- *Literaturgeschichte als Provokation.* Frankfurt: Suhrkamp, 1970
- 'Littérature médiévale et théorie des genres,' *Poétique* I (1970), 79–101
- 'Negativität und Identifikation. Versuch zur Theorie der ästhetischen Erfahrung,' in *Positionen der Negativität.* ed. H. Weinrich. München: W. Fink, 1975, 263–339
- *Untersuchungen zur mittelalterlichen Tierdichtung.* Tübingen: M. Niemeyer (Beihefte zur Zeitschrift für romanische Philologie 100), 1959

JOHN OF GARLAND. *The Parisiana Poetria of John of Garland.* ed. and transl. Traugott Lawler. New Haven and London: Yale University Press (Yale Studies in English 182), 1974

JOHN OF SALISBURY. *Metalogicon* I, ii. ed. C.C.I. Webb. Oxford: Oxford University Press, 1929. transl. D. McGarry. Berkeley: University of California Press, 1955

JOLIVET, JEAN. *Arts du langage et théologie chez Abélard.* Paris: J. Vrin, 1969

JUNG, MARC-RENÉ. 'Poetria: Zur Dichtungstheorie des ausgehenden Mittelalters in Frankreich,' *Vox Romanica* 30 (1971), 44–64

KELLY, FREDERICK DOUGLAS. *Sens and Conjointure in the Chevalier de la Charette.* The Hague: Mouton, 1966
- 'The Source and Meaning of *Conjointure* in Chrétien's *Erec* 14,' *Viator* I (1970), 179–200
- 'The Value of "Semantic Range" in Interpreting Medieval Writing,' *Tape of*

lecture presented at the 'International Conference on Medieval Grammar,' University of California, Davis, 19–20 Feb. 1976

KOSELLECK, R. and W.D. STEMPEL, eds. *Geschichte – Ereignis und Erzählung*. München: W. Fink, coll. *Poetik und Hermeneutik* V, 1973

KRISTEVA, JULIA. 'Le mot, le dialogue et le roman,' *Séméiôtiké. Recherches pour une sémanalyse*. Paris: Seuil, coll. *Tel quel*, 1969

KUENTZ, PIERRE. 'Parole/discours,' *Langage et histoire*. eds. Jean-Claude Chevalier and Pierre Kuentz. Special number of *Langue française* 15 (Sept. 1972), 18–28

LEFF, GORDON. *William of Ockham: The Metamorphosis of Scholastic Discourse*. Manchester: Manchester University Press, 1975

LEWIS, CLIVE-STAPLES. *The Discarded Image: An Introduction to Medieval and Renaissance Literature*. Cambridge: Cambridge University Press, 1964

LIPPS, HANS. *Untersuchungen zu einer hermeneutischen Logik*. Frankfurt a.M.: V. Klostermann, 1938

MALRAUX, ANDRÉ. *Les Voix du silence*. Paris: Gallimard, 1951

MAN, PAUL DE. *Blindness and Insight: Essays in the Rhetoric of Contemporary Criticism*. New York: Oxford University Press, 1971

– 'Theory of Metaphor in Rousseau's *Second Discours*,' *Studies in Romanticism* 12, 2 (Spring 1973), 475–98

MENÉNDEZ PIDAL, RAMON. *La Chanson de Roland et la tradition épique des Francs*. transl. I.M. Cluzel. Paris: A. et J. Picard, 1960

MOLES, ABRAHAM A. *Informationstheorie und ästhetische Wahrnehmung*. transl. Hans Ronge et al. Köln: Schauberg, 1971

MUKAŘOVSKY, JAN. 'Standard Language and Poetic Language,' *A Prague School Reader on Esthetics, Literary Structure, and Style*. ed. Paul L. Garvin. Washington: Georgetown University Press, 1964, 17–30

MURPHY, JAMES J. *Rhetoric in the Middle Ages: A History of Rhetorical Theory from St. Augustine to the Renaissance*. Berkeley: University of California Press, 1974

NIETZSCHE, FRIEDRICH. *The Portable Nietzsche*. Transl. Walter Kaufmann. New York: The Viking Press, 1954

– *Werke in Drei Bänden*. ed. Karl Schlechta. Munich: Carl Hanser, 1966

PATER, WALTER. 'A Study of Dionysus,' *Greek Studies: A Series of Essays*. London: Macmillan and Co., 1895

– *Miscellaneous Studies*. London: Macmillan and Co., 1895

PAUSANIAS. *Description of Greece*. With an English transl. by W.H.S. Jones. London: William Heinemann, New York: G.P. Putnam's Sons. 5 Vols., 1918–35

PÉPIN, JEAN. 'L'Herméneutique ancienne,' *Poétique* 23 (1975), 291–300

PETER OF SPAIN [Joannes XXI]. *The Summulae logicales*. ed. and transl. J.P. Mullally. Notre Dame: The University of Notre Dame Publications in Mediaeval Studies VIII, 1945

PLUTARCH. 'Theseus and Romulus,' *Plutarch's Lives*. With an English transl. by B. Perrin, v. I. London: William Heinemann, New York: G.P. Putnam's Sons, 1914

Poétique (1975)

POSNER, ROLAND. 'Strukturalismus in der Gedichtinterpretation. Text-deskription und Rezeptionsanalyse am Beispiel von Baudelaires "Les Chats,"' *Sprache im technischen Zeitalter* 29 (1969), 27–58

Qu'est-ce que le structuralisme? Paris: Seuil, coll. Points, No. 45, 1968

REISS, TIMOTHY J. 'Cartesian Discourse and Critical Ideology,' *Diacritics* VI, 4 (Winter 1976), 19–27

– 'Espaces de la pensée discursive: le cas Galilée et la science classique,' *Revue de Synthèse* (juillet-déc. 1976), 83–4

– 'Peirce and Frege: In the Matter of Truth,' *Canadian Journal of Research in Semiotics* (Winter 1976–7), 5–39

RENAUD, LAURENT. 'Le Problème de la signification chez Jean Duns Scot,' Unpublished thesis, École Pratique des Hautes Études, 5ᵉ section, 1968

RICHARDS, I.A. 'The Future of Poetry,' *So Much Nearer. Essays Toward a World English*. New York: Harcourt, Brace and World, 1968, 150–82

– 'Toward a Theory of Comprehending,' *Speculative Instruments*. London: Routledge and Kegan Paul, 1955, 17–38

– '*Troilus and Cressida* and Plato,' *Speculative Instruments*. London: Routledge and Kegan Paul, 1955, 198–213

– 'What is Saying?' *Poetries: Their Media and Ends. A Collection of Essays*. ed. Trevor Eaton. The Hague: Mouton, 1974

RIFFATERRE, MICHAEL. '*Paragram and Significance*,' *Semiotexte* (Fall 1974), 72–87

RICOEUR, PAUL. *La Métaphore vive*. Paris: Seuil, coll. L'Ordre philosophique, 1975

ROUSSEAU, JEAN-JACQUES. *Oeuvres complètes*. 4 vols. Paris: Bibliothèque de la Pléiade, 1959

RUBIN, EDGAR. *Visuell wahrgenommene Figuren: Studien in psychologischer Analyse*. Copenhagen: Gyldendal, 1921

RUSKIN, JOHN. *The Works*. Eds. E.T. Cook and Alexander Wedderburn. London: George Allen, 1891–1913

RUSSELL, BERTRAND. 'Introduction,' in Ludwig Wittgenstein *Tractatus Logico-Philosophicus*. eds. D.F. Pears and B.F. McGuinness. London: Routledge and Kegan Paul, 1961

SCHÜTZ, ALFRED. *Das Problem der Relevanz*. Frankfurt: Suhrkamp, 1971

SEARLE, JOHN. *Speech Acts: An Essay in the Philosophy of Language*. London: Cambridge University Press, 1969

SPERBER, DAN. 'Rudiments de rhétorique cognitive,' *Poétique* 23 (1975), 389–415

STEVENS, WALLACE. *The Collected Poems of Wallace Stevens*. New York: Alfred A. Knopf, 1954

– *The Letters of Wallace Stevens*. ed. Holly Stevens. New York: Alfred A. Knopf, 1966

STOCK, BRIAN. *Myth and Science in the Twelfth Century*. Princeton, N.J.: Princeton University Press, 1972

SURBER, JERE PAUL. 'Hegel's Speculative Sentence,' *Hegel-Studien* X (1975), 211–30

TILLOTSON, KATHLEEN. *Novels of the Eighteen-Forties*. Oxford: Oxford University Press, coll. Oxford Paperbacks, 1961

TODOROV, TZVETAN. *Introduction à la littérature fantastique*. Paris: Seuil, 1970
– 'La Lecture comme construction,' *Poétique* 24 (1975), 417–25
– *Poétique de la prose*. Paris: Seuil, 1971

TOPITSCH, E., ed. *Logik der Sozialwissenschaften*. Köln/Berlin: Kiepenheuer & Witsch, 1966. See especially Theodor W. Adorno, 'Soziologie und empirische Forschung,' 511–25

TUOMELA, RAIMO. *Theoretical Concepts*. Vienna/New York: Springer Verlag, 1973

VANCE, EUGENE. 'Augustine's *Confessions* and the Grammar of Selfhood,' *Genre* 6, No. 1 (March 1973), 1–28

VINAVER, EUGÈNE. *A la Recherche d'une poétique médiévale*. Paris: Nizet, 1970

WARNING, R., ed. *Rezeptionsästhetik – Theorie und Praxis*. München: W. Fink, 1975

WIMSATT, WILLIAM K. and CLEANTH BROOKS. *Literary Criticism: A Short History*. New York: Knopf, 1957

WHITE, HAYDEN. *Metahistory. The Historical Imagination in Nineteenth-Century Europe*. Baltimore: Johns Hopkins University Press, 1973

WITTGENSTEIN, LUDWIG. *Tractatus Logico-Philosophicus*. transl. D.F. Pears and B.F. McGuinness. London: Routledge and Kegan Paul, 1961

WOLLHEIM, RICHARD. 'Art and Illusion,' *Aesthetics in the Modern World*. ed. Harold Osborne. London: Thames and Hudson, 1968, 235–63

ZUMTHOR, PAUL. 'Rhétorique et poétique,' *Langue, texte, énigme*. Paris: Seuil, 1975, 93–124

INDEX OF AUTHORS

Bibliothèque de la *Revue Canadienne de Littérature Comparée* vol. 4
Library of the *Canadian Review of Comparative Literature* vol. 4

DIRECTEUR/EDITOR: M.V. Dimić, Alberta

SECRÉTAIRE DE RÉDACTION/EDITORIAL SECRETARY: E.D. Blodgett, Alberta

1   E.J.H. Greene, *Menander to Marivaux: The History of a Comic Structure*. Edmonton: University of Alberta Press 1977. Pp. 201; $10.00

2,3   M.V. Dimić, J. Ferraté, E. Kushner, R. Struc, eds, *Proceedings of the VIIth Congress of the ICLA* [Montreal-Ottawa, 1973]. Budapest: Akadémai Kiadó; Stuttgart: Kunst and Wissen; forthcoming. Two volumes

4   Mario J. Valdés and Owen J. Miller, eds, *Interpretation of Narrative*. Toronto: University of Toronto Press 1978